Following the Bouncing Ball

A FRAGMENTED AMERICAN LIFE

Following the Bouncing Ball

the

A FRAGMENTED AMERICAN LIFE

RABON SAIP

gatekeeper press™
Columbus, Ohio

Following the Bouncing Ball: A Fragmented American Life

Published by Gatekeeper Press
2167 Stringtown Rd, Suite 109
Columbus, OH 43123-2989
www.GatekeeperPress.com

ISBN (hardcover): 9781662918131

DEDICATION

This book is dedicated to those about whom it is written as well as to those for whom it is intended: Aerin, Arnelle, Austin, Batra Njana, Deirdre, Eric, Hue, Jade, Jamie, Jim, Kai, Kathy, Mary, Rachel, Ravi, and Zack. With special thanks to my friend Kathleen.

TABLE OF CONTENTS

INTRODUCTION

"You are living the life you choose to remember."
– Susan Musgrave

One of the great advantages of living for a long time is that we get an opportunity to make sense of our lives as never before possible. As elders, when we take on the challenge of writing about and re-thinking our life stories, we review our past experiences through the lens of the present, from the perspective of an older and wiser person, one who has learned to think with both the head and the heart. The integration of a fragmented life, with its various adventures of success and failure, especially through trials such as disability and addiction, can be an immensely rewarding process - reviewing, confronting, forgiving and healing. With the practice of re-thinking and re-storying, which does not at all imply changing the "facts," healing integration simply *happens*, it is a natural by-product of the process. Courage and adaptability are allowed to emerge where self-doubt and shame had prevailed. If taken to a fairly deep level of honest introspection, we will find within our own thinking the healing power of story, not only for ourselves, but as legacy for those we leave behind.

KILLER WASHTUB

I was walking down the dirt road from my grandparent's home to the only candy store for miles around – a filling station up on Columbus Highway. I had stopped a couple of times, to close my eyes and squish the silken pools of Georgia dust between my toes, like a warm dry liquid. The quiet summer world drifted through me without boundaries, my internal and external sensations a seamless playground of childhood imagination. I was easily distracted and forgetful of just how far I had to go.

Since leaving the farm house I hadn't noticed a parade of summer storm clouds that had been steadily building in the southern sky. Now, as the sun slipped behind the head of the tallest cloud, I felt a sudden chill and looked up. A gigantic black cloud was spreading its broad wings high above me. And, just as I looked up, a pinpoint of sunlight broke through the cloud, which was shaped like a grotesque Devil's head, in exactly the spot where an eye would be. Two thin plumes of cloud had even sprouted out like a pair of horns.

Breathless, tingling with a mixture of wonder and fear, I was totally thrilled. The idea of playing hide and seek with the Devil, with that same evil creature who lived in my grandfather's fiery sermons, was truly scary; but it scared me just right. With a rush of childhood omnipotence, I clenched my fist around the pennies in my pocket and ran to hide beneath the nearest tree. As I gathered the courage to look back up at the sky, large drops of rain were already blowing in my face.

The bright summer afternoon of just moments before soon disappeared into uniform darkness. It wasn't long before the wind and rain seemed to be coming from every direction at once. I hugged myself into a ball at the base of the large, sheltering pine and peeked down the country road toward Columbus Highway. What I saw there brought yet another ominous thrill.

A plodding, dim-lit figure was coming down the road toward me, his broad shoulders hunched forward as he struggled to keep pace. He wore bib-overalls, as I did, and a soaking wet, flour-sack shirt was plastered to his large muscles. He held a straw hat to his head as the wind threatened to snatch it away.

I had no sooner seen this figure than a totally unexpected sight whizzed past me on the road, hurtling toward the bent figure. A large, round metal washtub was careening down the dirt road on its rim, amazingly keeping its balance. I held my breath as it blew closer to the man. With his head down, I couldn't tell if he had seen the tub or not. I wanted to yell, but my voice stuck in my throat. All I could hear was the wind.

Then, by the fact he had stopped, was crouched down and moving sideways, I knew he had also seen the tub. But no matter which way he moved, left or right, the spinning washtub seemed to correct its course and continue to target him. During the last few seconds before impact, the man must have changed direction three times, but then, WHAM!

He sprawled forward, and for a moment it seemed he had pinned the washtub down; but, like a thing alive, the tub twisted to one side and continued to roll off into the distance. The wind was famous for instigating such unusual events, but I've never yet heard of anything quite like what I witnessed that day.

The man lay there without moving. I wondered if he was bad hurt, or even dead. But then he rose unsteadily to his feet, gripped his straw hat, which was somehow still in his hand, and continued on down the road in my direction. I sat very still, huddled tight against the trunk of the tree, waiting for him to pass me by. But just as he was pushing alongside my hiding place, he saw me and stopped.

The look on his strong, black face was severe. I felt guilty. I wondered if in my fearful excitement I hadn't actually sent that Devil of a washtub to collide with him myself; or, at the very least, maybe I had seen something I shouldn't have. He made a slight move, as though to come toward me. But I was poised to run. Then, he just stopped and stood there, clutching his straw hat to the side of his head and staring at me. The moment was stitched in time – a rain-soaked tableau - the little white boy and the big black man, motionless, like an illustrated page in the storybook of my childhood, ever waiting to be turned.

But then, the big man began to smile, and suddenly burst into laughter. His deep booming voice was the sound of joyful thunder. Just a moment before I had been frightened and alone, but now, I felt strangely warm and secure. I began to laugh with him, intoxicated by the embrace of his powerful spirit. The sound of our voices blended into the wind; the chirping child, the basso profundo, joined in our own secret duet. There was a fleeting bond between man and child that was far more important than my young heart could hold at the time.

Without a word, still laughing, he turned back into the wind and continued on down the road. The Y of the bib-overalls over his wide shoulders stayed in my mind's eye for a long time. And the lonely ache of a fatherless child that followed behind him after that rare moment of shared joy would stay with me for years to come.

OLD TIME RELIGION

I look back now with the realization that my early years in rural
Georgia were essentially spent in the 19th century. The language,
customs and implements of our daily lives had changed little since the
Great Civil War. The rural farming community of my forefathers was
like a living museum – an isolated piece of slow-moving history. Still
smarting from the agony of defeat, as though Sherman's march across
Georgia had just happened, the dark undercurrents in my family clan
were a toxic mixture of fear and rage, exaggerated Christian morality
and suppressed sexuality.

Convinced of their own sins, disciplined to the rigors of a hard
life at best, my relatives were perfect customers for an occasional,
exciting wave of Revivalism. Since the first Great Awakening in the
mid eighteenth century, several generations of backwoods farmers had
experienced the awful pressures of Biblical guilt. And it took a bit more
than small weekly doses of the holy spirit in our country church to
keep them safe. It took the catharsis of radical salvation, and even that,
in most cases, proved only temporary.

At the same time, generations of itinerant preachers had continued
to adapt and refine the techniques of Revivalism. It was obvious they
were paid performers who made financial deals with local churches,
but who can say what percentage of those preachers were charlatans;
and who really cared. What seemed to matter most was that a good

revival meeting always left some money and higher church attendance in its wake.

To my child's mind, there was no more arduous a task than going to Church on Sunday morning. I would rather have carried the chamber pot, or fed the hogs and chickens, or even pull weeds, than stand in that metal washtub and receive the thorough scrubbing that always preceded those agonizing eternities on a hard bench.

"Cleanliness is next to Godliness," said my grandmother as she applied the coarse washcloth behind my ears with religious zeal.

Our church was a rough wooden structure at the crossing of two dirt roads, deep in the piney woods. I remember the dust, churned up by the wagon wheels, that hung like a fine mist in the pine trees. And the mud, the red Georgia clay that seemed to reach out and stick to everything. Winter or summer, rain or shine, we always went to church. And there was always room in our family wagon for an occasional pedestrian along the way. Automobiles were still rare in that part of the country – novelties that few could afford – so the majority of people still traveled as they had for centuries.

Of all things common to that backwoods culture, going to church on Sunday came first. Those individuals who risked the condemnation of not attending, without good reason, were duly noted and shunned, so what chance did I have, a small child, of avoiding the senseless torture of attending church.

When I was first told to stop fidgeting, I looked down at my guilty little body and tried to catch a glimpse of what "fidgeting" was. Then, when I was also told to stop "squirming," I spent some time deciding the difference between the two and it wasn't long before I had mastered a combination quick fidget and slow squirm and no one ever told me to stop doing both at the same time.

Then, at precisely that moment when I couldn't take it anymore, when no amount of containment could prevent the horrible explosion of my overwrought little body; we were finally excused to Sunday School.

It was there, in a crude lean-to attached to the rear of the Church, under the careful tutelage of a loving but ignorant young woman, that I was first introduced to the black and white of it all. I'll never forget the pieces of speckled paper and black paper that were held up to represent the impure state of my immortal soul. Damn, I didn't even know I HAD an immortal soul, let alone that it had been given to me in such sinful condition.

As a child in the segregated South, the connection between paper color and skin color was all too obvious, and, easily explained by the greater degree of sin for which black people were being punished. From that time on, I always looked carefully at the adults in our congregation, to see if I could detect those among us who had once been black.

I'm not sure whatever else I was supposed to have learned in Sunday School. I remember the storybook pictures in our one tattered volume, of bearded white men who carried long sticks and wore dresses. They were usually posed in bright beams of light that came down from the sky.

Finally, when we returned from Sunday School to the main congregation, the end was in sight. Even some of the adults were getting restless. But, before we could leave, the Preacher had this weekly ritual to perform. It was always the same. He would reassure us that all the rich people were going to Hell, tell us about a heavenly eternal city where the streets are paved with gold, then ask for money and offer to save our souls.

This closing ceremony was a most puzzling time. While the offering plate was being passed, and the congregation softly sang "Oh Lamb of God, I Come, I Come," the Preacher would get really emotional, downright melodramatic, as he dared everyone in the church to walk down the aisle and get their ticket to Heaven. He would beg, he would scold, he would threaten.

I could feel the confusing struggle between him and the congregation, which was more like a half-hearted game. The Preacher did his best to make the people feel guilty and they did their best to deny him. This was ridiculous. Why were they all there in the first place, if not for the Prize – the Big Banana – the Brass Ring?

When just a few people broke down and went forward, some of them in tears, I could only imagine that they had done something really rotten. The rest of the congregation held back, smugly approving, or shamefully restless. I swear I could smell their fear. Afterwards, everyone would complement the Preacher on "such a fine Sermon" and then go home to eat fried chicken. There seemed to be this unspoken agreement between the people and the church. It was like they would continue to support the preacher so long as he kept available the promise of some last-minute Salvation.

*   *   *

It wasn't until I was seven or eight that I witnessed my first revival meeting. News about the event was spread around the countryside for weeks in advance. It puzzled me that so many people were actually excited about the prospect of going to church in a big tent. I knew for a fact that many of them didn't really enjoy going to church that much. But I sensed this would be something different.

The rough wooden benches were filled early. There was standing room only by the time my friends and I squeezed under the edge of the huge revival tent and positioned ourselves in the sawdust at the edge of the crowd near the platform. Everybody settled down with anticipation as one local preacher came out to introduce the famous Reverend, Clyde Bouchée, who had a reputation for preachin' up a storm." However, the pathetic little man who stepped out onto the platform wasn't at all impressive, in fact, he seemed to be embarrassed.

When he began to speak, there was a general rustle of disappointment. A few people yelled for him to talk louder.

"Please forgive me, my friends," he suddenly cried out, raising his arms. "But I am in pain." His straining voice was indeed filled with torment. And as he took a few steps across the platform, every movement described agony. There were tears in his eyes. The people up front were mesmerized by his pain.

"My heart is broken." His voice grew stronger. "Because I have sinned." Everyone could relate to that. All Brother Clyde needed was a slight grip on the edge of their guilt and he had them. Slowly, skillfully, he built up the intensity of their shame and remorse until it oozed like a thick, fetid stickiness. Many of the people were in tears. The little man played the crowd with a voice that could roar like a tornado or whisper like a gentle breeze. He somehow managed to be equally seductive and terrifying – a siren dance of sweating words. He could raise hope, or fear, as he chose.

The crowd loved it; they began to get crazed. When he held his breath, they held theirs; when he jumped for joy, performing a standing back-flip with stunning skill, they went wild. The emotionally charged atmosphere inside the big tent was like something between a carnival and a war-zone – an execution and an orgy. Drunk on Love and the Holy Spirit, folks managed to excuse their inhibitions. With calloused hands groping in crowded exaltation, they brought forth squeals of joyous suffering, and groans of passion. In later years I would come to understand that a lot of people would get lucky that night.

Meanwhile, some overwrought souls had spasms and fell down; some frothed at the mouth and spoke gibberish; still others just started yelling and running around. I remember that on the following day my grandfather actually did jump over a fence and start dancing. And sure enough, church attendance and offerings did increase; for a while.

* * *

It was dark and quiet as I stood in the back yard of our ancient farmhouse. The world was asleep, but I was awake and worried. The revival meeting had left me with some strange new thoughts. I had never before felt guilty just for being alive. I looked back toward the house, calculating the distance to the security of the back porch steps.

I looked out toward the field, searching for the confidence that God would protect me, even in the darkness beyond the out-house.

In the faint glow of starlight, sensitive for the slightest comforting sound of a familiar farm animal, I went to stand in the dark, open field. I looked down at the hand-made nightgown I was wearing, which my dear grandmother had fashioned from an old blanket. I remembered the picture book from Sunday School. With all my heart, I lifted my arms to Heaven and waited for a beam of light to come down from the night sky.

GRAND CENTRAL STATION

My earliest memories of twilight recollect the islands of illumination created by coal oil lamps. Everything that needed doing after the sun went down was done by their soft glow. And then one night, something new, a bright and harsh electric bulb of stark illumination hung down from the front room ceiling by a thin dark wire. It made so much brightness one could see into every corner of the room. Such bright light seemed overbearing to me, like an alien imposition into the cracks and blemishes of our rural, bare wood existence.

The coal oil lamps still carried pools of light to different parts of the house, where the wire had not been strung. And I noticed that Grandma seemed to prefer the old lamplight, as I did, even when she had sewing to do.

And then one day, a thing came into the house that would change all our lives. It was a mysterious and powerful piece of furniture, with large black knobs and a long row of numbers behind a shiny glass window. It was majestic. In fact, although I could not quite decipher it at the time, the word "Majestic" was emblazoned on its wide, wood paneled facade.

For those of us too young to have a say, instructions were clear. Only my grandfather and oldest uncle were allowed to touch those large black knobs. They would determine the miracles of modern broadcasting that blessed our excited evenings of family entertainment.

Amos n' Andy, Jack Benny, Fibber McGee and Molly, Allen's Alley, Gangbusters, The Shadow; how exciting and real they all were.

And how strong the memory, as we sat staring intently into that majestic piece of furniture, as though the images inside our minds depended on looking deeply into the fabric behind the thin wooden filagree covering the large speaker. In the dark recesses of that place, behind the bright, shiny veneer, was a magical world that sparked the awesome power of our imaginations. The sound effects were amazing; the crunch of gravel, the creaking door, the sound of breaking glass, and the wind storms. And how many times did I hear that same squeal of tires and the car crash that followed?

Then came the miracle of Saturday morning, a blessing from on high, as we listened to the offerings of Let's Pretend and Buster Brown. I can still hear the jingle about Cream of Wheat, "so good to eat," and "Pluck your magic twanger Froggy," which made me wonder exactly what his "twanger" was. Then, when I got just a little older, I even stuck around for the announcer's deep, sonorous voice calling out, "Grand Central Station! Crossroads of a million private lives! Gigantic stage on which are played a thousand dramas daily!"

Eventually, with the newness of this miracle beginning to wear off, I dared to approach that sacred machine for my own investigation. There was no one in the house. Grandfather and my uncles were gone hunting. Grandma was outside and my aunts were off someplace out of sight. I was careful to look around for my Uncle Sherrill, only a few months older than I was. I was concerned that he might tell on me.

I was holding my breath as I reached out for the big knob that turned the radio on. Click! Carefully, carefully, keeping the volume low, I manipulated the master knob that scanned the world of radio frequencies. Voices spoke about adult things that didn't hold my attention. There were the hillbilly sounds of the Grand Old Opry and stars like Roy Acuff, Earnest Tubb, and my namesake Rabon and his brother Alton, known as the Delmore Brothers. Then suddenly, a radio station in Atlanta changed my world forever.

It was as though all my life I had been living in a closed box and all of a sudden, the lid had been snatched away. The giant sound that poured into my brain was almost unbearable. I felt my head expanding, my body expanding. I felt strangely exposed. I had never even dreamed anything could sound like that; so full, so complete, so beautiful, like the whole wide world wrapped into one magnificent blast of harmony. Such was my first experience of classical music, from the Atlanta Symphony Orchestra to a little boy down West of Macon.

I became so excited I ran to tell others of my magical discovery. Big mistake. I had forgotten the rules.

PERFORMANCE

Most of my childhood memories make sense to me. Their time, place and experience come together with enough coherence to make a fairly clear and sensible memory, even with large doses of childhood fantasy thrown in. But this particular memory has a disturbing edge about it, beyond which I can only speculate.

It was 1942, I was near seven years old. My young mother and I were living with my grandparents and five of her siblings, three brothers and two sisters, in an old run-down farmhouse past the edge of town. Her two older brothers were visually impaired (4F) and not acceptable for military service, a fact that affected me indirectly because of my exposure to their anger and shame; and directly because I had also inherited the same eye condition (acute myopia plus achromatopsia).

My mother and both her sisters were employed at a local cotton mill (they carried but did not express the family eye gene) and I was left with grandmother and an uncle who was just six months older. Although we were family, I detected a difference in the way I was treated, especially by my grandfather, who obviously favored his own. His contempt for the young man who had deserted my mother made me an innocent target for his resentment. And when my father did come back and try to see me and my mother, my grandfather and older uncles chased him away with threats of violence.

As terrible as all this may sound, I was gracefully insulated from it by the protective shield of childhood innocence and adaptability.

These difficult facts would not become a part of my conscious awareness until some time later. Anyway, such was the background for my story, a story that doesn't quite fit with the crude outhouse and hand operated water pump in the back yard of the old farmhouse.

Regardless of our proximity to town, and even though some of the family found employment there, the poverty of our rural farming lifestyle was still prevalent. During the time I lived there, however, things slowly did get better. It was a time of enormous transition for all Americans and my family's gradual shift from the hardships of the country to the more technical, economic benefits of town was part of it.

A short walk up a dirt road to Columbus Highway and a lengthy bus ride brought us to downtown Macon, Georgia, the largest town this side of Atlanta. The film actor Paul Muni was starring in "Commandos Strike at Dawn," playing at the Bibb theater, and a local radio station was promoting an in-studio talent contest for children. Aside from the movie theater, the radio in those days was all the world - remember? Fibber McGee and Molly, Jack Benny, The Shadow, Jack Armstrong, The Green Lantern, Captain Midnight, The Lone Ranger, Superman, Buster Brown and the gang and Let's Pretend, Grand Central Station, I Love a Mystery; and so on.

At any rate my mother entered me in the radio contest and I was prepared to sing one of two currently popular songs. I don't remember how the decision was made, but I think it was concluded by a panel of her friends. My mother was prone to showing off her little boy's musical ability to anyone even slightly interested. It was decided I was to sing the song about war heroes and the Star-Spangled Banner.

I was scrubbed and dressed in my Sunday best and my mother and I took the bus into town for the big event. Macon was a fascinating place to me. The five and dime store, movie theater, drinking fountains and flush toilets, all were sources of almost magical wonder.

We eventually arrived at the studio along with several other participants. A couple of more affluent parents with musician youngsters began checking out the studio piano, another child had brought a violin, but most of us were going to sing. After several huddles of last-minute parent-child consultation, the radio announcer brought us all to order for a dress rehearsal. An elderly woman pianist who could back up the songs the singing contestants had listed was on hand to serve as accompanist.

A darling little girl in a plaid party dress, wearing pigtails, who curtsied to everyone, gave us "Don't Sit Under the Apple Tree with Anyone Else but Me." A well-dressed overweight little boy passionately pounded out "That Old Black Magic" on the piano. And then, when it came my turn, I stepped up to the microphone and delivered an obvious winner. It was not only the correct pitch and clear tones of a seven-year-old boy with adequate vocal equipment; it was the song. "There's a Star-Spangled Banner waving somewhere, in a distant land so many miles away. Only Uncle Sam's great heroes get to go there, where I wish that I could also live someday."

How could I miss? Our nation was in the midst of world-wide conflict and my song was not only patriotic, it was patriotically suicidal. After I had finished, moving through the words with dedication and passion, other mothers in the room looked at my mother with a compliment of resentment and envy. It really was that obvious. The three judges in the control room would have a hard time not going along with the Star-Spangled banner.

But then, when we went live, on air, with all our relatives and my mother's friends listening, the worst possible thing happened. I stepped up to the microphone and completely blew it. In spite of the elderly accompanist's strong lead in, I started singing the wrong song, in a disgustingly sassy manner. "Lonesome river, flowing in the moonlight." And after just another couple of lines, which I've gratefully forgotten, I ended with the dumb statement, "That's all I know."

I'm sure everyone was as dismayed by my reversal as I was, but probably not all of them were displeased. Without a word my mother grabbed me by the wrist and hurried me out of the studio, just as the kid who was next in line started to scratch out a violin solo.

My mother was silent as we waited for the bus and I was silent in return. She had let go of my hand and as I looked up at her stone-faced expression, I could feel the bitterness of her disappointment. At first, after the shock and my own dismay, I felt guilty about the terrible thing I had done. But then, in some strange way I felt good about it as well, which completely confused me. Until this day I wonder about the provoking complexity that came over me. It was as though another entity had taken up residence inside me and was giving voice to thoughts that were not my own.

Serves her right, it thought, for exploiting me the way she does, just to make herself look good. I should be more valued for who I am, not just for what I can do.

Several years later however, when I successfully belted out the beautiful Irish ballad, "Galway Bay," and took first prize on the stage at San Rafael High School, in California, with my mother in the audience; the incident at the radio station in faraway Macon was still a haunting memory. But now I had made up for my belligerent failure.

Nevertheless, even after all these years, whenever I get near a microphone, I have this strange impulse to grab it and tell whoever is listening to go hump themselves.

WINSHIP STREET

My early childhood did not take place in one home, or two, or even three. I have memory traces of living in several dwellings by the time I was eight years old. From the year of my birth (in Macon, Georgia), 1935, to the year I came to California, in 1944, I had gone back and forth between my young mother and her parents, with whom three of her five brothers and her two sisters still lived.

To my grandparent's family I was an add-on, a seventh child, included in the family mix and given a proportional share of food and shelter. And I must give special credit to my grandmother (whose maiden name was Mattie Hancock) for doing for me as best she could, considering the slave like labor that was her lot in life.

My mother and father were legally married, but he took off when I was six months old. Later, when he tried to mend his ways and return to care for us, my grandfather and older uncles threatened his life and denied him that possibility. I didn't know of his redeeming efforts until much later; in fact, it was after fifty years of separation from his side of my family when I learned the truth of it.

My mother married again, in the late 30s, to a charming, violent man who turned out to be a criminal and an alcoholic. And then, yet again in 1943, after another period of living within the strict domain of my religious grandfather. She married a soldier from Indiana, who was stationed at nearby Camp Wheeler. He would become the long-lasting stepfather who brought us to California.

*   *   *

There were two houses my grandparent's family shared with me - the poor country farm west of Macon, and the house on Winship Street, near the shanty town edge of that small city. I can still see the burly form of a young ice man striding down the bare wood hallway, his iron tongs biting deep into a dripping block of ice headed for the ice-box in the kitchen.

Winship Street was a dirt roadway that ran from a high point intersecting a paved street, down through an old, dry riverbed, and up to the other bank. Along the bank on the far side of the riverbed was Negrotown, pronounced Niggertown (I have such mixed feelings using the word).

The oldest houses on that dirt street, one of which my family clan occupied, were built on brick piers, three to four feet high, apparently left over from a time when the river still ran full and occasionally flooded (but was later diverted into a local reservoir).

I recently visited Winship Street with my grown son, Ravi. It wasn't easy to find, and when we did, I couldn't believe how much everything was still there and how incredibly small the area was compared to my early memories. That entire district of Macon has now become what we once called Negrotown. My son and I had an uncomfortable time with some of our Southern relatives when it came to racism; but we learned to tolerate those attitudes, which we obviously couldn't change.

The house of my childhood still stands, although greatly improved. The gaps between the old brick piers have been filled in with basement walls and the whole structure now has a decent paint job. I felt a temptation to knock on the door and ask for a tour of the interior.

I imagined the house was as much changed on the inside as it was on the outside after sixty-five years.

* * *

Pieces of Winship Street are scattered across my neurons with no particular regard to sequential time, but the images were deeply chiseled into the new marble of a child's mind. I am suddenly standing at the edge of the front yard, looking at the swirl of designs my grandmother leaves in the bare earth with her homemade brush broom. There are no lawns on Winship Street, only the bare sandy earth. Years later I will look at a book on Japanese Gardens, notice rake patterns in the sand and remember the beauty of my grandmother's designs. As a small child watching, I could tell she enjoyed a certain distracting reverie while making those patterns - a temporary respite from her hard life.

* * *

The family is gathered on the front porch (all the houses had front porches). A watermelon wagon has just gone by, only a nickel each. We are enjoying a flavor I haven't experienced since then, watermelons not hastily grown for profit. It is a quiet sunny day, not a cloud in the sky, when suddenly there is a loud, clanging noise from the back of the house.

Just as she does in the front yard, my grandmother has the habit of making sweep patterns in the bare earth of the back yard as well, starting at the outside perimeter and working her way back to the steps of the back porch, where she always stops for a moment to admire her work.

As we all round a corner of the house, everyone stops and stares at the six-foot wide, shallow metal cone standing on its short metal legs. It is well within the swirling designs of my grandmother's broom strokes, with not an interruption, not a footprint, around it. So, how did it get there?

I later learned that the contraption is an old-fashioned incubator, or brooder, common to farms with lots of chickens. It didn't take too long to unravel the puzzle. There was no other explanation. It must have been sent aloft by a storm, then drifted around until it landed in our back yard. The real mystery was: where and when had that storm occurred?

*   *   *

I am standing on the river bank next to a large pine tree on our side or the riverbed, waiting my turn. I watch as one of the boys ahead of me grabs the short length of pipe and launches himself from a low limb. Down, down, down he glides as the pipe travels the length of the cable. When he hits the sandy riverbed at the bottom, an older boy waits as he unwraps a thick piece of cloth from around the pipe. Friction from sliding along the cable creates considerable heat, so a rag around the pipe keeps it from getting too hot to handle.

After a moment, the older boy holds the pipe like a javelin and whips it back up the cable for the next ride. The boy who has just enjoyed the long ride down takes the rag with him as he climbs back up the bank to await his next turn. Such is the cooperation between the older boys, one at the top and one at the bottom, which allows us smaller boys to experience the thrilling cable ride.

Whose idea was it anyway, to wrap a cable around a tree high on the river bank and tie it to a long metal stake driven into the riverbed? I never knew. Such is the inventiveness of poor people long before Disneyland. One of my favorite toys is an old automobile tire which I've learned to control as I whip it along with a heavy stick. All our playthings are made out of whatever we can find.

*   *   *

It is night time along the wagon rut roadway that crosses the field behind Winship Street. My Uncle Glen pulls a wad of rags, tightly bound with wire, from a small open can of kerosine. He lights the kerosine soaked ball on fire and then swings it around and around before letting go of the wire handle. The fireball soars high up into the air. My job, along with a few other small boys, is to run to wherever the fireball lands and beat out the flames in the short grass with gunny sacks. Other teams of firebugs are scattered around the field, watching and competing with each other's homemade pyrotechnics. But no one bothers us. No alarm is sounded.

*   *   *

On the corner where Winship Street meets the paved cross street, there is a bus stop. Sometimes I go there to wait for my mother, who works in the cotton mill far across town. I'm standing there one day when an amazing thing happens. A man walks up and hands me a square of brightly colored cardboard with a toy pistol and mask attached to it. There's a picture of the Lone Ranger on the cardboard.

Excited by this stroke of luck, I thank the man and run home to show the family my unexpected prize. My grandfather seems angry. He takes the piece of cardboard from my hands and throws it into the fireplace, forbidding me to touch it. That evening, when the fire is lit, I turn away as the flame curls the cardboard into ashes. I didn't know the man at the bus stop was my absentee father, but my grandfather did. And I never got over my fear and resentment for that old man.

*   *   *

The dry riverbed at the foot of Winship Street is a place of many adventures. A major discovery for me is the gullies, a miniature badlands formed in times past when the river rose far above the riverbed. For a small boy the gullies are an other world terrain of deep chalky ravines.

I am playing there alone, hiding in the tight corners and steep canyons from an imaginary enemy. As I round a sharp outcrop, going from one ravine to another, I come face to face with a little black boy. He is also playing in the gullies by himself. Without a word of conversation, we immediately fall into play mode with one another. Our understanding of each other's imaginations is perfect. His play world and my play world merge into one exciting, shared experience. As we emerge from one of the sharp canyons into the dry riverbed, I suddenly hear one of my teen-aged uncle's taunting voice.

"OooWee, am I gonna tell on you," he calls. He is standing above us on the white folk's side of the riverbed. This abrupt change of mood causes the black child and I to suddenly see one another in a different way, a way we don't understand. Our crime is innocence. We didn't know any better than to play with one another. My uncle starts throwing rocks at the boy, one of which strikes him in the face.

"G'wan Nigger, get back to where you belong," my uncle shouts. We never did meet again, that black child and me, but I imagined his name was Leroy. And aside from the spanking my grandfather gave me, what I vaguely remember is that the incident involving the black child and my uncle started a brief confrontation between blacks and whites down by the dry riverbed. I had been restricted from going there, so I only heard about it.

The story was told about a black man brandishing a shotgun and yelling threatening remarks from the far bank. I vaguely remember the feeling that if this was Leroy's father, I could only be proud of him. Fortunately, nothing of any further consequence occurred. There were no "authorities" involved. Our dirt-poor neighborhood was generally ignored, beneath consideration.

* * *

There are no fences between the houses on Winship Street. My playmates and I run free through the row of yards behind the houses, past large cauldrons with fires beneath them, past wash tubs and clothes lines. I stop to look back the way we just came and time stands still.

My brain registers a cultural image that will stay with me for the rest of my life.

Behind each house women are occupied with one of several laundry day chores: tending the fire, stirring the clothes with a large wooden paddle, lifting the steaming clumps of fabric out of the cauldron with that same paddle and into the washtub for rinsing. Then neighbors take turns using the co-owned hand cranked roller wringer. It is an ancient, chatty and collaborative ritual. I stand there for a long moment, recording history, and then run on to catch up with my playmates.

EARLY TRANSITIONS

The year 1944 marked a major turning point in my young life. It started in Macon, Georgia and ended in San Rafael, California. Early that year I was still a part of my grandfather's large household clan, but my mother had dated and married a soldier from Indiana, so we moved to a nearby military base. And then, by the middle of October, we had moved all the way to California.

I don't know exactly when my mother married Daddy Bill, but their relationship was the beginning of major changes for me. It is perhaps an odd way to bookmark such a significant event, but what most stands out in my memory is the transition from an out-house to indoor plumbing. I don't recall ever using the indoor public toilets in the dime store or movie theater on one of those rare bus trips to Macon, although I probably did. But my first clear memory of indoor plumbing was in a brand-new housing unit at Warner Robbins Air Base, where my brand-new stepfather was stationed as a security guard.

The move from my grandparent's house to the housing project was a dramatic one. The housing units were still under construction and occupied as soon as they were finished, so we were the very first family in our new unit. I remember these places were constructed of brick, with freshly painted dry wall interiors. This was my first smell of new. And it had a much more secure and permanent feeling than the single walled, pine board construction with which I had grown up.

When I first went into our new home's bathroom alone, I stood there and repeatedly flushed the toilet. Then, I ran water into the bathtub, turning the facet on and off. I was amazed that these modern inventions were now going to be a part of my daily life. I vaguely remember being asked, through the closed bathroom door, just what was I doing in there.

My previous experience with taking a bath was in a round, galvanized metal washtub in the middle of the bare wood kitchen floor; nearest the wood stove in winter. It was the same kind of tub that was used to water the cows. Chamber pots and the small wooden structure set off across the back yard were all I understood of sewage systems, except that the outhouse also provided a place of privacy. It was also the place where I was once trapped by a determined old Billy goat who butted the door shut every time I tried to get out.

I don't remember ever using that outhouse with anyone else, nor seeing more than one person go in there at one time; but still, there were two holes. I never asked my grandfather why he had cut two holes in the rectangular wooden box above the pit; for what, emergencies? Many years later when I was in graduate school, a discussion came up about toilet habits in which it was determined that private stalls in public places were historically quite recent. Was my grandfather in touch with some traditional principles of a shared toilet experience. Clearly, in the bath houses of ancient Greece and Rome, truly public toilets were the norm.

At any rate we didn't stay long in our brand-new home at Warner Robbins. Two things happened simultaneously: my new stepfather soon realized that he had married the whole damned family clan, whose interference he resented; and, he got a chance for a transfer back to Hamilton Field, in Marin County, California, where he had previously been stationed. I later learned he had given my mother an ultimatum - stay in Georgia with her meddling family or come with him to California

*   *   *

On October 10, 1944, my ninth birthday, we had a brief layover at the train station in Chicago and my stepfather found a store where he bought me a cap pistol and a sheriff's badge. Then he bribed a conductor with a five-dollar bill to put us in a Pullman coach just ahead of the rush that quickly filled it. I remember such details about him with pride. He seemed like such a man-of-the-world to me. Passenger trains were always packed during those war years, often and mostly with military personnel.

The train ride was long and tiring, and, at the same time, exciting. Nevertheless, nothing could have prepared me for San Francisco. The walk along Market Street from the Ferry Building, where we were met by a couple my stepfather had known from his previous time in Marin County, still lives in my mind as such a special occasion. And the ultra-modern system of little serving windows in the Clinton Cafeteria on Market Street was indeed a high point in my transition. Over time I would become intimately familiar with San Francisco, intimate because so much of my growth experience during the next couple of decades would be framed within the myth and magic of this incomparable city.

My first crossing of the Golden Gate Bridge, on our way to San Rafael, would be followed by countless crossings to come. But first, I would live through the culture shock of a visually impaired kid who neither spoke nor understood much of the Yankee dialect that filled his strange new auditory world. My second-grade teacher, at B Street Grammar School in San Rafael, spoke the Yankee dialect with a slight lisp, which made most of what she said incomprehensible to me. After my first day in school, I walked back to where we were staying with tears in my eyes.

Over the next four years, I attended B Street Grammar (San Rafael), both Old Mill School and Park Elementary in Mill Valley, and then back to San Rafael and E Street Grammar. During my thirteenth summer, after finishing the seventh grade, I awoke early one morning with a plan that had been growing inside me almost without my conscious awareness. I would run away from home that summer, for no apparent reason, to hitchhike and ride freight trains and eventually wind up back in Macon, Georgia.

Recollecting my state of being at that time has not been easy, primarily because I must have been out of my mind. If anyone had asked me why I ran away, I could not have come up with a coherent answer. However, in retrospect, I can find plenty of reasons. First of all, that dangerous cross-country trip was a self-initiating rite of passage; a primal process. Then, as the seventh child in my grandfather's household, with an uncle just six months older, I had been, and still felt like, the least of all these. I was quite sure that crossing the continent alone and showing up in Georgia would give me hero status, and besides, it would also give me a chance to ask my grandfather, in person, about why he had cut two holes in the outhouse.

As with many of life's lessons, most of what I learned from my cross-country adventure didn't occur to me at the time, or, for some time thereafter. It was only in recollection that I would put together the lessons that fit my life's journey. At thirteen, I was blessed with the Power of Innocence. I was ignorant of my limitations and therefore not at all hampered by their existence. At that tender age, I operated on the edge of fantasy. The assumption that I was invincible loaned me an alternate reality, one in which I could survive any risk.

* * *

I had the most profound near-death experience on that trip, one that opened the doors of perception in such a way that still haunt me. Once, when jumping from the top of one boxcar to the next, like in the movies, I slipped and fell between cars and barely managed to grab hold of a worn metal ladder on the end of the forward car. From my hips on down, I could feel the suction of air rushing beneath the fast-moving train. As my fingers began to slip, and I dug them into the metal, my consciousness shifted.

I was suddenly lying on the back porch of my grandparent's house, years before, watching as my grandmother churned milk in an old wooden churn. The grain pattern in the wood was remarkably clear and detailed, illuminated by the morning sunlight and just inches away from my nose. At the very same time, I was having a conversation with my step-father; at the very same time, I was playing with the family dog; at the very same time, I was sitting in school. Endless scenes from my short lifetime began to materialize. And, in spite of their sense of "reality," their vivid individual detail, these things all seemed to be happening simultaneously, as though time were a still pool into which I had been dipped.

As I lay gasping on top of the boxcar, not sure of how I got there, the sounds of a freight train were transformed into powerful chords, a full symphony orchestra playing what I would later come to call Wagnerian music. I'd heard music in natural vibrations all my young life, ever since the mind-blowing experience of classical music for the first time on the radio when five years old; but this was different, more intense.

It's difficult to describe what happened after that initial encounter with such a wide spectrum of musical tone. As I moved about in my visually limited out-of-focus world, my auditory world took on a whole new clarity and dimension. I seemed to have my own private radio station inside my head, but it was one over which I had little control at first.

At times I would be quite distracted by the wheel of outstanding music that turned inside me, especially when it was triggered by harmonically complex external sounds; like machinery, or wind, or flowing water. Over time I learned that my own brain could gently filter and persuade the direction of the sounds I heard. So long as I maintained a delicate collaboration with natural harmonics, I could be a conductor and a composer all at the same time.

*   *   *

I have since held the awareness that what we understand as everyday "reality" is but one dimension of a greater whole, a greater truth. One cannot have such an experience without knowing this to be so. Why does this timeless review of one's life occur just at the brink of death? Is this experience common to all creatures, or exclusively the domain of human beings? And how can I explain the clarity and intensity of so much experiential detail in such a brief passage of time. It really was like re-living my short life all over again, in a flash. Does the "afterlife" consist of instantaneous access to all that has ever been or ever will be?

*   *   *

Eventually I made it to Georgia and thought I was pretty hot stuff for having done so. It would be years before I understood that having something to prove sometimes only proves that you have something to prove. Nevertheless, I did get a chance to ask my grandfather about the two-hole outhouse. It seems he just wanted to outdo his neighbor down the road who had only a one holer.

At any rate, I didn't stay too long in Georgia. I missed the advantages and growth I had found in my new home. I came back to California, but this time it was because I myself had made the decision to do so.

A WARTIME STORY

Call it "shell shock" or "battle fatigue" or PTSD; many good people have suffered, often without a lot of help or understanding, with this condition. I've never been in battle, but I was almost in the Army. I memorized the eye chart by listening to the guys in front of me at the induction center (in Oakland, CA) and could recite the first six lines by the time it came my turn. Until my deception was found out, I guess I was in the U. S. Army, more or less, until they sent me home.

Watching Ken Burns production about the Second World War recently has brought back lots of memories. In 1945 both my stepfather and mother were working at the Marin Café, on Fourth Street in San Rafael, which was a 24-hour hangout for both the local police and military from all branches.

A group of young, homesick servicemen had adopted my family and loved to come to our simple home in Tiburon Wye, right off a then two-lane highway 101. The core of our house was in fact a remodeled railroad car, left over from an era when trains ran all over Marin County. The car had apparently been left on a siding and eventually became the property owner's project for wartime rental housing. A couple of bedrooms had been added to one side of the old Pullman coach, which was long and wide enough for a living room and kitchen.

It was a rare weekend gathering when both my parents were home at the same time. I was ten years old and loved to be in the midst of servicemen friends during party time. There was a group of us in the kitchen and I had been allowed just one sip of bourbon.

Next to the kitchen door was one of those old-fashioned refrigerators with a coil on top. Just as a young soldier came through that door with his girlfriend, with an outstretched hand ready to meet my stepfather, the refrigerator coil turned on with a rat-tat-tat sound not unlike a nearby machine gun.

What happened next has lived in my soul as a vivid memory for all these years. The young soldier hit his girlfriend hard in her back, shoving her under the kitchen table. He then dove to land almost on top of her, to protect her body with his. Then, the whole scene stopped, like a movie frame stuck in a broken projector.

Out of that frozen tableau, with whiskey glasses and beer bottles held tight, came the sound of a gasping sob as the young man realized what had happened. His body was trembling as he pulled his girlfriend to her feet and choked out a whispered apology. The refrigerator coil went silent and no one else said a word.

In that moment our kitchen became a deeply eloquent, sacred place. Although I couldn't fully comprehend it at the time, I could feel the deep and silent bond of compassionate understanding between those young men close around me.

VJ Day

I was almost ten years old on VJ Day, 1945, and a truckload of pears turned over near where I lived (Tiburon Wye, Marin County, California). The driver was unhurt. He sat by the side of the road, drinking from a pint whiskey bottle and merrily inviting passers-by to help themselves to all the pears they wanted.

A number of cars came slowly driving through, honking horns of victory and crushing the spilled fruit beneath their tires. Standing in the midst of all those pears scattered across the pavement, eating as many as I wanted, I absorbed the relief at the end of world war. I felt great pride and joy. I was part of the greatest nation on earth.

As I speared a pear with my pocket knife and held it above my head, waving at the honking cars. The part of my being that records history clicked in and I was suddenly aware that I would always, always remember this moment. G.I. Joe and G.I. Jane had just handed the whole world to the U.S. government on a silver platter. Voices of great joy and optimism filled the air.

FOLLOW THE BOUNCING BALL

I don't recall exactly the year, maybe 1946 or 47, not too long after WW II. Something that had been a part of my childhood experience came to an end one day and the memory of that event still haunts me.

I was sitting in a movie theater in San Rafael, California, listening to an invitation I had heard many times before. A cheerful voice invited me to: "Follow the Bouncing Ball." Yea, a community sing along. The screen lit up with a lively rendition of "Shine on Harvest Moon" and, enter left, the bouncing white ball. I was mesmerized by this little character, by the way it bounced over the syllables along the bottom of the screen, keeping time with the music; by the way it would pause over just one syllable now and then for a double or triple bounce.

Just as I always had, I started to follow along, joining in with a few others. But most of the audience just looked on in silence. Seeing this, those of us who had opened our mouths gradually fell silent. It was strange. Images of a moonlit countryside continued to show up on the screen and "Shine on Harvest Moon" continued to play; but, for the first time in my experience, most of the audience seemed oddly opposed to the sing along. And, after all these years, I still wonder.

There were undoubtedly some in the audience who just didn't want to be reminded of the painful associations they had with this once popular sing along? So many friends and relatives had not come home from that war. Were they just wanting to forget? Were there still others who were simply indifferent, or to whom the bouncy little character was un-cool, passe, part of a more innocent, backward time? Some might even have felt a little embarrassment for the theater management. Didn't they know the war was over? America had won, let's move on. Was this continued showing of the bouncing ball simply an oversight?

I felt inhibited, and a little confused. I leaned back in my seat and imagined my disembodied spirit flying circles around the beautiful Art Deco chandeliers high above, banking and swooping, observing the audience. I imagined a young voice asking why couldn't we still have a community sing-along, even without a war?

I had mostly known WWII through the experience of the adults around me. From the time I first heard an awe-struck whisper that the "Japs had just bombed Pearl Harbor" until VJ Day, I could feel the anxiety, the uncertainty, the unspoken pain. I remembered the ration books for butter and sugar, gasoline and tires. I remembered the patriotic war songs and movies, the Nasties and the Japs, the Movietonews and the battle scene photos in the newspapers.

Now, as an impressionable youngster, still attached to the telepathy of childhood, I could feel a subtle undercurrent moving through the audience around me. The collective heart, which only beats in the company of others, and knows so much more than any one heart can hold, was awakened. As we all sat in silent witness to that little bouncing ball, each wrapped in the spell of his or her own relationship to it, there was a brief moment when the most tender and loving wave of compassion swept over us.

We had followed the little bouncing ball into history, through fear and sacrifice, strength and grace. We had learned a lot about ourselves, about our capacity for love, and for hate, during those recent war years. Patriotic Americans had united a whole nation with the single purpose of ultimate victory. There was no alternative. Our huge national family was made humble and intimate as we shared so much of the same hope, the same pain, and the same grief. What the war had taken away could never be restored; but, at least, the world had begun to learn a better way: Or so we thought at the time.

To my knowledge that was the last time the bouncing ball made an appearance in the Rafael Theater.

PROGRESS

When I was a child in grammar school, a memory was put in place that I have occasionally recalled with some puzzlement. There was a graphic in one of my textbooks entitled "Progress" which strangely disturbed me. The graphic itself was not so remarkable, with its late 1930's automobile, streamlined locomotive and airplane (all drawn with angles and speed lines indicating rapid forward motion), with a set of smoke stacks in the background. What was remarkable was my reaction.

As I stared at this graphic, located at the head of a chapter page, I felt a profound sadness. Maybe it had something to do with missing my grandmother, who was far away in rural Georgia. Maybe on that particular day I was especially in touch with some mysterious realm of childhood wisdom. I distinctly remember the feeling that something was wrong with devaluing the past the way I felt this picture was doing, as though everything that had gone before needed to be improved. This thing called "progress," it seemed to me, was like a bully on the playground.

*   *   *

We human beings have survived and proliferated as no other species. We populate the planet in every corner of the globe, adapting to all climates and conditions. It is this adaptability on every level (physical, mental, psychological) that accounts for so much of our success. And, at the foundation of all this, according to a recent study of ancient skulls (teeth serration), about thirty-five thousand years ago we started living well beyond the age of procreation, to the ripe old age of thirty and beyond. This allowed the first grandmothers to assist in childcare and passing on of practical skills to older children, which facilitated younger women to have more babies and older people in general to contribute to the establishment and passing on of culture.

Over time our accumulation of culture and adaptability to change has served us well, but now, I wonder if this same ability to adapt to any circumstances might not also be our undoing. We live at a time when trust and compliance, the path of least resistance, have been increasingly manipulated by an ever more sophisticated communications technology. To anticipate, and even mold, our thoughts and feelings has become a powerful science.

Our willingness to push buttons and listen to endless recorded messages has gradually increased. We have adapted to a world wherein the majority of our choices have already been calculated, wherein grotesque incongruities between espoused intentions and actual outcomes have become strangely acceptable.

There will come a day, in the not-so-distant future, when the last person alive who remembers a world before television will pass away. Will that day be noted? Will anyone bring attention to such an historical passing? Probably not. In a world of time simultaneously shared by several generations, the importance of time's passing is a relative value. But the loss of the oldest among us, with their memories of a more balanced and grounded existence, in relationship to a more beloved and bountiful Earth; this may be a far greater loss than we can now imagine.

A SIERRA MOMENT

When I was a boy I loved to wander alone in the woods. My freedom in that natural setting was based on instinct, away from adult authority, away from any awareness of age or social standing, I could be as boys have been in the woods for all time; a creature among creatures, with a sense of belonging I didn't have to understand to enjoy. I look back now in deep appreciation for the bliss of that joyful ignorance, which is also perhaps our greatest wisdom.

What I'm about to describe happened more than once, but with varying degrees of intensity, and I'm sure it has happened to others as well. So, let me begin with this question: Have you ever been in the woods and come upon a special place that seemed to hold a memory of its own, a landscape with mysterious power?

I was maybe eleven, exploring and mind-mapping in the woods near Mill Valley. As I happened upon a small clearing, I felt a sudden chill - a psychic flash of some long-ago human activity in that place; it was unmistakable. For that moment I seemed to exist at two different times. My young fertile mind conjured up a compliment of ancient people. In that imaginal space, I could almost see them. I could almost hear them.

As I look back, I recognize the influence of youthful imagination; but still, even though my own ancestral memory might have been evoked, something was definitely there to inspire the experience; some powerful residue. It was as though I had touched upon an energy inside the landscape itself. Years later, when I first read the poetry of John O'Donohue, I completely understood his notion about the "consciousness" of certain Irish landscapes.

A few years after that, when I was camping with a Boy Scout troop in the Sierra, another moment of wonder entered my lifelong album of treasured memories. A group of us had gone off for an overnight trip away from the main camp. I had managed to get off by myself, away from our temporary campsite, to enjoy the wilderness solitude. I had walked for about ten minutes, careful to notice the landmarks for my return, when I came upon a sight that spoke directly to my soul.

I had wandered to a spot high above a long and wide canyon, receding away into the distance. Enormous flat top boulders, like stepping stones for a race of giants, were staggered but evenly spaced down from where I stood, down into the late afternoon depths of shadow. Tall sentinel trees, like cathedral pillars on either side of the canyon, suggested an architecture so grand, so colossal, it was far beyond anything that could be achieved by man's desire. And the low orb of the sun, perfectly centered at the far end of the canyon, casting its light through distant trees, formed a stained-glass appearance so beautiful, so appropriate, my eyes brimmed with tears.

As I stood there, mesmerized, I experienced a longing, an ache, that was nearly unbearable. And although I would later come to understand its source in a different way, I knew then exactly what the ache was about. To experience such beauty as I was given in that moment was one thing, but to share it with another would have made it perfect. I was overcome with a strange loneliness, an initiation into another mystery of the human condition. Seeking to occupy that perfection in later years would occasionally consume all my attention.

AND JELLY BEANS

Sometimes it's hard to accurately locate oneself in times past, to determine exactly what year or what month when something happened. For me it helps to first remember the environment; what house, what school, what else was happening. During the year I'm thinking about we had moved from Tiburon Wye to Shaver Street in San Rafael. I'm not sure if I had yet started E Street Grammar School, so maybe it was in the summer of my eleventh year.

I had a bicycle, one for which I had taken on a newspaper route to help pay my share of its cost. And it was when I pulled up in front of the house on Shaver Street, with my right pant leg rolled up to avoid getting it tangled in the bike chain, that a neighbor noticed some purple spots on my leg.

It was never determined how I contracted Henoch's Purpura, a blood disorder resulting in purple spots from broken capillaries, especially on the lower body and legs. But, within a few days, the spots were joined by a high fever and severe abdominal cramps.

An advantage of having fallen prey to this unusual disease was that by the time I got to Stanford Lane Hospital, in San Francisco, it had been determined that my parents would not have to worry about any medical bills; provided I could be viewed as a research specimen.

I had been a pretty hefty kid, so at the time I became ill I probably weighed around 125 lbs., if not more. Within weeks, however, I was down to barely 82 lbs., a figure I well recall from one of the most embarrassing events of my life.

As a research specimen, I was dutifully wheeled into an amphitheater, wearing nothing but a skimpy bridge cloth to cover my genitals; and, in front of a crowd of young medical students, I was lectured about by an old guy who pointed at me with a stick.

I was indeed severely ill and received a lot of penicillin and morphine. The stomach pain was so intense I damaged my right hand from pounding on the wall next to my bed one night while I was delirious. I couldn't keep food down and so had to be fed intravenously.

I became weaker and weaker, I later learned that I came close to having my spleen removed. Then, finally one morning, for no apparent reason, the crisis was over. When I awoke, after a fateful night of concern for my survival, the first thing I said was, "I'm hungry." This was apparently a good sign. I remember broad smiles among the white coats gathered around my bed.

I remained at Stanford Lane for another couple of months after that for convalescence and observation. For weeks I would go down to a lab on the first floor and have small amounts of concentrated material - animal, fruit or vegetable, from all over the world, infected just under the skin on my arm. They were apparently looking for anything to which I might have an allergic reaction, anything that would help to explain how I'd been infected. But nothing was found.

During most of this time I was held to a pretty strict diet, a lot of pills, cottage cheese, white rice and biscuits. That's when I started dreaming about bananas, marshmallows and jelly beans. I was recovering nicely and became a kind of hospital mascot, allowed to move about with relative freedom. I enjoyed trying to make myself useful by getting involved with chores for sexy young nurses.

Finally, after additional weeks of medical observation, I was released from Stanford Lane Hospital. Although a bit more is now known about Henoch's Purpura, the cause for me remained a mystery at that time.

I sometimes wondered if my close association with servicemen friends of my parents, returning from distant places after WW II, might have had something to do with it.

*   *   *

Anyway, some weeks after my release from the hospital, I carefully planned an event for which I still have fond and proud memories. I rigged up a hammock with an old blanket in the back yard for privacy, went alone to a local market with ten dollars and bought an outrageous amount of bananas, marshmallows and jelly beans. I took it all into the hammock and got ridiculously sick - but it was wonderful.

VENICE AND THE BIG BARN

I always enjoyed the way wet pavement, dripping ferns and Redwoods, seen from inside the comfort of my passing car; somehow became a whole worth far more than its parts. There's the faint musk of primal vegetation, the slicing sound of tires cutting across water-soaked cement, and the tingle of inner warmth as I look out through the windshield at the cool, deep green, misty world. How special that deeply felt, soulful alchemy, a delicious subtle mixture of something so vague, yet so important, this is how it feels to dream awake.

When I was in high school, I would spend many hours driving around the streets of old Marin County towns, soaking up the serenity and security of quiet neighborhoods, lush landscapes and stately homes. It was somehow as though my mere exposure to these symbols of stability could take away the fragmentation and uncertainty of my childhood. In later years I would go for long walks past stone pillars and wrought iron gates, where I could imagine I once belonged.

Perhaps it was because I had witnessed the dirt road poverty of rural Georgia in my early life that my later youth in Marin County was so saturated with promise. But it was a haunted, illusive promise, an obscure feeling I could never quite completely articulate. I was somehow balanced between two worlds: the one of fear and biblical damnation, hard work and bent bodies; the other of a vague and foreign culture that was insulated by the ease of casual wealth.

In 1947 my family bought a home in Santa Venetia, just north of San Rafael, on the corner of San Pablo Road and Mabry Way. How amazing to think of it now. There were two baths and four bedrooms, two of which (with bathroom) had been added above an attached garage with a flight of stairs leading up from inside the dining room. It was a great buy at five thousand dollars.

As I understood later, the original home had been the gatehouse to a wide, wrought iron gate that had extended all the way across Mabry Way. There were still two smooth concrete blocks, about three feet square by seven feet tall on each corner, which had anchored the gate from either side of the street. These blocks had been decorated with inlaid designs and were topped with what remained of ornate light fixtures. I believe they still stand today.

Over time I would discover other remnants of past glory, all that was left in Santa Venetia of real estate developer Mabry McMahan's grand scheme. Between 1914 and 1916, he invested enormously in plans for a luxury development styled after the city of Venice, converting marshes and creating canals and levees along the long, natural canal from San Pablo Bay that ran just north of Santa Venetia.

Aside from the structures he built, when the Panama Pacific International Exposition closed, in 1915, he acquired several structures from that great event and had them brought over to Santa Venetia by barge. He also planned to import authentic gondolas from Venice. But the entire plan eventually failed, first due to the interruption of WWI and then the economic downturn that followed. Nevertheless, Mabry McMahan did have a festive Grand Opening in August of 1914. The event was attended by three thousand people, many of whom were ferried up from San Francisco and into the canal along the north edge of Santa Venetia.

His various activities left some very exciting discoveries to accompany my adolescent and high school years. After later securing my own outboard motor boat, I would pass by canal walls with their ornate light posts many times on my way out through the canal to San Pablo Bay. But, by far my favorite discovery was the old barn, all that was left of Mabry's expansive estate a short distance away in the hills.

The mansion itself had long since burnt down, leaving bits of overgrown foundation and a few short flights of cement stairs which led nowhere. It wasn't until this very week that I finally saw an old photograph of that mansion, in an online internet collection from the Anne T. Kent California Room in the Marin County Library.

* * *

My freedom to roam as an adolescent in Marin County was a unique and historical asset, a kind of freedom not nearly as much enjoyed by the majority of 12-year-olds in our culture today. So long as I was home around supper time, my where-abouts during the day was of no great concern to my parents. Perhaps it had something to do with our coherence as a culture during the Second World War. Perhaps that shared experience of uncertainty and personal loss brought all of us closer together in the unspoken trust of extended family. Whatever the case I remember long days of freedom, to walk or hitchhike around the countryside at will.

In due time I would meet and team up with several friends around Santa Venetia, but I was alone on the day I discovered the old barn. There was a general store then, where San Pablo Road took a sharp left turn toward the old flight strip and China Camp. There actually had been a small airport on San Pablo Road, just at the bayside edge of Santa Venetia. At that time two dirt roads took off from the bend by the general store: one leading up to Black Canyon (at least that's what we called it), the other in the direction of the old barn.

I could think about it all day and still not be able to gather all the ingredients surrounding a 12-year-old boy exploring Santa Venetia in 1947. For sure it was a simpler world, with fewer people, and it was also a world with much greater evidence attached to its past. But there was yet another element that catches my mind, another element related to my experience of youthful freedom - the element of risk.

Again, perhaps it had to do with the great war that had just past, and the conditions through which young soldiers had come into manhood. But I remember, in spite of my protective mother, that I and my peers were generally allowed to take risks for the sake of learning how to take care of ourselves. Of course, this was also a time before the plethora of insurance companies, therapists and attorneys who would later learn to exploit issues of child endangerment and law suits in general involving children.

For better or worse, the family was still the core authority for child raising. Even so, my buddies and I never told our parents about how we would go over to Turrini's Junkyard, just up 101 north of Santa Venetia, and aggravate the wild pigs who roamed among the old wrecks near the edge of the marsh. The game was to wait until the last minute before jumping up on the old cars in order to avoid the charging pigs. The joy and tension of my freedom to explore was like a pure, sharp crystal edge, made all the more meaningful and exciting by the possibility of cutting myself.

As I walked along the unknown road that day toward the old barn, the first hint that something different lay ahead were the tops of several neatly lined up and out-of-place palm trees. As I got closer, there was a vaguely visible intersection with the long-abandoned estate driveway and I saw the brick wall, with its evenly spaced brick pillars topped by elegant but headless light posts. This sturdy wall ran alongside the drive. It was so incongruous with the surrounding countryside it appeared like an old stage set which had been planted there and forgotten.

As I negotiated the long overgrown, eroded driveway, I caught glimpses of a huge wooden building through the trees and bushes ahead. Entrance into an ancient lost city or an Egyptian tomb could not have been more exciting. I could tell this was no ordinary building. It was a huge three-story structure, which reflected the grand scheme of its builder. And now, on a quiet sunny day many years after its usefulness, there was something ominous about its silence.

I hesitated by a small stand of young Eucalyptus trees across the yard from the front of the building. There were two huge sliding wooden doors for the bottom floor entrance. The wide-open mouth of an empty doorway at the center of the second story told me nothing, nor did the small window openings beneath the slant of the third story peaked roof.

Suddenly I felt like a trespasser, a modern-day Peeping Tom gawking at the naked corpse of a ruined past. What if there was still someone inside? That thought brought even greater excitement. As I approached the wide doors and peeked through a crack at one end, the hairs on my neck bristled. I was doing a damned good job of scaring myself. But it was fun.

I pushed sideways with all my strength and was rewarded as rusty wheels squeaked in a rusty track and the massive door rolled aside. Daylight fell across a smooth cement floor, a large lobby-like room where carriages would have been pulled inside. Through an open doorway in the back of this large lobby I caught sight of a gold braided rope with tassels hanging down across the tops of what I could see of several horse stalls.

Even after the abandonment of so many years, there was still a formal elegance to it all. I held my breath at the thought of what might have transpired here. I imagined guests arriving in sleek coaches and attendants putting their horses into the fancy stalls. My mind's eye danced with their arrival, in a horse drawn world that would soon give way to the coming of more and more automobiles.

A staircase at one end of the fancy stalls took me up to the second floor. There was still evidence of straw in the dirt on the wooden floor. There were some scattered and rusty tools, and partitions for smaller rooms that had been damaged in a way as though someone had gone berserk with a sledge hammer. Another set of narrow stairs led to the third floor. There I found an old single sized set of rusty bed springs, some wooden boxes and a crude old chest of drawers, evidence that someone had once lived between the slanted walls of the roof.

There were broken out windows at the back of the building on every floor. These overlooked a steeply cut creek bed downhill behind the building. Continued exploration a little further uphill from the barn revealed the overgrown foundation of the grand old home of Mabry McMahan. In later years, when I first saw the Wolf House Jack London had built near Glen Ellen, I would think back to this moment.

Although there were assorted items strewn about the stately old barn, like old tools and wooden boxes, I took nothing from there; then or ever. Over time however these things would disappear as others discovered the place. But I like to think I was one of the first, if not the first, to enter that old world edifice after all those years.

*   *   *

I couldn't tell you how many times I returned to the barn over the coming years. It eventually became a play house for a small gang of us and was also the place where we outgrew such play. Our activity turned from hide and seek war games to youthful philosophical conversations that would eventually carry our minds into the larger world. On a few occasions we decorated the "lobby" on the first floor and held lantern lit teen-age parties. I had my first sexual encounter with a high school girl of easy access and later brought other female companions there to share romantic interludes, though not necessarily sexual.

The important thing about that barn to me now, which has long since disappeared, is what it meant to me as an historical site, both in the world and in my life. And my single regret is that I did not secure the gold rope with the lovely tassels that hung above the fancy horse stalls.

LITTLE BLACK BEARS

It was cold. He was thirteen. The darkness of the Nebraska night seemed to be filled with silent breathing, like that of a gigantic black animal, as big as the dark night; expanding, contracting. He could feel it's slow pulse and smothering weight as the moonless night descended around him. He dared to take a deep breath, a conscious effort to rouse himself from too much fear. It was all he could do to guard against his own imagination.

He concentrated on the comforting sound of his boots as he scuffled along in the loose gravel. How long had he been walking? How long since he'd seen a car? He was scared; but he was also angry with himself for being scared. He was old enough to know that the smile on the service station attendant's face, back at the crossroads, had meant that he was just kidding about the little black bears here-about; but he was still young enough to see fleeting evidence of those same creatures in the inky shadows of every bush and tree.

He began to whistle, softly at first, then louder, hearing the words inside his mind.

"Froggy went a'courtin' an' he did ride, uh hum. Froggy went a'courtin' an' he did ride, oh yeah (double scuffle gravel shuffle). Froggy went a'courtin' an' he did ride, he had a sword an' a pistol by his side, uh hum."

The dark night receded a little. He was encouraged by a struggling sense of his own importance. What the hell, he thought, might as well let them know that the California Kid is here. His grip tightened on the hilt of the surplus Marine knife that he carried. Suddenly, dramatically, he crouched and wheeled in a tight circle, extending the heavy knife before him like a saber.

"C'mon, you little black bears," he whispered. "I ain't scared of you."

He stopped turning and remained perfectly still, staring defiantly into the darkness. He held his breath as vague beastly shapes began to form out of the shadows and move toward him. He felt the deepening grip of an overwhelming terror. This was it! There was no other way! He gathered up all his courage and regretted for the hundredth time that he'd forgotten to bring a flashlight.

"Ayeee!" He let out a primal war cry and lunged forward.

"Ayeee!" He was impressed by the power of his own performance. As he boldly stabbed the air, the beastly shapes began to vanish into the night. Presently, he was alone again. The silence that remained assured him that there was nothing around now that was any bigger or more dangerous than the California Kid.

He began walking again, at a more leisurely pace. The sound of his whistling and his boots on the gravel were like an invisible shield. He knew that he would be invincible so long as he believed that he was invincible. He heard a dog barking in the distance; he stopped to listen. When the sound came again, he felt a warm tear eroding the dirt on his face. He helplessly thought about the big, friendly mongrel that he had left behind.

"Go home, Poker!" He had tried to sound rough as he half-heartedly threw a small rock toward the confused animal.

"I'll be back to get you, I promise." Old Poker just stood there, his head lowered, his tail hanging limp. The look of hurt betrayal was more than the boy could take. He dropped to his knees and invited his friend to a final hug. Then, the same pitiful process of gently thrown rocks started all over again.

Now, a thousand miles away, he reached out at the thought of the dog's warm body beneath his hand. That memory triggered other images of home, comforting pictures that sought to replace the cold Nebraska night. He thought of his mother and step-father, asleep in the morning light as he had quietly gathered lunch money from the pile of coins on their dresser. Some nights his mother would bring home as much as twenty-five dollars in tips, especially if there was a banquet, but he never took more than four quarters from the pile.

Just as he started to leave, she stirred in her sleep. He hesitated at the bedroom door. He felt pulled upon not to go through with his plan, but he was also filled with a mysterious resolution. He went around to retrieve the knapsack he had lowered from his bedroom window. As he slipped it on, he looked toward the distant hills that had, until today, been a boundary to his world.

A sudden commotion in the brush alongside the road yanked his startled attention back to the present. He jumped out into the middle of the pavement, instinctively crouching with the knife before him. A very large body was moving through the brush, breaking dry stalks with an incredibly loud noise.

He stood his ground. Somehow, the reality of something that he had feared so much was almost a relief. He didn't feel as frightened as he thought he should be. Whatever it was, it sounded really big, but he refused to run. Just as he was trying not to imagine what it would be like to be torn apart, the beast made a soft "moo" sound. He straightened up and cautiously moved toward the noise. After all, how could he know for certain that it wasn't a bear trying to imitate a cow.

"Here, Betsy," he called. He peered into the darkness. He was startled by an even louder crashing as the cow moved away from him. He stood still, alone and disappointed. He had wanted so much to touch the animal, to put his arms around its neck.

* * *

The two-lane highway had remained silent and empty throughout the long hours of darkness, but now, with the first glimmer of dawn on the pavement, he heard the distant, familiar sound of an approaching car. His dirty white sailor's cap was turned down to cover his ears. Above the surplus army boots and khaki pants, he wore two sweaters and an army field jacket, which gave his small body the appearance of more bulk than was actually there. The dirt-laden fuzz on his chin made him look older.

He stared at the U.S. Marine combat knife still clutched in his small hand and looked around at the soft glow of the frosty fields, orderly fenceposts and squat, innocent trees. A rooster crowed from somewhere in the fuzzy distance. He raised his arms, still holding the knife, and threw his head back to crow like the rooster. But the sound that came out was more like the sound of screeching brakes. He could feel his laughter releasing the shadows of a long night.

Like an Indian with his ear to the railroad track, he cocked his head to catch the vibration from way off down the road. He slipped off his knapsack and bent down to put his saber out of sight. There was an ache in his hand that he hadn't noticed until now. As he pulled a clean t-shirt halfway out of the knapsack to wipe the darkness from his thick glasses, he contemplated the two cans of spaghetti and an accordion-like loaf of squashed Kilpatrick's bread. His stomach growled at him as he realized he would hold off till later in the day.

From the corner of his eye, he caught the distant halo of headlights coming along the road behind him, maybe a soft ride in a warm car. He stood up, smiling.

"C'mon, you little black bears," he whispered, sensing an internal change that the night's experience had made. "I ain't scared of you."

The Friendly Inn

Tired, bone tired, but young enough to keep going, I trudged on down the tracks. Daylight was fading into twilight. I could barely make out the dim lights ahead. Damn, I had jumped off the train too soon, mistaking the whistle as a signal it was pulling into a freight yard. I couldn't remember all the signals, but I thought for sure that three blasts meant the train was pulling into a freight yard.

The idea was to get off the train before getting caught by the "bulls." When I first heard this term, I actually imagined these animals were turned loose in the freight yards to watch out for illegal passengers. I only later realized the term was another name for railroad detectives.

"If they ever come after you," I was told. "Make sure to run through mud, or weeds, or even blackberry bushes. They're usually kind of dressed up and wont chase you. But, if they do catch you, you'll wind up being free labor for the county."

It was exciting, but scary, to be on my own again. The guys I had teamed up with back in Nebraska, where I first started riding freight trains, had all gone their own ways. The four of us had parted company in the huge Chicago freight yard.

"Take care, Kid." Gray haired Fred had done his best to teach me all he could about riding trains. He understood my vulnerability far better than I did. Fred was on his way back to a home he had left one day, over a year before, when he told his wife he was going out to buy a pack of cigarettes.

Curly headed Nick (the Greek) had bragged about how he knew a route of transfers, all the way across Chicago, on just one ten cent trolley fare, all the way over to the east side freight yard miles away. He was on his way to Boston.

And there was Don, dressed in new khaki work clothes and carrying a new pack, who had argued about the difference between bums, tramps and hobos.

"Bums are like beggars," he said. "And usually boozed up. Tramps are guys who don't work. You guys look like tramps to me. I'm a hobo. Hoboes are guys who ain't afraid to work." Nick was offended at being called a tramp, so he challenged Don to take it back, which Don only did after Nick had him pinned down and was getting his new clothes all dirty. Fred made them shake hands.

I got the feeling Don was on the run, in some kind of trouble. Old Fred privately called him a "Yegg" (a criminal). I especially didn't like the way Don had laughed at me when I first learned about how freight trains take up slack. You could hear the sound coming closer, as each car was jerked into motion, but I didn't know. I was standing in the middle of the boxcar trying to roll a cigarette and got knocked on my ass. The other guys laughed too, because the experience was like an initiation, but their laughter wasn't cruel.

The lights along the tracks ahead turned out to be the edge of Kankakee, Illinois. After walking a couple of miles more, I found myself in that neighborhood known as "the other side of the tracks." It was 1948. The bar in the middle of the block was actually called "JOE'S," and was surrounded by an assortment of run-down buildings. I passed a couple of dirty doorways, with stairs to sit down on, but it was getting cold. I needed a warm place to rest. I went into Joe's.

The horseshoe shape of the bar filled the room, with little space between the bar and the side walls. It was crowded. I headed around the right side and found an empty stool near the back. I was only thirteen, but I looked a lot older. I needed a haircut and the peach fuzz on my face was black with soot, giving the impression of a beard.

A surplus army field jacket, backpack and combat boots completed my outfit.

"What'll it be?" asked a beefy man wearing a dirty apron. His face was red and his grin was from ear to ear. He appeared to have been sampling a lot of what he was serving. I looked around at all the beer mugs on the bar and ordered the same; I was thirsty. Then I noticed the small basket of peanuts and pretzels already on the bar.

"Help yourself, Kid," the bartender pushed the basket in my direction and went to draw my beer. As I settled onto the stool, with my pack at my feet and my elbows on the bar, exhaustion and hunger competed for attention. I dug into my pocket for a dime and then into the basket for pretzels. I had almost eight dollars left, but I hadn't seen a store for a while. Then I became aware that the guy sitting next to me was staring. He was propped up against the wall and was really drunk.

"You son of a bitch," he glared at me. "You leave my girl alone." He was an older guy and didn't look all that tough, but my fight or flight response was aroused and it woke me up like a shot of adrenalin.

"I don't even know your girl," I said, "I don't even know you." I was ready for anything. But the old guy obligingly passed out against the wall. As I turned from that brief exchange, I saw the bartender pull a pistol from a drawer under the cash register and hand something small to one of the men across the bar. He raised the pistol and pointed it.

"Alright Sam Snyder," he addressed a man down the bar. "Say your prayers. This is it." His declaration was quickly followed by a loud bang. Everything stopped. The sound of the firecracker he had slipped to the other customer was followed by gales of laughter as Sam checked himself for bullet holes and then tried to climb over the bar. The noise and energy of the place was scary, but I was fascinated with this "rough and tumble" adult world. I drank two glasses of beer and what I didn't eat from the basket on the bar I managed to slip into my jacket pockets. The guy against the wall remained passed out.

I left the bar and pushed on down the tracks, exhausted but stubborn. I was driven by the desperation of not knowing what to do.

I came to some empty boxcars on a siding and crawled into one of them, thankful for the pile of smelly straw in which I tried to get warm. I dozed off, but was awakened by a passing train. It was cold. I started walking again. After a while I found myself standing on a bridge above another set of tracks, watching a train that was passing beneath me.

I was exhausted to the point of delusion. I actually thought about jumping onto the top of that moving train. I knew it was headed south and that's where I was headed. I had learned that friendly brakemen routinely left doors open on the ends of empty boxcars. I found myself calculating the speed and distance to the top of the train passing beneath me. Fortunately, my guardian angel spoke up and I stayed alive to share this memory.

A little further down the tracks I came to the railroad's crossing a major north-south highway. There was occasional highway traffic so I turned south and started to hitchhike, a more familiar activity than riding trains.

"I'm goin' as far as Terra Haute," said the friendly driver of a big rig. What a relief. It was warm inside the cab. After a brief exchange with the man behind the wheel, I made a pillow of my pack in my corner of the cab and was soon asleep. If the driver had wanted someone to keep him company, he was out of luck. It was nearly dawn when I was awakened.

"End of the line, fella," said the driver. "I hafta unload near here. Anyway, you're pretty much down town." With profuse thanks and an apology for sleeping through the whole ride, I climbed out of the high cab and onto the early morning sidewalk of a small town that had not yet awakened. Being awake before others had always given me a sense of power, but as I looked around at that moment, all I felt was homesick. I quickly swallowed the feeling. I had to keep moving.

As the semi-trailer pulled away, I took a moment to stretch and yawn, and then, just as I was pulling on my coat and picking up my pack, a policeman on a three wheeled motorcycle suddenly appeared.

"Hey you, where you headed? You got any ID?" I just stood there, in shock. Where the hell had he come from?

"I'm headed for Atlanta," I replied. "And I don't got an ID."

"Then you follow my directions," he ordered. "And don't try anything funny." There was nothing funny about it. He kept pace with me on his motorcycle while I followed his directions and walked myself to the police station.

"Hold it right there." He took my pack and ushered me inside. I gave them a phony name and told them I was headed down to Georgia to visit relatives, which was true. The cop going through my pack found my surplus Marine combat knife.

"Whadaya use this for, Kid?" he asked. I thought about it. So far, I had used the knife only once on my trip, so I told him.

"To spread mayonnaise," I timidly replied.

"So, you wanna be a wise guy, huh?"

"No, Sir," I stumbled. "I'm just being honest."

"What was your last address, Hotshot? How long did you live there?" Another officer joined in,

"We gotta coupla unsolved crimes around here, y'know."

"Where did you say you were from?"

When it became apparent they weren't going to just let me go, I broke down and told them the truth.

"I ran away from home," I confessed. "From California, I'll give you my parents address and phone number."

When it was determined that I was telling the truth, they did call my parents; collect. I spoke with my mother and step-father, who were thankfully more relieved than upset, and they spoke to the police. It was agreed that I would continue my trip on down to Georgia.

But I was not released. I was taken from the adult jail to a juvenile facility called "The Friendly Inn." This was an old three-story brick building in a residential section of town, right next to a school playground. The building had apparently once been a part of the school complex, but now stood as a symbol of what happens to misbehaving students. I was taken to an empty "cell block" on the third floor. There was a total of six individual cells (floor to ceiling cages), three on each side, with a large day room and long wooden table and benches in the middle. At that moment I was the only inmate.

The Friendly Inn did not live up to its name. The hard and hefty woman who let me into the cell block was not at all friendly. And the little old man who later brought me a dry baloney sandwich made me stand at the far end of the room while he put the sandwich on the floor just inside the door.

The empty cells, with their narrow bed frames, were all locked. So, the only place to sit was on a bench at the long table. I could dimly hear the sound of children in the playground. I quickly noticed that every wooden surface in the room - the table, the benches, and even some parts of the wall, were literally covered with the carved initials of former residents, with dates going back to the early thirties. These had all been painted over, leaving a monotone hieroglyphic effect. I passed the time by going over every inscription, but the only name I remember from that proud gallery was one George "Flash" De Long. His name stands out because I later saw it in one of those True Detective magazines. I guess George finally made it to the big time.

Although I felt certain I would not be held for very long, when the iron matron came in and unlocked one of the cells, it was apparent I would be there for at least overnight.

"I have no news for you," she said, before I could ask. She placed a straight back chair, with a towel and a couple of blankets on it, just inside the main door.

"There's a shower down there by the toilet," she said, pointing to the only door at the end of the room. "Use it. And remember to put your clothes on this chair when you go to bed." Her voice was cool and indifferent, devoid of emotion. Unfortunately, I made the mistake of bringing the chair into my cell and placing it by the narrow bed. I was exhausted. I neatly folded my clothes on the chair and quickly fell asleep.

Whack! At first I just felt it, and then I heard it. The matronly jailer had just whipped a leather belt down on my backside, pretty hard. I guess I'm lucky I wasn't sleeping on my back.

"Dammit," she scolded. "I didn't say you could move this chair. You just put your clothes on it and it gets taken out, overnight."

"Yes Mam," I managed. I couldn't believe it was just me. She must have something against all boys my age. That night was the first time since I'd left home that I allowed myself to cry. The next day was many hours too long. I only saw the old man.

"When am I getting out?" I asked, as he sat a food tray inside the door.

"I don't know nothin'," he replied. He did seem a bit simple minded, which underlined what he said.

My cell was on the side with windows overlooking the playground three stories below. As I looked down through the bars, I could see and hear some kids not much younger than I was. I felt strangely detached, even benign, like an older brother who had gone off to sea and came home much the wiser. I had pushed myself over two thousand miles, on a quest for something I later realized could only be found inside my own soul.

I didn't understand it at the time, but the drive to leave home, even though everything was fine with my family, was a dramatically self-imposed teen-age initiation. Had I been a Native American boy, my tribe would have provided such a thing, but without the benefit of tribal tradition, I had devised my own rite of passage.

On the second day an overweight detective named Tony from the Terra Haute police department came to take me out to a barber shop, where I received a short and proper haircut. He then drove me to the train station. After a brief discussion with the conductor, to whom he gave my train ticket, the detective handed me an envelope containing roughly fifty dollars, which had been sent by my parents.

"Don't ever come back to Terra Haute," he said, with unquestionable authority.

The conductor escorted me to an old passenger car at the very end of the train, which was full of drunken soldiers. I wondered what the detective had said to him. The soldiers were on their way to a base in

Florida and were celebrating a few days of relative freedom. After I had stashed my pack above one of a few empty seats, I sat down and took a deep breath. Wow. I looked around. Here I was just out of prison and led directly into the company of a troop of fighting men. Their rowdy behavior, with open bottles of alcohol being passed around, was totally exciting.

"You're not part of this outfit. Where you headed?" asked the young soldier sitting next to me, nursing a fifth of bourbon.

"Camp Wheeler," I lied. "That's down near Macon." I was relieved when he didn't pursue this line of conversation. He handed me the bottle and I took a drink, only to start choking. He laughed and slapped my back. I took another drink, just to show it was no big deal. The shabby old passenger car was alive with all the testosterone, exuberance and bravado of young warriors. I was thoroughly impressed to be there. I listened to them with rapt attention, longing to really be a part of such a brotherhood. I proudly accepted a drink from every bottle that came my way and it wasn't long before I passed out.

When I awoke it was just about dawn and almost all the soldiers were asleep, except for one guy who was collecting empty bottles into a cardboard box.

"Hey pal," he said. "Wanna have some fun." There was no caboose on our train and we were in the last car. Beyond the end door was a small balcony like platform. Gary, the young soldier collecting bottles, took them out onto the platform and started finding creative ways of smashing them.

"Here, c'mon," he said. "There's plenty for us both." My head hurt something awful and I felt sick, but watching him having fun got me going. I started out just dropping bottles onto the track that whizzed by beneath us. The shattered glass was quickly left far behind. Gary was taking aim at things alongside the tracks. He even managed to hit a couple of telephone poles. I joined him.

Then he tried to hit a large black woman who was walking along by the tracks. The bottle smashed right in front of her, sending shards of glass in every direction. But the scene went by so fast I couldn't tell if she was hurt. An image of her remained suspended in my mind, the exploding glass resting in midair. I tried to see her face. Was she okay? Was she injured? Suddenly I felt like a criminal, like what we were doing was very wrong, and what Gary had done was even more wrong. I stopped throwing bottles and went back inside the passenger car full of hungover young soldiers.

Eventually the train pulled into the train station in Macon, Georgia and I began yet another chapter of my initiation journey within the parameters of my family clan.

INTO THE SWAMP

The most remarkable thing about my cross-country trip in 1948 was that I survived it. My lack of experience, my innocent ignorance, was my best defense. I remember some close calls, and there was no doubt a few of which I wasn't aware; but somehow, I managed to stay alive. Considering the stupid things I did, especially in learning how to ride freight trains, the trip was proof enough that guardian angels do exist. At the time, however, the glorious credit was all mine. I swaggered back into my Southern family clan as though not a dragon was left alive in my wake.

I'd traveled from Northern California to Central Georgia, a distance in both time and space, from the marvelous new world of the San Francisco Bay Area to a land still conscious of its defeat in the Civil War. I'd been gone from the old farm house, where once I had lived (with my grandparents, my mother, her three brothers and two sisters), for a number of years, which seemed even longer because of the variety of my experience since then.

In 1943, my mother had married a serviceman who had previously been stationed at Hamilton Field, in Marin County, California. He'd fallen in love with the San Francisco Bay Area and wanted to return. He managed to finagle a re-assignment back to California; and, one magical day the following year we boarded a west-bound train.

My mother and grandmother had been pregnant near the same time, so I had an uncle who was barely six months older. Although

I wasn't really conscious of it at the time, it was because of him, and because of his father and older brothers, that I'd been so determined to make my way back to Georgia in this heroic way. I had been the little runt, the misfit, the scapegoat - the occasional target of older relatives who had a tendency to tease. But now I was back, an adventurous, privileged young hero, seeking righteous recognition of my manhood. I must have been insufferable.

In fact, I *was* insufferable. I still wonder if my Cousin Tom had been bribed to invite me out on a boat ride, to get rid of me for a while. He was a couple of years older, and chronically quiet. I didn't remember much about him from childhood, but I was told we had been playmates. My idea of a boat ride assumed we would be going out on a lake, or a river, but we wound up in the Okmulgee Swamp; a really weird place.

The mirror smooth surface of the black water reflected the dense tangle of vegetation all around us, rendering perfect images of upside down, gnarly Cypress trees with long streaming beards of moss. It was difficult to tell what was solid and what was reflection, and oddly disorienting to see almost exactly the same view in every direction.

We took turns at the hinged paddling device attached to the aft end of the boat, quietly sliding deeper into the watery labyrinth. I had to ask if Tom was sure he knew the way out. He just nodded, his demeanor more like that of a stoic old man than a teenager.

Around mid-afternoon it quickly became much darker. Heavy rain clouds came up and we were suddenly caught in a thunderstorm. Tom pushed hard on the back-and-forth paddle and sent the flat-bottomed boat sliding toward the nearest shore. We pulled the boat out of the water and went looking for shelter, crouching low through the heavy rain. Then, just around a turn in the shoreline, we came upon a couple of boats tied to a crude dock, with a path leading away from the water.

The cabin was so weathered into the landscape it was difficult to see at first. It was perched on thick pole-like stilts, about six feet off the ground. There was one small broken window on the side nearest us, covered from inside with cardboard, and across the front of the cabin was a screened in porch. Tom remained silent as I called out "Hello the house" through the rain. There was no response.

Without hesitation, I began to climb the built-in ladder leading up to a screen door. Tom moved to hunker down under the cabin, out of the rain. I grabbed hold of a handle on the door jamb, climbed up, pushed the screen open and entered at one end of the covered porch. To my right was another doorway, now open, into the interior. As I peered into the dimly lit cabin, I slowly discerned the outline of a large black man seated in a heavy wooden chair, slumped over to one side. He was sitting next to a small, potbellied wood stove. The pale stubble on his head and chin seemed to glow with a light of its own against his dark skin. It was hard to tell, in that first moment, if he was breathing, but then he stirred and mumbled.

"Mister," I called out. "You okay?" He opened his eyes and looked in my direction for a long moment before he actually saw me.

"You better keep down," he muttered. "You're making a damn good target." A chill went through me. Did he have a gun? Then I realized he was still half asleep. He blinked several times, sat up straight and reached for the whiskey bottle on a wooden box next to him. He took a drink and stared at me as though trying to decide if I was really there.

"Welcome to Shangri-la," he finally said, lifting the bottle in salutation.

"We got caught in the rain on our boat," I said, wiping the water from my glasses with my shirt tail. "My cousin's down below."

"I have a few relatives down there myself," he chuckled, revealing a lot of white teeth. I didn't get his reference to the underworld right away because I was so surprised at how much his cultured voice, with its perfect diction and no Southern accent, didn't go at all with his appearance. I had never heard a black man talk that way, especially one wearing worn out overalls and a faded plaid shirt.

As my eyes became more accustomed to the dim light, I looked around. The stove and heavy wooden chair were at the center of a cluttered cave. There were tools and boxes, a jumble of odds and ends on a crude kitchen washboard, and, in one corner a bookcase filled with numerous volumes.

"Would you care to partake?" He tipped the whiskey bottle in my direction.

"Sure," I responded, with youthful bravado. He let out a mildly surprised grunt and handed me the bottle. I boldly took a gulp of the harsh bourbon and shuddered all the way down to my toes. He motioned me toward a crude wooden stool next to the stove, across from his chair. After I sat down, he tipped his chair back at what seemed to me an awfully precarious angle, and, in spite of his drunken state, carefully looked me over.

"You're not from around here," he said, with only the slightest hint of a slur. I had automatically leaned forward, ready to grab his chair if it actually did start to tip over.

"I'm from California," I said, wondering how he knew. "Visiting relatives for a while." I started to call out to Tom, but changed my mind.

"You don't sound like you're from around here yourself," I continued. Some animal part of me warned that his casual manner could be deceptive. In spite of my inexperience, I had gained some sharpening of my wits while on the road. In Illinois, I had ducked and spun around just in time to see a man quickly raise his blackjack again. I made a quicker escape.

"I was gone for quite a while," the black men said. He was looking at me as though trying to make up his mind about something.

"Where to?" I asked. He brought his chair forward with a thud. I jerked back. He stood up and stretched his arm to reach something on the wall. He handed me a framed photograph. Six young and proud black men, in U.S. Army uniforms, stood smiling into the camera. He was among them, and looked to be the oldest.

"I was in Europe," he said. "Killing Germans." There was anger in his voice, old and tired anger. "Protecting your little white ass," he suddenly added, in a harsh tone. Although his anger was directed at me, I somehow understood it wasn't about me personally. Even so, I was afraid. He was an awfully big man. But he quickly slumped back into his chair, becoming smaller, less threatening.

"I'm sorry, Kid," he sighed. He took a short pull from the bottle and sat quietly for a moment. Then, as though he had decided it was okay to tell me his story, he opened up.

"Sure, I was excited to go overseas, until they stuck my ass right up on the front line, in the middle of hell, along with my friends there." He nodded toward the photograph. "And now I'm the only one left." It was apparent he blamed himself. I could feel the weight of his remorse. But, at the same time, although struggling to keep my bearings, my composure, I was quite excited by this encounter. What a story I would have to tell. On impulse I asked him an obvious question.

"But why did you come back here?" He took his time answering.

"I thought I had something to prove," he said. He was quiet again. There was only the sound of the rain on the cabin roof. His answer echoed in my mind.

"When they found out I had a knack for languages," he continued. "Hell, I picked up a lot of German and French in no time. They pulled me back from the front for special duty. And I lost contact with my buddies." He paused. His eyes glistened. "And then," he said, with a deep sadness. "When I trained myself to talk like a white man, I lost something else."

At that moment Tom came part way up the ladder.

"C'mon, Rabon," he called. "The rain's beginnin' ta slack off."

"Just a minute," I responded. "In fact, c'mon up."

Tom continued up the ladder and entered the small porch, but his body language made it clear he wasn't coming any further. He was a tall, awkward teenager, with a large frame yet to fill out. And when he spoke, it was an imitation of the older, up-tight white men in his life. He peered into the dim room and shook his head.

"You shouldn't be in there," he said, with adult authority. His face bore such an expression of judgement, and disgust, I was embarrassed for him. It was ugly.

"This is Cousin Tom," I began.

"Yassuh Massuh." The large black man underwent a transformation. "Muh name's Red," he said, with a cockeyed grin. "Red White, an' sometimes ah sangs da Blues. Har Har." The articulate veteran was gone. In his place was this clownish buffoon. Tom stared at the black man without humor and then addressed me.

"Wait'll I tell yer folks," he said, pointing a finger at me. Tom also seemed different. He was vindictive. I wondered what I had ever done to him. Then, just as suddenly as he had disappeared, the articulate veteran was back. He glared at Tom.

"You'll keep your fucking mouth shut, you arrogant little prick," he said, quietly, distinctly. Tom stared in disbelief. White became whiter as the blood drained from his face. He stammered. He clenched his fists. This large, articulate black man was a racist's nightmare. Tom stared, holding his breath, the agony of indecision contorting his young, freckled face. Then, suddenly, he let out an angry cry and bolted out through the screen door. I don't think his feet touched the ladder on his way down. The veteran and I were left facing one another.

"Sorry about that," he said. "But I couldn't resist. If you'd like to take a swing at me, go ahead. I won't stop you."

"No," I replied. "But I better catch up to him."

As we parted company, the black man and I slowly shook hands. There was something gentle in his expression at that moment, a kindness of compassion that actually bothered me. I felt as though he knew me, or something about me, and that made me uncomfortable. It seemed to me there was nothing we had in common. But I would review our visit many times on the long Greyhound bus ride back to California, and then, at times in the years to come.

"Don't ever let 'em get-ya down, Boyo," was the last thing he said to me, with a delightful Irish brogue.

OF BULLETS AND BAND-AIDS

Boys will be boys - but what does that mean? Judging from many of my boyhood memories, it means that boys will be freaking idiots. I'm surprised more of us didn't get killed. It seems to me there must be guardian angels who follow ignorance around and hand out a large number of beginner's passes. But once you've exceeded the limits of first-time privilege, danger increases. The guys I hung out with in high school devoted a lot of time to figuring out the next most dangerous thing to do. Even when danger was not intended, we still had a knack for finding it.

My pal Buster and I were out crusting one Friday night when we met up with this red headed guy named Jerry, whom we knew from school and who had two fifths of Jack Daniels he'd taken from his dad's liquor cabinet. With all due respect for the Law, we took our drinking out of town. We drove all the way out to Sam Taylor Park, where we could drink and howl and urinate our way through the Redwood Forest.

Then, with our bolstered manhood aroused, we wound up driving toward Tomales Bay on Highway One looking for where the Portuguese sisters lived. They were especially good looking, and, living so far away from school, were something of a mystery. We just figured that sexy looking high school girls who live in the country must get lonely. We stopped at a pay phone in Point Reyes and Jerry gave them a call. He was in a class with Eileen, the older sister, about whom he had raved a few times before. She said we could come on up, but that we should be quiet about it.

We were in Buster's '39 Ford Coupe. Jerry sat in the middle. Every time he handed the bottle to me or to Buster, he'd take a drink himself, which meant he was drinking twice as much as we were. I was impressed with how well he could hold it.

"It's a dirt road," said Jerry. "Goes up a hill past this huge old building." The building he mentioned was the abandoned Marconi Hotel, a remnant of the historic Marconi Wireless Receiving Station near Marshall. The father of the Portuguese sisters apparently lived on the property as a caretaker.

"There it is." Buster saw the road ahead and turned without slowing down. We hit the rough dirt and started bouncing. Jerry let out a stream of curses as the whiskey bottle jumped out of his hand and Buster joined in as Jack Daniels splashed over his right foot. The car stopped. Buster tried to squeeze out his sock while Jerry and I took a leak.

Up the hill, a little beyond and to the left of the impressive old building, were two smaller buildings. The only light on the property came from the porch of one of these. "Whiskey Foot," Jerry and I climbed back into the coupe and continued on up the rough road passed the deep shadows of the empty three-story structure.

Eileen was on the porch waiting for us. She was barely sixteen, had a grown woman's gorgeous body and delivered a smile that said "what are you waiting for" and "don't you dare" at the same time. She wore a flimsy blue house dress and looked delicious under the dim porch light.

All of a sudden Jerry seemed really drunk, more than he had been a few minutes before. Maybe all the alcohol he had consumed was just hitting him, or maybe he was just showing off.

"Hey babe," Jerry called. He struggled out of the car past me and stumbled up the porch steps to slip an arm around Eileen's waist. He hadn't seen the way she put a finger to her lips and warned him to be quiet. She gracefully side-stepped his arm and took his hand. She wasn't being unfriendly, just making it clear that she would decide who put his arm around her waist.

"Hi, I'm Eileen," she said to Buster and me, keeping her voice barely above a whisper. "You guys need to be quiet."

"I'm Ray," I softly responded. "And this is my pal, Whiskey Foot. Is someone asleep?" Buster looked embarrassed and lightly slugged my shoulder.

"Yeah, my father," she continued. "He's passed out in the kitchen. You don't want to wake him." She paused, looked us both over and said: "Maybe we could all go over to the big haunted house." Something in her voice filled me with carnal excitement. I'd seen her around, but this was my first chance to admire her up close.

At that moment Anna stepped quietly out on to the porch. She was a petite version of her sister and just as attractive. Unfortunately, Jerry re-focused his passion onto her and we weren't close enough to grab him. With another "Hey babe" he drunkenly closed in on the pretty young girl and tried to embrace her. She immediately brought her knee up into Jerry's groin. He let out a loud "Jesus Christ" and staggered into the wall by the front door, still cursing. Then, without warning, the barrel of a rifle slipped out from behind the screen door and jabbed him in the ribs.

"You loud mouth sonva bitch," said a gravelly voice. "Waddaya doin out here wit my dottas?" Jerry was still trying to catch his breath as he backed across the porch. He was drunk, but he wasn't crazy enough to argue with a man who had a rifle leveled at him. Without a word or hesitation, Buster and I helped Jerry back into the car and were soon bouncing back down the dirt road to Highway One. Buster and I mercilessly picked on Jerry until he passed out.

*   *   *

I didn't see them again until school the following Monday. We gathered at lunch time under the trees in the big dirt parking lot. Jerry and I simultaneously noticed the three band-aids stuck onto the trunk of

Buster's Ford Coupe. They were in stark contrast to the pretty blue paint job.

"What's this?" I asked, pulling aside one of the band-aids. There was a small bullet hole underneath. The Portuguese sisters' father had apparently stood on his porch firing his rifle at the car as we drove down the hill. The dirt road had a switch-back which had brought us closer to the house again, but a little way downhill. He must have been drunker than we were. Even with a 22 caliber he could have killed someone, or possibly have blown up the car. Lucky for us he didn't use a more powerful rifle.

"Jesus Christ," exclaimed Jerry. "I damned near got us all killed." I felt that he was a lot more excited about it than he was sorry. I was just grateful that we hadn't been caught later on with the girls in the old hotel. Buster's usual easy-going attitude and wide grin were noticeably absent. He looked worried. His worst nightmare would be answering to any authority, especially his parents, about the bullet holes.

"I need you guys to help me quietly get my car into auto shop after school," he said. "I gotta patch it up." The three of us stood silently staring at the band-aids for a long moment. Then, all at once, we were overcome by fits of uncontrollable laughter.

SANDRA

I type her name in the search bar while I'm on the internet now and then. I see that along with her work in the San Francisco Mime Troop, she also acted in two films. And I read the praises written by Peter Coyote, a writer who responded profusely to her beauty and talent. His mention of her as a genius of an actress warms my heart. I dearly remember the lovely fourteen-year-old who quietly mused about her acting ambition as we sat on the lawn in front of San Rafael High School.

Even then, the quality and depth of her beauty was an obvious forecaster of things to come. I remember our drama teacher, a tall, balding man with the unlikely name of "John King," who one day mused aloud about what he called her "dark beauty." I automatically assumed he was referring to her Mediterranean skin tone, but perhaps he also saw something deeper.

I wish I could remember her face more clearly. I've tried to locate a photo of her on the internet, but none are available. I do remember the large and liquid midnight eyes, and the soft olive skin. I do remember the small, gentle hands I loved to hold now and then. I do remember the shapely, graceful body of a girl-child becoming a woman. One minute she would have the giggling demeanor of a child playing jacks, the next she would raise her head and cast a bewitching glance with all the impact of Aphrodite.

Did I love her? The obvious answer would be yes. But that's not nearly enough of an answer. Over those high school years, I both grew up with her and painfully apart from her. Sometimes I felt like a man with a Ford bank account staring in the window at a Ferrari. I was the odd-ball friend who shared more with her than most, but I was never exactly a boyfriend.

Although we came close to some kind of consummation parked at night in the hills near San Rafael, some idealistic, chivalrous part of me managed to interfere and keep her unattainable, on a pedestal. I later cursed that part of me as pretty stupid, but I also knew all along that the real value of our relationship was a different and somehow deeper kind of sharing.

I don't recall she ever went "steady" for any length of time with anyone. Although she was sought after, it was more as though she was a shared ideal, more than any one boy could deserve. But it was me with whom she dreamt aloud of a future wherein I would write and direct and she would star in our movies.

My most treasured memory is the moonlit night I drove us down to Golden Gate Park from Santa Venetia. I introduced her to Shakespeare's Garden, a small area off to the side of the Natural History Museum that I'd discovered, where a bust of that legendary playwright stood in a little stone alcove. Then, we laughed and played as we made our way through the dark pedestrian tunnel under the roadway and on to the central grove next to the classical bandstand.

We danced in the moonlight among the Greco-Roman columns of that large and elegant structure, humming and waltzing and whirling in the magical world bubble of teenage imagination. It's hard to believe there ever was such a time, when a couple of kids could drive into Golden Gate Park late at night and enjoy such enchantment, in a private and safe cocoon.

In spite of all that romantic wonder, our relationship remained platonic. There was an unspoken boundary from that first night I'd hesitated, a little too long, in a parked car. Some years later, in a class at Sonoma State, I would learn more about the "invention" of romantic love in the Middle Ages. Chivalrous love was usually indulged at a distance and always required an obstacle. Romeo and Juliet, Lancelot and Guinevere, such examples of forbidden romance can only hint at the tension I willingly harbored because of Sandra Archer.

Her family moved to San Francisco shortly after she graduated high school. The last time I saw her I was attending Marin Junior College, taking theater arts of course, and she was becoming involved with the little theater scene around San Francisco. At some point I invited her to a nighttime beach party in Marin County with some of the students I'd met at the JC. Her beauty and intelligence were just as impressive as I had hoped. I was so proud to be seen with her.

I don't remember all we talked about on our way back to the city. After we parked across the street from her parent's house, where she still lived, we sat in silence for a while. It was a comfortable silence. Now, all these years later, I wonder if some part of us might have known that night would be the last time we'd see one another. That was around 1955.

Now, in mid-February of 2007, I sit with the scant leads resulting from my internet detective work. I've learned there's a man living in Sebastopol to whom she was once married. I have his name and phone number, but I can't bring myself to construct a call. Two films she acted in, "Funny Man" 1967, and, "Hacer Que?"1970, are apparently not available.

Finally, I can only say this: "Dear Sandra, even though I would love to sit and talk about our lives and what we've learned over the years, there's a part of me that just wants to keep you as that pure and beautiful fourteen-year-old I once knew and loved so deeply."

* * *

A few years later (2010) I was surprised by an article in the SF Chronicle that informed me of her death, due to cancer, and much more information about her life. But it wasn't until recently, as I was reviewing files for this book, that I saw her in a documentary about the

SF Mime Troop, a further video of her memorial, and even the movie "Funny Man" in which she appeared. When I learned of her work as a high school drama teacher, I was so proud she had followed her heart in that direction. Her dedication to youth and theater gave me a sense of shared spiritual intimacy, which amplified memories of our shared high school experience.

And then, by what I can only consider an act that was destined to be, I managed to get the very last 1973 Press Photo of her from Columbia, in Chicago: "Sandra Archer is a creator of Magic. The two-week workshop offered by the Columbia College Theater Center. Photo measures 10 x 8 in."

On the center back of the photo is a faded short article about Sandra's youth workshop; and, in the lower right-hand corner, she had written her name, address and phone number at that time in San Francisco.

Thank you, Sandra, I finally got the message.

THE LAST CRANE

I had a number of jobs during and after high school. Mid-fifties America was booming and jobs were easy to find. During high school I had summer jobs like construction labor and a season with the California State Forestry, Firefighting Service, stationed near Booneville (a true gift to the maturing process of 16-year-old boys).

After high school, during a period of attendance at Marin Junior College, in Kentfield, I worked for a company making fiberglass luggage (all the rage) and then in a candle factory that filled my senses (all night long) with the delicious flavors of perfumed candle wax.

My next job, working for Northwestern Pacific Railroad, at the Tiburon freight yard down by the bay, was wonderfully historic. Next to where tourists now load onto ferry boats for Angel Island, there was once a rail connection for huge industrial barges, with sections of track on them, that hauled freight cars across the bay.

Much of Tiburon's yard operation was devoted to diesel engines and locomotive maintenance; but, on the far side, away from the bay and against the hill, was a string of buildings known as "Stores." I don't remember the exact year, but it wasn't long before NWP and the Tiburon freight yard would shut down forever. As I understood it, they were a victim of rising real estate values and Southern Pacific's greater growth and power.

After I had been hired to work in Stores, an old Swedish guy with an abnormally broad right shoulder (from many years of right-handed labor) took me aside to give me the real lowdown. The first thing I had to learn was to set aside at least a half hour of work, to make a good impression in case the guys in suits from on high showed up.

My favorite set-aside was to wheel empty fifty-gallon drums up and down the wooden platform on a hand truck. Next, just in case there wasn't a convincing half hour of work to be found, I had to locate a really good place to hide. And, if you were dumb enough to ask, there was always bagging coal, a really dirty job, supplying what little need still existed for burning coal. Nevertheless, although business for NWP was rapidly declining, an occasional freight car would be set on our siding to be loaded or unloaded.

One morning I joined about a half dozen men who were standing around on the platform next to an open boxcar. The foreman, Louis, was scratching his head and studying the prospect of unloading a long set of heavy metal cabinets from inside the boxcar. Tape measurers were out and a discussion about the size of the cabinet and the size of the sliding boxcar doors went on for a while.

Louis, the foreman, was either utterly stupid or incredibly brilliant. Only an idiot or a genius could have directed six men for three hours to do the work that two men could have done in ten minutes. For the whole three months I worked there, this slightly built gray-haired foreman with an Italian accent remained something of a mystery.

One morning, before the eight o'clock whistle blew, I had an extraordinary run of luck at winning the pre-work pastime; pitching pennies. Only at this time we were pitching nickels. Unfortunately, I didn't know that when Louis was playing, the other guys would usually let him win.

Without malice, as a matter of form, my gambling success was rewarded with a short trip down the tracks to bag coal. But I didn't mind. It was good exercise. And besides, if I hadn't gone down the tracks to the coal shed on that particular morning, I might not have been blessed with a close-up view of that amazing piece of belching, wheezing, fiery antique machinery that had rolled in from somewhere.

It was a sky-high steam powered crane, right out of the Nineteenth Century. I was awe struck. The large open cab, along with the locomotive sized steam engine behind it, both swiveled around on a massive undercarriage to counter-balance the crane's gigantic lift. The operator was a tall skinny man who danced on the foot pedals and pulled the numerous levers with incredible skill. He was an artist.

The huge round electro-magnet at the far end of the cable, powered by an on-board diesel generator, was lowered into a mountain of scrap metal. Many ragged tons were carefully lifted and released into a half car (gondola) he was loading. His control over the awesome power of the magnet, and that huge piece of equipment, was ironically delicate and precise.

I later learned that this steam crane was the very last one of its kind. And the operator, whose name was Jerry, was one of the very last guys who could handle the many controls of that complex monstrosity all by himself.

The next time I saw the crane, there was a great hook on the far end of the cable and Jerry was loading bundles of railroad ties onto a flat car. As I stood there watching the process, with my mouth hanging open, Jerry couldn't help but notice me. He soon brought the operation to an idle and called me over.

"You work here, don't you?" he asked.

"Yeah," I responded. Not sure what was up.

"You think you could do that?" He pointed to where another man had been hooking up the bundles.

"Hell yeah," I exclaimed. Jerry signaled to the other guy and I went out to take his place.

After I had hooked up a couple of bundles and jumped off so that Jerry could swing them over to another guy on the flat car, I hooked one up and stayed on top of it. My unspoken question to Jerry was obvious. I waited. I was aware that he would probably be breaking some railroad regulations to give me a ride, but I was also aware that he knew how much I wanted it. And then, as I heard the engine's increased puffing and the cable tightened, I was lifted into the sky. That thrilling ride, including the high arch of the ride back, as I casually hung onto the thick cable with one gloved hand, and one foot stuck into the great hook, was definitely a high point of the summer.

Over the many years since then, every time I've gone to Tiburon, I get to look over to that long ago place where I once flew.

MARIN MEMORIES

When I was a youngster, Southern Marin County was like a world apart, a full-blown Domain, separate and complete. At its western boundary the impressive shoreline of the Pacific Ocean dramatically carved away at the foothills of a deeply wooded Mount Tamalpais. And the view from that mountain's top was far more pristine than it is now. To the east the sparkling waters of San Francisco Bay reflected the quiet coves of Belvedere-Tiburon and the long wooded hilltop of Angel Island. It was a time when my family could still safely eat the fish we caught in the bay.

From the residential waters of Belvedere and Tiburon to the artful village of Sausalito; from the Redwood hills of Mill Valley and over Mount Tamalpais to the summer-time towns of Stinson Beach and Bolinas - this was the "kingdom" of my youth.

After the Native Americans, who named the mountain and a few other locations, came the Spanish, who left many more names and their cultural Missions in Sonoma and San Rafael. As my Southern Marin kingdom was later settled and connected by ferryboat, it became a master bedroom for San Francisco, protected by wealth and the dominance of its natural beauty.

When I arrived, as a child of nine, Southern Marin was still quite rural and well defined. The shipyard (Marinship) just north of Sausalito would soon shut down and the Second World War would soon be over. But the natural beauty of Marin would stick in the minds of many who were passing through, as it did with my serviceman step-father when he was stationed at Hamilton Field in Northern Marin. He brought his brand-new family back to Marin County from Georgia in 1944.

* * *

There were still secret places in that rural setting where it seemed to me nothing but the moccasins of Native Americans had ever set foot. During that first year, when I walked to school from Tiburon Wye, a couple of miles east of Mill Valley, I discovered a short-cut through a small wooded area that still seemed to whisper the misty breath of a long-ago primordial age. There was "something" there for me, something that stirred a vague, dream-like memory and a deep longing.

As I snuggled into my secret resting place among the tall ferns, my school books and lunch bag at my feet, I tingled with an awesome feeling - a strangely powerful sense of belonging. My personal security was somehow linked to the ancient permanence around me. I felt more at home in that little grove of trees than in the comfort of my own bed. For the first time in my short and tumultuous existence, I had made a confident connection with the grand, sweet mystery of my own being.

I was enraged when my parents told me we were moving again. I had suffered so many moves in those early years. I went to my secret place with a determination to stay there, to hide there, but eventually my courage gave way to pangs of hunger and I went home. The move was just up the county to San Rafael, where my step-father worked, but to me it meant another new school with yet another new world of difficult adjustments.

* * *

It would be quite a while before I re-discovered the sacred land of Southern Marin. As a student in San Rafael High School my first automobile hardly ever came to rest. I would wait for my family to go to sleep so I could sneak out to drive around all night. I got into trouble for nodding off in class, but those midnight journeys, alone in my car on deep night deserted roads, were adventures of discovery well worth the hassle. There wasn't a back road in all of Marin County where my wheels didn't roll.

Sometimes I would get lost in the hills of Mill Valley or drive to the top of Mount Tam and see the whole bay area at my feet. Sometimes I would drive down to the Golden Gate Bridge, at dawn, to walk out on the span and watch departing fishing boats leave curly wake patterns drifting across the calm water - a delicately artful web I still hold in the memory of a breathless moment.

One morning, when I returned to where I had parked, on the Sausalito side of the bridge, there were two highway patrol officers looking at the road flares on the inside rear window ledge of my coupe. When I told them what I was up to, they granted that I obviously couldn't blow up the bridge with road flares, smiled and drove off without asking for any identification. That would be in late 1952.

*   *   *

By the time I moved there on my own, Sausalito was still in a post-war cultural transition. After the shipyard shut down and many of its workers had gone, a deep sigh of peace filled the land. Then, gradually, the authenticity of several local artists and the influence of a Bohemian houseboat community (along with the resurgence of 1930's folk music) evolved into an even broader non-conformist subculture. The antithesis of that counterculture was represented by an ever-increasing volume of tract home developments for nuclear families, with modern appliances and a newly emerging army in grey flannel suits.

*   *   *

Business was good; America was booming. The great wartime machine that had out-produced every nation on earth was now focused on transforming its output into the latest and most innovative material desires for a vast new American market. But the similarity between tract home development, mass produced products and the people who bought them seemed to some of us to represent a growing trend toward an equally mass-produced mentality.

There was a nagging cultural hunger prowling through our population of rebellious, dissatisfied youth - amorphous, persistent, hinting at something better, it told of different times, richer and more fulfilling times, when a depth of culture had carried everyone to a higher plane of existence. I learned to play chess, listened to Mahler and Mozart, read Nietzsche and Schopenhauer, although my limited experience didn't offer much of a hook upon which to hang European philosophy.

I learned that the Greeks of ancient times had looked back to even more ancient times, to what they called a "Golden Age," when greater human beings had done greater things. For those of us in Sausalito, looking out beyond our cultural comfort zone, bordered by Corte Madera to the north and the Golden Gate Bridge to the south, there seemed to be a vast movement in America that wanted all of us not only to look alike, and live alike, but most of all to think alike.

And so, we reacted with our beloved non-conformity, with our books and berets, our jargon and our jazz. Like the ancient Greeks we looked to a time we thought must have been better, although we didn't quite know exactly when, or where. What we dreamt was more like a cultural essence, an idea, a Great Waltz of the mind - the vague memory of a way of being that no one could even be sure had ever existed. Perhaps all the great cultures we'd ever heard about were only reflections of another time that never was.

But by whatever we were doing, and the environment in which we were doing it, we soon became an oddity to those we regarded as outsiders. I remember one particular Sunday afternoon, walking with a small group of friends along Bridgeway (Sausalito's main street) when there were suddenly too many cars in town. We thought maybe there had been an accident up ahead. But no, it was the beginning of tourism in our beloved Sausalito. And the following weekend, it was even worse.

After Herb Caen gave us the name, "Beatniks," we became something of a tourist attraction. From Sausalito to North Beach in San Francisco, there was a time and place to enjoy classical music, engage in meaningful discussion, play chess and watch the tourists watching us. But with the coming of the so-called "Hippies," a different breed was moving into our former territory. The quiet depth of life we had borrowed from Bohemian culture was replaced by "rock and roll," both in music and in behavior. By the time I left town, in 1964, the focus of counterculture had moved to the "Haight" in San Francisco. Some of us followed the flower children, but others of us were turned off by what we saw, as it seemed in its own way just as brainlessly banal as the conformity we had earlier resisted.

*   *   *

I guess in a way it's all still there, beneath the slow-moving layers of history, for those who come to enjoy the atmosphere and buy into a piece of the myth. But for those of us who saw the old bait shop on a tumbled down pier in the middle of town, and knew everyone we saw on the street, Sausalito was something else. Then, at some point during those early years, in one mysterious unrecognized instant, that which was becoming, became, and was past. Myth embellished memory, and so remained - a lasting banner to be draped from the walls for another generation of tourists to see.

THE VISIT

The magical route I once drove no longer exists in the way I knew it then - across the Golden Gate Bridge, out along 19th Avenue to the turnoff a little beyond San Francisco State, out to the ocean and then south on Highway One, past Devil's Slide to Half Moon Bay, past the far reaching luminous arms of the lighthouse at Pigeon Point, waving like an old friend gathering lonely travelers halfway through the night, on down to Santa Cruz, around the bay past Fort Ord and Seaside to Monterey, beyond Pacific Grove, New Monterey, Carmel and Carmel Valley, on to the raw beauty of Big Sur, with Palo Colorado Canyon, Nepenthe, Murphy's Hot Springs and up the many dirt road mysteries along the way.

With youthful optimism, always ready for the next adventure, I traveled this route back and forth many times. Some of my peers were of the same nomadic inspiration, wandering and wondering, as I did, if perhaps there might not be a more exciting, fulfilling world somewhere along this magical route. And so, we journeyed, from Sausalito, North Beach and Mill Valley, all that way down that magical drive to Big Sur. And somehow, we knew we were still in the same neighborhood, living makeshift in one another's lives, renting our way to higher ground, boys and girls in playland. It seems amazing that more of us didn't suffer the ravages of VD, although, most of us came from the disinfected world of middle America in the mid nineteen fifties.

We also came from the Judeo-Christian values of that world, which seemed to us more like a prison than a way of life. We resented what little we knew of ourselves and our heritage. We only wanted to escape into the future, into the unknown, on to a clean slate, to a tabula rasa upon which we could write our own destiny. And so, we experimented with everything in our reach; words, ideas, poetry, politics, drugs and relationships. We danced on the edge of excitement and mystery, looking for our own kind of meaning in what seemed to us a meaningless, materialistic world.

*   *   *

I hadn't seen Ron or David since they had ventured down to Big Sur a few months before. All I had were directions to a property at the upper end of Palo Colorado Canyon. One of the great advantages of those years (the late fifties/early sixties) was the availability of living space. There were still older homes for rent on the edges of rural communities, affordable historicals where young nomads could land for a while.

The situation Ron and David had moved into was fairly common to roving young men at that time. Looking back, the failed marriages and loose sexual alliances between young people were at the least careless, if not immoral. One result was a large number of young women with small children, women too young to "settle down" and too inexperienced to make the best possible choices for themselves and their children. I don't know how it may be for that same segment of the population today, but back then many of these women were easy targets for those loose young buckoes who were looking for love with built-in temporary housing. Such was the situation my friends had found in a large old rural house located in a beautiful setting high up a canyon in Big Sur.

I pulled off the road just south of Carmel Valley and looked again at the letter I'd received from Ron some weeks before. After refreshing my mind with complicated directions up the appropriate dirt roads,

I resumed my journey. Strange to remember a time before cell phones and e-mail, when not even everyone had what is now called a "land line." Our communications then depended a lot on word of mouth, on news of our friends passed from person to person.

*   *   *

It was a warm and beautiful summer morning. The great expanse of ocean to my right was in a softly sparkling, gentle mode. As my car climbed up from the Redwoods along the floor of the canyon near the ocean, I remembered to take the right fork a little beyond the hard left curve. I slowed to negotiate the deep ruts and hollows of the dirt road and eventually came to a shady grove of oak trees. There were a few dusty vehicles parked under the trees. As I stopped and climbed out of my old Chevy, I noticed an odor of dust in the air and one of the vehicles was making the crackling, cooling sounds of its recent arrived.

To my left was a steep downward path beyond which I could see a large wooden deck. As I made my way down the path, beneath low-lying oak limbs, I thought I could hear voices. As I stepped onto the deck, I noted a large rustic house tucked into the hillside to my right. From the deck one could see past the steep forest all the way to the Pacific. It was a wildly beautiful, impressive view.

Ron and David were standing in the wide front doorway with their backs toward me. And, although I didn't recognize their back sides right away, I did recognize Ron's voice.

"Just tell me the truth, Darlene," he implored. "Look me in the eye and tell me you want me to go." There were other voices from inside, but I couldn't distinguish what was being said. Regardless, the aura of tension was unmistakable.

Suddenly a young woman pushed her way between my two friends and took Ron's arm. As they walked away from the door, Ron acknowledged my presence with a somewhat bewildered glance and a nod, but continued across the large deck with the young woman. At that moment another young man, wearing a brightly colored head band, appeared in the doorway and watched the couple walking away. Then he and David began sizing one another up like two mongrels circling on the sidewalk. This seemed like a good time for me to intervene.

"Hey David," I loudly announced my presence. "What's happening?" I could tell from his expression he hadn't noticed me until that moment. As he came across the deck toward me, another couple appeared in the wide doorway. Neither the attractive young blonde woman nor the tall skinny guy beside her were familiar to me. My friend David put his arm across my shoulders and I could feel the weight of his tension. His dark eyes moved quickly from Ron and the girl at the far edge of the deck and back to the trio now standing in the doorway. Across the deck, in an enclosed yard next to the house, three small children were quietly playing.

David leaned close and began speaking in a low, hurried tone.

"Ron and I just got here," he said. "We were in jail until this morning. Served twenty days for shoplifting groceries in Monterey."

"That was pretty stupid," I interrupted.

"Which," he responded, with a slight smile. "Shoplifting or getting caught?"

"Both," I replied, and I meant it.

"Anyway," he continued. "We had been living here with Sandy and Darlene, but when we got back a little while ago, we found these other two guys staying here. Damn it, we still got all our stuff in the house."

At this point the trio in the doorway were moving further out onto the deck and Ron, with his arm around the slender red headed girl named Darlene, was steering her back toward them. Sandy, David's former girlfriend, was looking toward him with tears in her eyes. David squeezed my shoulder and then moved toward her and the group, now forming in the middle of the deck. I stayed planted where I was.

I will always remember the image of the two young women and four young men as they milled about on the large wooden deck in that beautiful forest setting. But more, I will remember the powerful undercurrents moving through and around them. On the one hand, just beneath the surface, were the raw primal elements of dominance and territory, violence and sexuality, an ancient mode of being where women were to be won in battle. On the other hand were the intellectual, non-violent claims of the growing subculture to which we all belonged. After all, we were the leading edge of a movement that would soon become known for its message of peace and love.

It occurred to me to leave at that point, but the conflict involving my friends was still unresolved and I felt the need to be on hand, just in case. Then, at the very same instant I had decided to interject and introduce myself to everyone, Ron broke away from the group and came over to me.

"Hi Ray," he said. "Sorry we're in the middle of this up-tight situation. Did David tell you what happened?"

"Yeah, you poor criminal," I smiled. "What can I do here, crack some skulls?" I knew David could take care of himself in a fight, but I also knew that Ron, gentle poet and scholar, abhorred violence. Nevertheless, looking at the expression on his delicately handsome face right now, I imagined he might even surprise himself.

"Just please stick around," he said. "We're going inside to work this out."

As the group of six went into the house, I wandered across the deck toward where the three toddlers were playing. I was impressed by how quietly occupied they had been during all that was going on. As I approached the small gate to the play yard, the little huddle of two girls and one boy separated. It was then I noticed the little boy, probably around four years old, was holding something in both hands.

At first I thought it was a realistic looking toy, but as I came closer, the object appeared more like what it actually was, a 32 caliber, stub nosed revolver. I'm sure that every hair on my body stood straight out. A rapid succession of worse case scenarios flashed through my mind.

"Hey buddy," I said, keeping my voice as soft and calm as I could. "Mind if I take a look at your...toy?" It was then I could tell it was loaded. The little boy clutched the 32 to his chest, with an expression that clearly said "Mine." Oh my God, I thought, what do I do now? I kneeled down on my side of the two-foot-high wire fence and gently extended my hand.

"Oh, pretty please," I cried, making myself as small and unthreatening as possible. "I'll give it right back."

It was with profound relief that I accepted the weapon and then tried to explain it to the child. But he wasn't having any. I had taken his toy and he wanted it back. There was nothing I could do as he began crying, with gusto. Almost immediately the small, attractive blonde girl named Sandy came out a side door and into the yard. Her expression was angry.

"What the hell's going on," she demanded, in a voice that was larger than she was. I stood up as she came toward me.

"The little boy was playing with a loaded pistol," I said. "Do you know who it belongs to?" I held the weapon out before her. It took a moment for this information to sink in. Then her face went pale and I thought she might faint. She kneeled down to hug the crying little boy and looked up at me with an expression somewhere between shock and gratitude.

"Will you please come back inside with me," she said. Her voice was now soft and shaken.

"You bet I will," was my response. I was almost certain the weapon didn't belong to Ron or David. And it was clear to me from Sandy's response that neither she nor Darlene owned it. That left the new boys in town. I held the pistol carefully, without placing a finger through the trigger guard.

Sandy was still holding her little boy. She went to Darlene and whispered something in her ear. Darlene let out a sharp gasp as her two little girls climbed up into her lap. Everyone was seated, I remained standing. I held the pistol out in plain sight.

"Who wants to take responsibility for this?" I asked, in my most dramatic tone. "Who wants to take responsibility for endangering the lives of these kids?" The room remained silent. Looking at them now, folded into a large fluffy couch, the presence of the two young male strangers seemed diminished.

"Alright then," I continued. "I'll take it with me." As I carefully slipped the pistol into my pocket, I could see the jaw muscles of the young man wearing the head band tightening, but he said nothing.

"Ron, David," I concluded. "When you guys get things sorted out, I'll be up in my car."

I had an urge to drive away, but then preferred the responsibility of my friendship with Ron and David. After a while I heard the sound of Bill Haley and his Comets coming from the old house. As I got out of my car and looked down the embankment, the whole gang came out onto the large deck.

After profound and painful peace and love negotiations, the girls had decided to reinstate Ron and David's residence if they wanted it. The other two nomads had apparently only been there a couple of days and relinquished their "squatters" rights without objection.

I went down to join the parting of ways and awkward pretense of no hard feelings. The tough guy with the head band held out his hand as I emptied the little revolver, put the shells in my pocket, and handed it to him.

PARTY TIME

I'm sure that more than a few of us have experienced the power of party time - that high flying, altered state usually brought on by a special occasion (a wedding, a birthday, or New Year's Eve) and liberal doses of some social lubricant or other, usually alcohol. My saturated party time got launched in high school and lasted until the day I died, many years later, and was born again into grateful sobriety. For the majority of us who drank too much, the heavy-duty party time of dangerous overindulgence was a phase, in high school or college, which tapered off as we grew older. But, for others of us, the party was never over. The following story is about one of what I later identified as 'binge parties,' an ongoing high time that could last for days.

*   *   *

It all started in Elie's closet. Her mom had passed away a few months before and Elie had brought home a huge box of the clothes she remembered her mom wearing when Elie was a child.

"Look at this bonnet," she laughed, pulling out a hat that looked more like a flowerpot in full bloom. She had not talked much about her mother's death since it happened, but we all knew it had been doubly devastating for her. Her laughter and sharing now were a welcome relief. As Elie and Trudy dug deeper into the large box of vintage clothing, I went into the kitchen, opened another beer and joined my friend Dean on the back porch.

Trudy and Dean were a young couple I had known and partied with for a while. They were intelligent and fun loving, in a cultured and subtly humorous way that had drawn me to them immediately. Elie, quite a bit older, had a house near Mill Valley, loved to drink her troubles away and surrounded herself with lots of company. She had suffered two great losses in the past year. First, her beloved husband, Joey, had been swept overboard from a fishing boat in a storm at sea, and then, her mother had passed away.

"Hey, you guys, look at this," Trudy announced as she stepped through the kitchen door onto the back porch. As Dean and I turned around, she made a slight bow and extended her arms back toward the door in a dramatic pose. Trudy was petite, blonde and pretty, with a theatrical flair that served her well. "Ta Dah," she continued, with appropriate emphasis. "May I present the one, the only, Lavinia T. Buggers."

As Elie stepped through the door, we all melted into cascades of laughter, as much for the ridiculous name Trudy had made up as for Elie's appearance. Her costume was a mismatch of styles and colors, which included the flowerpot bonnet, an odd pair of high button shoes and a fox stole wrapped around her neck.

I didn't notice during those early years just how addicted I was, not only to substance, but to the very experience of escape into party time. With alcohol (the great dis-inhibitor) at work, most people were able to do things they wouldn't usually do, with a culturally acceptable excuse that somehow made even the wretchedness of our toxic hangovers into funny stories.

Some of us were so strenuously devoted to party supplies we stayed in, or close to, the kitchen. This was usually where the bottles and cans of alcohol were kept and someone had to make sure we didn't run out. Taking up a collection and making a late-night liquor store run was hard core insurance.

Elie, Dean and Trudy, and a few others besides myself, formed a contingent of heavy drinkers who could be counted on for a good time almost any time. Now, as I look back to the back porch of that little house near Mill Valley, I'm inspired to smile in spite of a veil of painful memories. Regardless of the ignorance and danger we shared, there was a deep, loving bond that struggled to follow us through the eventual disasters of our lives, as we collectively and individually fell apart.

At that moment, however, when Trudy came through the kitchen door and Elie followed in her costume, we were still in the honeymoon phase of our shared addictions. As we continued to practice the existential high art of alcoholic delusion, with a gross appreciation for just how special we thought we were, we proudly indulged in the clever, arcane humor and symbolic language of an exclusive little club in our own fantasy world.

Those of us who managed to show up for the jobs that helped to support our party time were not always available, but we always knew where the party was. And when we showed up with fresh supplies, we were welcomed as heroes. The name Trudy made up, "Lavinia T. Buggers," became a part of our language and that day at Elie's began a Dada period of costume dress-up. Shortly thereafter, with visits to the rich wardrobes of affluent Marin County second-hand stores, we achieved the height of our shared insanity one day at Muir Woods State Park.

Somehow a group of us, drunk out of our minds, in a variety of costumes (ridiculous and sublime), wound up taking a drive over the shoulder of Mount Tam one foggy morning to the parking lot at Muir Woods. There was Dean and Trudy, Elie and myself, as well as Peggy and Laura, a lesbian couple who occasionally joined in our parties.

As we noisily piled out of my 51 Chrysler sedan, with its beautiful midnight blue paint job, white sidewall tires and rear mounted radio areal, we might have been mistaken for some United Nations delegation out for a good time. Dean was dressed in a quasi-military uniform, complete with an officer's shiny brimmed cap and bedecked with braid, ribbons and medals; Trudy was wearing a fringed and sequined flapper's gown from the Roaring Twenties, which fit her perfectly; I had on a worn (but presentable) full dress tuxedo, complete with tails and spats, but topped by a cowboy hat: Elie wore the same vintage outfit from her mother's clothes box; Peggy, a tall and elegant red-head, had found a World War One pilot's outfit, complete with ear flapped leather cap and a beautiful white silk scarf. Her partner, Laura, a gorgeous little brunette, wore a long black gown, slit up one side, with high boots and a black cape. Her face was made up like Vampira. We were indeed an outrageous menagerie.

The events of that day are so memorable because of the paradox in the quality of their lasting impressions. On the one hand, I feel shame for the naked and ugly parts of my past addicted behavior. At the same time, I am fascinated by some aspects of what I witnessed. The behavior of six drunken fools is easy to explain; however, the behavior of three park rangers and a number of tourists is not so easy to explain.

It didn't take long for us to realize we were operating in a protective bubble. It was as though we were invisible. And the more outrageous we became, the more invisible we became. Nobody wanted to deal with us. People would either laugh, look away, or stare straight through us. It was dangerously empowering.

There's probably a name for this phenomenon, but I'm not sure what it is. Unfortunately, it must be related to how people can witness a tragedy, like the woman who was beaten to death in front of a crowd on a New York sidewalk, without interference. In our case I think the aversion was so great that even the park rangers were willing to defer reaction until we actually did disappear. In fact, when we came to the large, burnt out, cavernous Redwood tree trunk in the midst of the park and crowded inside to light up a joint, one elder ranger came by with a few tourists, stared straight at Dean, who raised the lit joint as an inviting salute; but, without a hint of acknowledgement, the ranger casually moved along with his little group of tourists, who also ignored us.

Why am I telling this story? If these memories are so embarrassing, even though I haven't had a drink in many years; why go there? Part of the reason is my inability to deny the mysterious and magical power of the unconscious, no matter how it is accessed. Through the use of alcohol and other substances, my friends and I actually did tap into a reservoir of power and creativity, a wellspring of things mysteriously beautiful and sublimely human. But, as we continued to engage in the juvenile practice of undisciplined, unholy access, without the wisdom of spiritual direction; as we reveled in uncharted territory, where one's soul can easily be hijacked by demons; we learned that such unlimited access always brings the wax wings of one's ambition up against the dazzling heat of one's madness - a necessary and deadly limitation.

We danced barefoot on a knife edge between life and death and didn't seem to suffer a scratch. That was the enticing danger of our shared insanity. However, regardless of the power of party time, eventually Dean would die from an overdose of heroin, Trudy would be found dead in her apartment of undisclosed causes, Elie would die in an alcohol related auto accident, Peggy would commit suicide, and I never knew what happened to Laura.

*   *   *

I have deeply complicated feelings about outliving, for so long, so many of those I loved who died young. But I am nonetheless grateful that I get to hold these memories, ridiculous and sublime, of that long ago morning in Muir Woods.

JOAN

It would be difficult to describe Joan with a few words, as I would attempt to describe others I've known. I hardly even knew her well enough to say she was a friend, and yet, we shared some incredibly intimate moments when our lives touched after many years absent. But that one encounter, unexpected and isolated, was there for those moments and gone. She knew, better than I did, that it could have been no other way.

My earliest memory of her went all the way back to Grammar School, to a time of first awakening. She was ahead of me by only one year, but the distance between the sixth and seventh grades was much greater than the passing of a single summer, especially for a girl who looked like Joan. The full early blossom of her womanhood was all the more striking in that noisy environment of children who looked so much younger.

The most lasting impression I have of her from that time occurred one Saturday morning, on the playground, as our school band prepared to take part in a parade. Tall and blonde, softly beautiful, she already stood out conspicuously from the other children. But on that occasion, the usual loose blouse and plaid skirt had been replaced with a tight and revealing majorette costume.

I was confronted by feelings that I can only now decipher. I was outraged! The parade was just too flimsy an excuse for the school, and her parents, to undress her that way. The strap that supported the bass drum I carried pulled tighter around my neck. Her round womanly thighs and clearly defined breasts were totally out of place beneath the innocent young girl's face. They were a secret best kept for a while. I wanted to protect her – to re-conceal the glorious mystery that was so suddenly, and unforgivably, on public display.

But, being who I was, a misplaced immigrant from the deep South, in my fourth Grammar School, I was too insecure to ever approach her. I watched her from the safety of my private shell. In my fantasy world, however, where boys-will-be-men, Joan Anderson was the main attraction.

Then, suddenly, shortly after the day of the parade, she was no longer in school. Among adults the story was whispered with clucking tongues and juicy concern, but for those of us who didn't read the newspaper, it only gradually trickled down. Joan had apparently received a bit too much attention from Mr. Hofstadter, our paunchy, bald-headed school principal. The resulting scandal had sent him to jail and her to another school. I died inside. I didn't get to see her for a long time thereafter.

Our separate high-schools were miles apart and had a long history of rivalry. The recent war with Germany and Japan had interrupted the football tradition, but it was being revived with an all-American passion. Once again, boys were sent out onto the battlefield while the older men watched from the side-lines. In a world gone peaceful, excited with relief, the high school football games became a county wide focus on better times. The honking color draped car caravans brought community smiles and became a familiar ritual. The Friday night stands at the high school stadium were always packed.

I saw her a couple of times, across the field among the rival cheerleaders. The woman's body and child's face no longer stood apart. She had blended. She was a magic more beautiful than my imagination - a goddess who could only be known to heroes. Indeed, the inter-school gossip mill had it that her boyfriend was not only the football star of Tamalpais High, but also a Senior.

Beneath the bright lights of the stadium, in the chill night air, amid the yelling, whistling, thudding and clapping; I stood by a fence closer to her side of the field and filled my private shell with quiet longing. As I watched her movements, framed in bright color, so much more graceful than the other girls; my sweet agony was strangely resolved - a martyr came to roost. It had to be enough just to see her, if I never saw her again.

*   *   *

I remember the years right after high-school as one long quest for quick and easy fulfillment. I couldn't understand why my ability to create the perfect stage set didn't automatically achieve the feelings I wanted to go with it. Just having a job and a place to live was boring, never enough. I became expert at new beginnings.

But I always returned to Sausalito, time and again, until I finally stayed. The place was a focal point for my generation of searching souls and I didn't want to miss anything. After a while it didn't seem to matter exactly what we were searching for, the quest became one long party that looked for itself. We were the Beat Generation - lean and hungry young puppies who correctly pronounced the names of foreign composers and philosophers. We habituated the bars and coffee-houses that couldn't have existed without us. Behind a mask of existential angst, I searched for dope and picked-up on young ladies, some of whom wore far more sophisticated masks.

Unfortunately, my early discovery of alcohol and drugs set me free. I had lived for so long without social confidence that the shock of being at ease with people, when I got loaded, was like an introduction to reality. For the first time in my horny young existence, I enjoyed a sex life that was the envy of some of my peers; and, for better or worse, I could bullshit in tight circles with mysterious, unkempt wisdom.

In all that time, I'd hardly ever thought of Joan. I heard the name once or twice (if it was the same Joan Anderson) and got the feeling that our circles might over-lap someday, but it was quite a while before I saw her, at a party.

An Era was ending, but the hang-outs were hanging on. The folk-singers didn't quite know they had become passe: the chess-players were pushed off into a corner: the poetry and literature group had grown smaller, but still attracted a fair share from the ever-increasing crowd of impressionable new-comers. And then, certainly, there were those of us who had seen it all and still didn't know very much.

There was no hint of recognition in her eyes, but she was unmistakably a gorgeous older Joan. And still, she was a glowing magic at the far end of the galaxy - out of my league. She was gracefully at ease among an elite group of successful older artists and jazz musicians. I kept an eye on her while I mingled with a more accessible group.

To my surprise it was only a week or so before I saw her again, on a Saturday afternoon in the Old Town Coffeehouse. I was sitting at a crowded table with my usual group of lean and hungry young poets when she walked in the door. She was stunning. She wore a deep lavender dress, snug, with sheer stockings and high-heels. Every eye in the room, male and female, followed her to the women's room.

There was an attempt to continue our conversation, but we all kept glancing toward the door that had closed behind her. When she re-appeared and headed straight for our table, I felt myself slipping into shock. We stared up at her - an odd-ball assortment of leering young stallions. She met every leer with a sweet knowing smile and then laid her hand on MY shoulder.

"Well, are you ready to go," she said, in a soft voice that sounded as smooth as she looked. Dismayed as I was, I take pride in my quick recovery. By the time I stood up, I could act as though I was in control.

"Sure," I said, slipping my arm around her waist and leading her toward the front door. My backward glance at the table I'd been sitting at revealed some priceless expressions.

We paused on the steps of the coffeehouse and looked toward the bay, less than a block away. The afternoon was grey and gusty. Across the street, where several cars were parked, the windshield wipers had been left on in a late-model Buick and my VW Bug had its headlights on.

We regarded the scene, looked at each other with the same question, and broke into laughter. They were our cars. To this day I wonder how such a "coincidence" could have happened. Did Joan leave her wipers going on purpose? Had she seen me driving the VW? I never asked her. Anyway, it was a fun and magical beginning.

After she had turned off the windshield wipers, collected her coat and a large leather bag, we got into my VW and drove up-hill. The high back-streets held little traffic and gave up some wonderful views of the bay. Our windows were open to occasional puffs of wind. Long strands of golden hair danced around her softly glowing profile. I could hardly believe it! The unreachable Joan Anderson, the girl of my dreams, was riding next to me; at her own request. She was at ease, comfortable in a trusting way that made me feel confident. I thought about a majorette costume that might have been almost the color of her dress.

I drove the steeply manicured residential streets until we reached Waldo Grade and then turned onto Highway 101. She looked back, and down, at the flecks of white sail on the bay.

"That's really something," she said. "Thanks, Ray. I never knew there was such a beautiful back way out of Sausalito." I glanced at her, still amazed that she was there.

"Back roads are a hobby of mine," I said. "How do you know my name?" She responded with a special smile that I would never forget.

"I asked someone at that party the other night," she said. "You were staring at me, remember?" I nodded, but I had hoped she would remember a long time ago.

She was quiet as I took the Mill Valley exit, but then, as I rounded the curve toward Tam Junction, she answered an un-spoken question as though I'd spoken it.

"I did have a date in the city," she said. "But maybe I can break it." She paused, watching me closely. "God knows I could use the money." She laughed. "But I could also use some time on my own." I said nothing.

When I pulled over to the public phone booth at Tam Junction and dug into my pocket for some change, she accepted the coins without a word and got out to make her call. The implication about her prostitution did bother me, but I was riding too high to let it bring me down. Maybe, I thought, it was for the best.

"All settled," she said, getting back into the car. "They can get someone else." I hesitated before starting the car again. Her boldness back at the coffeehouse had been impressive and thrilling, but I was accustomed to taking the initiative.

"Why did you pick me?" I asked. But the question didn't come out right, it sounded more like a challenge. I hoped I hadn't damaged our bubble. Her steady blue eyes, all the brighter through her expert make-up job, didn't waver from mine.

"You weren't the only one looking around at that party," she said. Her soft honey voice made me feel warm. "I like the way you move when you dance," she said. "And your gentle way with people." She paused. "You're like an iron butterfly."

Damn! She really got me. My face must have been bright red when I quickly looked down to the ignition and started the car. With a throaty laugh she leaned over to lightly kiss my cheek.

"I'm certainly not after your money," she said. "Anyway, sex between us would probably ruin everything." There was a game in her voice that I wasn't sure I knew how to play. Her bright boldness had some sharp edges.

As we drove on toward Mill Valley, she busied herself with removing her make-up. She had everything she needed in that big leather bag. My occasional glance bore witness to an amazing transformation. When she finally turned to me, she was younger, even more attractive.

"So much for THAT painted hussy," she laughed.

*   *   *

When the season is right, there's a great little waterfall in the hills of Mill Valley, but even when the creek is dry, the location offers a secluded and romantic park. I had automatically driven us there, to a familiar stop on my usual trail of assorted conquests. Joan surprised me by suddenly pulling up her dress to remove her stockings. I glanced out the window, away from her beautiful legs, and tried to act casual. She was messing up the protocol of my practiced Casanova routine. She produced a pair of flats from her bag and we strolled up the wide easy trail. Her sleek lavender dress seemed out of place; but she wasn't. She breathed deeply, absorbing the environment.

"Oh God," she beamed, "this is wonderful!" She stretched her arms and looked around at the steep hillsides of lush fern and young redwoods. "This is just what I needed."

She skipped along the trail ahead of me, moving easily in spite of her snug dress. She was almost my height, but the smooth and sensual, perfect proportions of her body made her look smaller, more delicate than she actually was. She paused by the rough wooden bridge that crossed the creek until I caught up. For all I could tell, she was twelve years old again.

"I want to build a house right here," she said. "And stay forever."

"Wait till you see the waterfall," I said. "It's not far."

Her child-like excitement was contagious, encouraging. I wanted to show her all the secret places that I knew. I wanted to share secret thoughts. Whatever my doubts had been, they blew away as we easily joined hands and walked on. The humus packed earth, spongy as a mattress, added to the softness of our touch. She started skipping again, hanging onto my hand so that I joined her.

Sound waves don't travel very far in such surroundings, so both the sight and the sound of the waterfall occur quickly; along with a slight drop in temperature. Joan was delighted as she backed up to snuggle against me, to receive my arms. But the touch of her body against mine made me jerk away from her. And that reaction confused me. I was suddenly embarrassed. She had left her coat in the car, so I hurriedly took off my light jacket and placed it over her shoulders.

From the first brief touch of her back-side against me, I felt as though our bodies could fuse - like hot, incandescent spoons. The

sensation was like an electric shock. I couldn't handle it. The great
Casanova was baffled. I had wanted to hold her, to tell her for how long
I had wanted to hold her. But instead, I walked away a few feet and
leaned against a small redwood.

Joan just sat down where she stood, arranging her dress and pulling
my wind-breaker around her. She gazed at the fifteen-foot cascade of
water for a moment, and then turned back to look at me. Her eyes
insisted on contact.

"I'll bet you've brought a lot of girls up here," she said, raising her
voice above the sound of the water. Her smile was a little inquisitive,
but open and honest. Regardless of my embarrassment, she made me
feel more at ease.

"As many as were willing," I said truthfully. "But never anyone like
you."

She gave me her special smile and then looked back toward the
splashing water. She hugged her legs and rested her chin on her knees,
seeming at peace to watch the falls. Since the coffeehouse she had
constantly surprised me, and now, as I watched her, I saw something
else. In spite of the long blonde hair and sexual beauty, there was a
certain "maleness" about her - a shadowy presence of masculine
strength. She possessed some complicated quality that was a mystery to
me, a subtle dignity that wrestled with my chauvinistic view. Sad to say,
I was only dimly aware of some of the revelations I would eventually
encounter in my quest for the company of woman-kind.

My painful infatuation with her had been long buried, but now,
I was experiencing it all over again. Why couldn't it be simple? I was
angry with her. She had betrayed me; she had betrayed herself. This
beautifully pensive young woman who had been the star of my boyhood
fantasies was a paid whore.

With a reflex to pain, I reached into my shirt pocket for the little
packet of three joints that I carried (just enough to eat if I had to). I lit
one, took a long pull, and moved over to hand it to Joan. She brushed

my hand away. I was surprised, but then I noticed her quiet tears. I gently put my hand on her shoulder, but she shrugged it off.

"It has nothing to do with you," she said. I withdrew from her and sat with my back against the young redwood. Screw her, I decided. I was ready to drive her back to Sausalito without a word. Presently, she got up and started back down the trail without me. That's just fine, I thought. But she was again waiting by the little wooden bridge when I caught up.

"I'm sorry, Ray," she said. "I really do appreciate you bringing me here." She tried on a smile. "I guess I should have warned you that waterfalls always make me cry." She held out her hand, which I accepted. I was sorry too. Maybe if I had just been honest with her, I wouldn't have made such a fool of myself.

"I'm really amazed that you haven't been here before," I said. "Tam High is just down the road." I was having trouble getting my thoughts in order. She looked at me with a puzzled expression.

"Damn," she said, shaking her head. "You're being a little weird. If you have something to say, say it."

I blurted it out.

"I had one hell of a crush on you at E Street Grammar School," I said, a little too loud. Her eyes widened. I'd probably said the last thing she'd expected.

"Christ," she softly exhaled. "I was just thinking about those years, but..." She looked into my face. I nonchalantly leaned down to pick up a twig and toss it into the rapidly flowing creek.

"It's no big deal," I lied. She pulled me closer.

"Yes, it is," she said, reading my face. "You were hurt, and I don't even remember." I tried to maintain my nonchalant appearance.

"I wore glasses then," I said. "I wear contacts now."

Suddenly there was a connection in her eyes and she started laughing. I pulled back, trying to break her grip, but she tightened her arms around me and welded her body to mine.

"You were in the band," she said. "You were the kid with the bass drum." She chuckled in my ear. "I wanted to talk to you, a couple of times, but you were so shy it was painful." She leaned back to see my face, still holding me tight, and then gave me the kiss I'd never had.

From that moment on, beauty prevailed. We seemed to share some special talent just for being with each other. Our flirtations were sweet and delicate, playfully bordering on passion. I knew that we would sleep together that night, but it no longer felt like an objective.

We talked and talked. All the way up the coast to Jenner, where we stopped to eat, and then back down along the Russian River, where we found an old motel. We never shut up. Our commonalties were exciting. We shared a growing trust, a way of being as though we had known each other for all those missing years. We talked about everything from the size of the universe to her feelings about being a high-priced call girl.

"I've wanted to give it up," she said. "But the money..." She paused. "No, that's not all of it. I like the clothes and the make-up, and the acting, like being on stage." She was quiet for a moment and then spoke with sudden bitterness.

"I like the power," she said. "I control them, they don't control me. That way I feel safe."

Our grammar school principal had been just one of many older men who couldn't keep their hands off Joan. Some of these she had blackmailed, out of vengeance, but it eventually became just a matter of money. Younger men, to whom she was attracted, were often afraid of her, or would become dangerously obsessed, or both.

As I listened to her, I heard the confusion and fear of a little girl being molested. There had even been a couple of older relatives who came to her in the night. She'd never had a chance at childhood. I began to experience some guilt for my own lustful feelings toward her. I wondered if I could just sleep with her.

The little one-room cabin, vintage 1920s, had seen better seasons, but it was clean. Joan checked out the bathroom and then sat down on the squeaky bed to rummage through her leather bag. I noticed a couple of empty nails stuck in the bare walls.

"This place could use some decoration," I said. I went out to the car and returned with a colorful Hawaiian shirt that I'd tossed in the back seat a couple of days before. I hung it on a nail above the bed. Joan looked up and smiled. She pulled a bright blue scarf from her bag and hung it on another nail, opposite the bed. We looked at the result for a second and then moved to switch the items in silent accord. It was plain to see that the scarf belonged above the bed.

Then I noticed the partly burned candle and small glass candle holder that she had placed on the night-stand. I tried not to stare at it, but in spite of our understanding, I wondered where and when she had last used it. By now I realized that the large leather bag was her call-girl kit. She somehow caught the direction of my mind and quickly moved to embrace me.

"Please," she whispered. "That has nothing to do with this. I love YOU, my iron butterfly."

When we got into bed, I was almost overwhelmed by her intensity. I felt her offering me something that I believe few men had ever received. It was her essence, her trust, her sensitive and intelligent vulnerability - a private, spiritual innocence that transcended a life-time of abuse and guilt.

Her deeply sensitive kisses and soft, alert body made me a part of her secret self. I was swept from awareness of all that I thought I knew into a place where I could only discover. There was no separateness, no performance. We carried each other in the same body, sustaining an incredibly delicate balance – an intricate duration on a tight-wire stretched across a boundless ocean of tenderness. We worshiped each other to death, until the God in her and the Goddess in me became one unconscious, androgynous mess.

We had breakfast in a small coffee shop, and laughed. We smoked a joint, and laughed. We still coincided as we had the day before, but then she began to change. With every mile back from the Russian River,

I could feel her growing distance. As we passed Fulton Road and came within sight of Highway 101, she began to apply her make-up, paving over the authentic beauty that had been like food to my soul. I was stuck on the feeling of her. I didn't want to let go. But there seemed to be nothing I could do. Her retreat was non-negotiable. I knew that if I pushed too hard, it would only spoil a quiet ending to our perfect interlude.

*   *   *

After I'd taken her to her car, and she sat with the motor running, I stood on the street with my hands on the car door and tried not to let my feelings show. I wanted to be as detached as I thought she was, but only the anger of my hurt came through.

"Well," I said. "Thanks for the freebie" I was immediately sorry for that remark and expected her to be upset, but she looked up at me with soothing understanding. Her beautifully honest blue eyes actually shared my reluctance to let go. There was pain in her smile, and love.

"We had it all, Ray," she said. "And that's all there is."

Then she was gone.

*   *   *

When I heard the painful news about Joan's suicide some time later, I went back to the waterfall in Mill Valley and stayed for a long time. I needed to see her there - to feel her presence, to bury her there in her happy place. I needed to know if there was anything I could have done.

WHIFF

I was recently walking down the sidewalk in Petaluma, California, totally wrapped up in my own thoughts, my autopilot fully engaged. I had no conscious connection with my surroundings. But then, there was this faint odor.

Suddenly, without warning, I was five years old again, standing in an aisle of F.W. Woolworth's, in Macon, Georgia. I was fascinated by the money tubes that occasionally flew across the ceiling, up or down the wires between clerks on the main floor and the cashier's cage high above. I was barefoot, but in calloused comfort on the narrow wooden floorboards, hypnotically decorated with grain pattern landscapes to get lost in and worn to a dull satin finish.

The air was thick with the odor that had brought me here – that popcorn, powder puff, chewing gum, marshmallow, cotton candy, comic book odor, with an intoxicating whiff of peppermint fading to chocolate, an undercurrent of gunny-sack dust and the faint occupied musk of sweating bodies. I was totally present, transported through time and space on the wings of an alchemy that only noses can know.

Then, suddenly, I unexpectedly stepped off the curb back in Petaluma. The jolt woke me up. I got a few worried glances from other pedestrians as I went back and forth on the sidewalk, sniffing the air and trying to find that odor again. I became completely obsessed with finding the source of something I hadn't smelled in over seventy years

– that exhilarating downtown five-and-dime smell of my childhood dreaming.

I went from store to store, still sniffing the air. I even told a few people about my experience. That brief moment was not enough. I wanted to go back again, back to that wonderful innocent time, to see the world purely as possibility again.

The clerk in the drug store was alarmed when I asked if I could come behind the counter and sniff around. As I started to tell her my story, I got another faint whiff from somewhere outside. I quickly turned back to the sidewalk.

A Morning Walk

I pause on a residential street corner during my morning walk and notice an amazement of things. I notice the blazing star that warms my face and lights the world with its colossal fire. How does it do that, hanging out there in space for billions of years; burning, burning, burning? How does it stay the same size?

I notice how the trees are designed to drink the sunlight and wonder about the issue of Evolution versus Creationism. Who designed the trees? Couldn't the trees have designed themselves, through a long, long process of finding out what works, and still have been created by God? Whatever works, whatever promotes life, isn't that what God wants? The conical evergreen, a study in optimal exposure; the spread of the oak tree as it displays its boughs full of leaves, reaching up and out to catch the sun's early rays.

Life's answer to life's needs, from the smallest blade of grass to the giant Sequoia, apparent symbiosis, an exchange of interdependent functions, an infinite network of intricate, loving relationships; yes, loving, like the exchange of gasses between me and the plants I keep in my apartment, as we feed one another the breath of life.

I notice the blunt buildings around me, the wires and telephone poles, the man-made things that are gathered beneath the flickering birds and the reaching trees. I look toward the humming freeway a few blocks away, obscured behind the trees and thickets alongside it, and wonder about the tenacity and adaptability that allows that vegetation to survive.

Evolution? Creation? Aside from the biblical context, and a lot of monkey business, these words are mostly a reflection of man's natural tendency to polarize? I remember Carl Jung's saying that everything is defined by its opposite. But even that relationship implies a continuum, a connection, which means that everything, in some way, also contains its opposite.

> "Navaho dogma connects all things, natural and experienced, from man's skeleton to universal destiny, in a closely interlocked unity which omits nothing, no matter how small or how stupendous."
> – ("Navaho Symbols of Healing" by Donald Sandner)

I look down at the ground, at a bare spot of earth next to the sidewalk, and try to imagine that unity. I try to imagine the world around me as it might have been long ago. The ancestors of the native Pomo people lived here for ten thousand years and never left a mark. And yet, their technology provided for their survival, in balance with the natural world around them. I remember the words of a Sioux Chief, Luther Standing Bear (1868-1937):

> "I am going to venture that the man who sat on the ground in his tipi meditating on life and its meaning, accepting the kinship of all creatures, and acknowledging unity with the universe of things, was infusing into his being the true essence of civilization."

That makes such sense to me – the true essence of civilization defined as civility toward all life, toward all things, without violation, in harmony with the planet. So, who exactly are the civilized?

Recently, while looking through some of my old writings, I ran across this little snippet I had written:

> "In an effort to explain everything, to understand the world by taking it apart, our culture has become dedicated to the

division of the whole into its parts. But does a dissected bird reveal the essence of its flight?"

I was deeply moved by Houston Smith's imagery in "Forgotten Truth," about the experience of Native Americans:

"They watched a landscape dismantled, a physical landscape of almost magical richness. Untapped, unravaged, its grains of soil had been to them beads in the garment of the Great Spirit; its trees were temple pillars, its earth too sacred to be trodden save by soft skinned moccasins. Across this un-paralleled expanse of virgin nature there poured hordes possessing a capacity so strange that they seemed to the natives to represent a different breed; the capacity to look on everything in creation as material for exploitation, seeing every tree only as timber, deer only as meat, mountains as no more than potential quarries. For the victims of this 'civilizing mission,' as the predators chose to call their conquest, there could only be, in the words of a former U.S. Commissioner of Indian Affairs (John Collier), 'a sadness deeper than imagination can hold - sadness of men completely conscious, watching the universe being destroyed by a numberless and scornful foe.' For the Indians had what the world has lost... the ancient, lost reverence and passion for human personality joined with the ancient, lost reverence for the earth and its web of life." (From "Forgotten Truth" By Houston Smith)

When I first read the above quotation, I was filled with sadness and shame. My race, the white race, has been cursed, and blessed, with brains and power, with energy and curiosity; and, with all the assumptions of entitlement. We have traveled the world and conquered the world. And I wonder; could we have done anything different?

Our religious mandate gave us the mission of spreading the Word, of converting the world to the one true God; while our military and industrial technology gave us the means to exploit the world, to take whomever and whatever we wanted. Manifest Destiny was such an eloquent misnomer for the fact of brutal conquest.

Have we in fact gone astray; and from what? Has our devotion to power and technology, to growth and progress, led us to a crucial imbalance with our natural habitat, even with the God we so proudly proclaimed?

If the pendulum of technical science has indeed swung out of control, how can we hope to correct it? Obviously, the material benefits have been monumental, but what have we given up in the process? Can we even know? Are we hopelessly lost in the seductive intoxication of technology? Have we completely abandoned the guidance of natural morality?

*   *   *

We already know about the dwindling environment and the dead seas, the polluted air and the disappearing species. We are accomplished at pointing fingers and looking for quick fixes, for the promise of eventual solutions. But what would happen if we stopped looking outside ourselves and started looking within ourselves. What is the condition of our internal environment? The degradation of our external world is obviously taking a toll on our physical being, and that of our grandchildren, but what about our ecology of soul? Are we living beyond our means there as well?

Are we really some sort of cosmic experiment? Will our species' dominance on this planet end in disaster, or will we wake up to our responsibility as stewards of our own survival? I remember a friend who once reminded me: "You Can't Save The Gold Fish If You Can't Save The Bowl."

As I walk down the block on Eleventh toward Cleveland, my heart once again holds the words from Houston Smith's book: "...the ancient, lost reverence and passion for human personality joined with the ancient, lost reverence for the earth and its web of life." I don't want to unduly romanticize Native Americans, they certainly had their faults as well; but, there's a key for me there, in the way indigenous peoples accepted their place as a part of something far greater than themselves; in the way they looked to the organization of nature for their answers. In our so-called civilized world, it seems that God is dead while fundamentalism flourishes.

I pass the old boarded up warehouse on the corner of Eleventh and Cleveland and turn toward home. There's a thought at the edge of my mind so elusive that it fades out of focus as soon as I try to look at it, like the logic of a dream that fades in the light of day. The passing of a large truck creates a momentary breeze, disturbing the leaves on the hedge next to my head. Then, as the morning traffic increases, I wonder about the system that drives so many to work so hard for the ultimate benefit of so few, but I resist going there. Power and surrender are a complicated relationship at best. I want to resume my previous train of thought, if I can find it.

*   *   *

We have created a world that is separate from nature, that lights up the night and supports whatever conditions we choose. For the most part we look out the window at a world that no longer holds us hostage, except for occasional natural disasters. If humankind was created in the image of God, as we are told, and has the power of creation; then, by the very nature of this magnitude, we must also contain the power of evil, at least of deliberate self-destruction.

It is not so much the point that God loves us, as do we love ourselves? On the surface we are able to disown our evil and project it onto others, onto the convenience of enemies; but, in the depth of our heart's wisdom, we know they are us, brothers and sisters in spite of the differences in culture and geography.

I wonder, do we also hold the power to forgive ourselves? I wonder if this apparently hell-bent world we have created is the result of our own self judgment? Are we punishing ourselves for not deserving to have it any better? If we cannot love ourselves enough to save the bowl, then what about loving the gold fish, our grandchildren?

I turn the key that opens my front door and regret that I felt I had to lock it when I left.

GO BACK TO TOLUCA

From 1955 to 1965 was the decade of my twenties, a span of time during which more things happened in my life than now seem possible. Perhaps the experience of reflecting upon those memories, replayed and examined for meaning, contributes to my sense of compressed, extended time. And, it's also true that if I cannot locate an experience in its appropriate chronological order, I usually claim that it must have happened during the early sixties, when everything else happened.

Memories of those years are punctuated with a number of spontaneous trips into Mexico, the longest and most extensive of which I made with a beautiful, red haired woman named Kathleen. She was older than I was, by a few more years than I knew at the time.

Kathleen was brilliant, and a little strange. I remember her now as a gentle, self-absorbed Druid Queen, a soul out of place and time, always seeking to find her way back to a distant and mythical home.

She knew a lot about an odd variety of things; ancient art and religion, herbal medicine, nutrition, astrology and health food. But some of her knowledge was so esoteric it sounded like science fiction. She told me strange things, but in such a matter-of-fact way they almost seemed plausible.

She claimed that in the far distant past, when people had lived for a much longer time, women had carried their children in the womb for up to three years. So that when the children were born, they were already capable of language and mobility. I would listen and nod and wonder where she had heard such bizarre ideas. She also confided that she belonged to an ancient, secret society, but, in her beautifully smiling, mysterious way, would say no more.

Our trip to Mexico started in Pacific Grove, California, where I spent some time with a young madman – a kamikaze mechanic who was usually loaded on Methedrine. We took my VW bus engine completely apart and put it back together again. And I must admit, it did run perfectly for many, many miles, back and forth across Mexico, usually at Kathleen's direction.

One of our most memorable side trips was in quest of a place called Valle del Bravo (Valley of the Brave), where Kathleen claimed some friends of hers from Europe had a home. She had no address or phone number, only the memory of a conversation she'd had with them a few years before.

How she could be so sure they were there was a mystery to me, but we were off to find them anyway. Coming from the north, Valle del Bravo appeared on the map in the mountains some distance southeast of Toluca.

We drove into the city of Toluca late at night, apparently in the midst of a power outage. The boulevard light poles were dark silhouettes, so any road signs that might have been helpful were invisible. Since we slept in the VW bus and Kathleen wanted to push on, my job was to find the road out of this darkened city that led to Valle del Bravo. In other words, to find somewhere to ask directions.

Driving around in the darkness, looking for signs of life, I noticed the headlights of an old Ford sedan moving slowly along the street. I was somehow encouraged by the sight of a huge hairy arm holding a full-sized stringed bass onto the side of the car.

"Adonde esta el camino para By-yay del Bravo," I managed. After a brief discussion among the occupants of the car, I was told to follow them, which I did. However, a short time later, I began to suspect we were being set up to get robbed, or worse. We traveled through some dark residential neighborhoods and then into an even darker industrial section. Finally, the Ford stopped and I pulled up alongside, ready for anything. The driver smiled and pointed to the dirt road before us.

"Valle del Bravo," he said. I looked at the rough dirt road and didn't believe him, but I quickly drove on anyway. Maybe we were getting off with just a dirty trick. Then, to my surprise, I was soon driving on smooth pavement, on a well-kept country highway we would never have found without that car load of mariachis. After a while I pulled over and found a level spot a little off the road to get some sleep.

The following morning revealed that we had parked in a beautiful spot high above a lush, agricultural valley. Even the surrounding countryside had a trim, park like appearance. Kathleen left the bus before I was out of bed and was sitting on a grassy hillside just across the road from where we had parked.

As I joined her, I could see she was mesmerized by the landscape, her blue-green eyes focused on fantasy images that I couldn't see. I was enchanted by the air of child-like anticipation that often came over her. There was a breathless excitement, as though her dream castle would appear in this magical landscape at any moment.

"This is just how I remember it," she said, with a sweeping, slow motion gesture of her delicate hand.

"What, you've been here before?" I asked. She smiled, in that charming 'I've got a secret' way.

"It just seems so familiar." she replied. "Like memories from another lifetime, as though I have been here before, a very long time ago."

I had learned not to press too hard in such conversations, unless I wanted to hear more about the ancient world that lived inside her mind, with its temples, costumes, and rituals.

We presently returned to the microbus and were just finishing our usual morning routine of camp stove coffee and granola when I heard the sound of many boots slapping the pavement. At first, I couldn't figure out what this out-of-place sound could be, and then, I was startled as a troop of about thirty Mexican military came marching around a nearby curve in the highway.

Their tempo seemed to become a little smarter when they saw us, but aside from that, we could have been invisible. As they marched on by, their rifles over their shoulders, I was puzzled that such a well-kept highway seemed so devoid of vehicle traffic. Not a single car had gone by us all morning.

Then, just after the soldiers had passed out of sight around another curve, we heard some yelling and a couple of gun shots. Somehow, I knew the ruckus had been made just for our benefit. But as we traveled on down the highway, there was no sign of the soldiers. They had disappeared, most likely to march cross country.

After a while a few cars did pass us, going the other way. And I noticed they were new and expensive looking cars. At the bottom of the hill, at the foot of the rich, agricultural valley, we came upon a picturesque little hillside village, a perfectly arranged post card. Kathleen was excited to visit the place, so we turned off the highway and up the main street.

Here and there I caught glimpses of a dark skinned, dignified looking people all dressed in white, some of whom carried rifles. Most others in the village could have been dressed right out of a Sears Catalog. I saw leather jackets, Levi's and boots. Unlike everywhere else I had been in Mexico, there was no sign of poverty here.

*   *   *

Looking back now I am grateful we got through that trip without any more serious incident. What a pair we were. The regal red-head in blue jeans, who moved about as though she was on stage, or dancing under water. And the young stud in the Army field jacket, with a wide brimmed hat, khakis and boots. I hadn't been conscious, at the outset of our trip, that I had created a costumed identity, but, after a number of Mexicans had called me "Comrade," I got the picture.

It was interesting to watch the old women as they responded to us, most especially to the red haired "bruja" in their midst. Some made the sign of the cross, others would place a finger high on their cheek and pull down, forcing the eye more open, which I understood as an older, more pagan sign.

It didn't take long to realize how out of place we were. As Kathleen went to "ou" and "ah" at the vegetables in the small outdoor market place, I was approached by a small group of men, mostly older, with one old white whiskered spokesman. He advised me to buy some "membrano," as though it was my destiny to do so.

When I understood that he was talking about alcohol, I assumed I was being asked to buy a round. But, as it turned out, these gentlemen were simply intent that I should buy a bottle of an orange liquor, a local product, and leave town. In fact, just before I got the exact message, White Whiskers was showing signs of agitation.

Minute by minute we were attracting more of a crowd, and Kathleen didn't seem to understand they weren't exactly admirers. I gently engineered her toward the VW bus. I wanted to leave. But as we rolled down the main street toward the highway, she insisted that we had to find a telephone. She wanted to find out if her friends had any kind of listing.

She saw a likely looking tienda and put up a fuss to stop. I kept the VW running, parked right in front of the little store, and encouraged her to hurry up. Aside from my para-military outfit, I had been so wrapped up in creating my macho image, I'd done something quite stupid, which wasn't made clear to me until that very moment.

As I sat in the driver's seat, there was a large Bowie knife, in fringed buckskin scabbard, that hung on the interior wall of the VW bus a little way behind my head. It was in plain sight, but I had never intended it to offend anyone. I was just playing my game.

At that moment, however, I understood enough Spanish to hear that one young man in a passing group was indeed offended, and he wanted to talk to me about it. I was greatly relieved when his friends pulled him along with the group. They headed on down the street toward the highway at the bottom of the hill. I honked the horn and called out for Kathleen to hurry.

As we rolled on down the main street, I got a better view of the growing crowd of people at the intersection with the highway. Just as we came to a stop, a human chain was being formed across the highway to our left, blocking us from the direction of Valle del Bravo. Several people were pointing in the direction from which we had come and one clear voice called out in perfect English.

"Go back to Toluca."

KIVA

The girl behind the souvenir counter was startled.

"I didn't think anyone else was here," she exclaimed, quickly looking me over. As she set her Romance magazine to one side, I explained that I had been so engrossed in reading at one of the display cases, I hadn't noticed when everyone left.

"They've only been gone a few minutes," she encouraged. "And that's the last tour of the day. If you hurry..." She seemed genuinely concerned, but also anxious to get back to her magazine.

It had been a deceptively long drive from the main highway. The impressive flat-topped mesa had seemed to stay right in front of me, just a short distance away, mile after mile. There was a kind of timeless slow motion to the great distances one had to travel in this country, and the ever present, quietly lethal, heat of the sun.

Fortunately, the afternoon was cooling off rapidly on top of the mesa. The trail ahead slanted downward and was partially shaded. I opened my senses to the earth around me, entertaining myself with images of an ancient world, of a time when human beings were just a small, inconsequential part of this vast landscape, where one had to master a very intimate, but respectful, relationship with Mother Earth.

By the time I caught up with the tour group, they were already spread out along the narrow ledge at the base of the little cliff dwellings. A tired, elderly park ranger sat on a bench of stone shelf that had been weather worn into the side of the mountain. He was puffing on his pipe, taking a break. For the moment he seemed fairly unconcerned with his collection of tourists. He looked up at me through the shade of his straight-brimmed hat, his blue-gray eyes as indifferent as fragments of sky.

"I paid at the Museum," I told him.

"You ain't missed nothin'," he said. The pipe-stem clicked between his teeth. "Take a look around, but please leave things the way you find them. I'll be lettin' you folks go down into one of the kivas in a few minutes."

I walked further out onto the ledge, beyond the other tourists. In the distance I could see other island mesas rising from the heated mists of a desert sea. I thought about what I had read back at the museum; how there had once been a language of soft smoke that curled above those distant, tribal islands, and signal fires at night that could be seen for a hundred miles.

I turned back to the cliff dwellings. The slant of afternoon sunlight that cut across the silent little structures offered an irresistible impression of broken teeth in a narrowly open stone mouth, set deep beneath the lip of an over-hanging cliff. Darkened corners had begun to gather in the long shadows of afternoon.

My image making was interrupted by the voice of the old ranger, calling the tour group back together. As I turned and started back along the ledge, I was startled by the sight of an amazing trio of tourists - a holy trio - as out of place as penguins in the desert. How could I have missed them? Where had they been hiding? Their dark formal costumes were remarkably stark against the bare earth and among the brightly clad tourists. Although it had cooled off quite a bit, I wondered if they had been dressed like that all day.

It was amazing just to see them there, and even more amazing were the adoring glances the younger nun was casting at the handsome young priest. The other nun, old and thin, regarded her two companions with a face that was as changeless as the cliff wall behind her.

The park ranger stood by the top of a smooth wooden ladder, which extended down into a kiva. He had removed a Keep Out Warning sign.

"Only four at one time," he said. "Ladies first goin' down; gents first comin' up. Please be aware that others are waitin'."

As the elderly ranger droned on about the history of the ruins, I worked my way closer to the holy trio. I was hopeful they might volunteer to go down the ladder. At least the young priest showed signs of being interested. I stood close by as a family foursome emerged from the kiva, with comments and questions that brought a few well-practiced responses from the old ranger.

"Yep," the old man seemed to have gotten his second wind. "When a Native boy turned twelve or thirteen, he would stay alone in the darkness of the kiva for a long time, 'til he had a vision...."

When the priest moved forward, the young sister was quick to respond and I followed along with the watchful old woman, who silently made it clear they were going no place without her. The elder nun moved quickly ahead of the other two and mounted the ladder with careful dignity, dismissing the old ranger's move to give her a hand. Her expression conveyed that she would sacrifice this decent into a Pagan hell-hole only because it was her duty. With an unseemly giggle, the younger nun followed her down the ladder.

There wasn't much to see inside the dim little chamber. I had been inside a kiva before, but just being there with this holy trio made it a totally unique experience. My Southern Baptist childhood had conditioned me with a mis-trusting view of Catholics, who were generally more influential and wealthier than my tenant farmer clan.

The four of us stood in silence as we became accustomed to the soft, bare earth glow of illumination. I thought of the generations of wonder and worship that must have gone on inside this once sacred place, and then, the generations of abandoned silence. The small earthen fireplace next to one wall had been a long time cold and the curious glances of a thousand tourists hadn't left a trace. The dirt floor that had known the tread of soft moccasins or bare feet now knew the boots and tennis shoes of a conquering race – a strangely disconnected race.

The old nun stood rigidly by the ladder, her darkly clad arms like folded wings beneath her thin white face. Her inscrutable expression somehow managed to convey that she was ignoring the other two while watching them at the same time. The younger nun seemed oblivious to her elder sister. With a strangely awkward gesture, she exclaimed that this was "really something" and fixed her gaze on the golden halo of the young priest's curly hair. She moved closer to him, obviously using the cramped quarters as an excuse. I could have sworn she was drunk, or high on something.

With a quick glance at the old nun and an embarrassed half-smile in my direction, the young priest stooped down to examine a small opening set low in the wall.

"A neat piece of engineering," he said, in a tone that was slightly forced. "I read about it at the museum. A separate ventilation shaft that goes right through to the top." He looked toward the old woman as the younger nun exclaimed, "Oh, how interesturing!"

The old nun made a quick sign of the cross and stared straight ahead as her rasping voice came across like metal saw-teeth on stone.

"This was obviously a place of devil worship," she said. The pious judgement in her tone made me feel anger toward her, and a greater degree of sympathy for the young priest. But then, as I paused to take a mental snapshot of the whole strange scene, I felt a sudden impulse to burst out laughing. What the hell was going on with these people anyway?

"There are still Kivas in use today," I said, "and I know for a fact that devil worship is strictly forbidden." The old woman and I exchanged a glance of dead-pan acknowledgment. The young priest chuckled at my statement and extended his hand in greeting, pulling away from the young nun.

"I'm Father Bishop," he introduced himself. But before I could respond, the old nun, her hand still on the ladder, made a loud guttural noise, signifying her impatience. As we shook hands, it was clear the young priest was trying to hide a pained expression behind his smile. He gave the old nun a hard look as he passed her to climb the ladder. The girl in nun's clothing quickly started to follow him, but the old woman put out a stiff arm so that I could pass first. I engaged the younger woman's eyes for an instant as I slipped by her. There was an odd, unfortunate emptiness in her blissful expression.

As soon as they emerged from the kiva, the young priest moved quickly through the scattered tourists toward the trail that led back up toward the gift shop. The younger nun moved just as quickly to follow him, but the old woman stopped and silently stood at the foot of the trail.

When the young priest turned and looked back, his demeanor visibly changed. He stood regarding the old woman for a long moment before he came back down to gently take her arm and slowly start back up the trail. The younger nun took up residence on the other side of the priest.

I had an intense desire to follow, to learn more about them, but a mixture of reverence and respect, both for them and for myself, allowed me to let go of this strange holy trio. I had to accept, without a doubt, that whatever was going on with them was none of my business.

*   *   *

As I approached the main highway in descending darkness, I tried to find a story that fit this strange trio, especially after noticing once again the beautiful, shining black, mid-fifties Cadillac hearse still in the parking lot when I left. This had to be the vehicle they had arrived in. I couldn't help laughing out loud. What a bizarre and perfect disguise for a trio of bank robbers, or some other criminal enterprise.

By the time I turned west onto the main highway, I had given up trying to frame the holy trio, or the experience, into a coherent story. And in time to come, the memory of this bizarre experience would remain with me as some kind of mysterious blessing.

FIRST MEETING

My visits to Nevada to see friends in Carson City got paid for at a local casino. By the time I'd get bored with the people and the noise, I'd have won enough to cover the trip and still get back home with some money left over. Strange how little that meant to me at the time. I never had more than fifty or sixty dollars on me anyway, so what difference if it came from my counter job at the Deli in Sausalito or from the slot machines and blackjack tables in Carson City.

It was only after a few trips and consistent, casual good luck that I got the stupid idea to win some "extra" money on purpose. I really believed I could, as simple as focusing my attention on the process. However, after my naive endeavor proved to be a disaster, I was too embarrassed to ask my friends for money and had to sell my jack and spare tire just to get home.

My young life had flowed from one exploration to the next, usually involving some form of spiritual quest or other, which usually involved some form of drug use or other. I had lots of company in these pursuits, and the mixed blessing of ignorance and energy enough to pursue a perfect world.

As a lean and horny young poet, working behind the counter at the Kettle Delicatessen in Sausalito and part of the "beat generation" social scene in North Beach, I lived in a spiritually elite domain where I was one of the insiders; depending of course upon the location of that sometimes illusive "inside." The trick was not to care too much and make it up as you went along.

The cultural bonds of childhood had been broken, or so I thought at the time, and I was a free agent in that beginning discovery period a few years before the now famous Sixties.

* * *

My friends Mark and Karen had moved their young family to Nevada as part of an early exodus from Marin County of those who saw the coming crowds on the horizon. The charming village and houseboat community of Sausalito that we'd all had the good fortune to find a reasonably priced residence in was rapidly becoming an expensive tourist attraction.

After a couple of months in Nevada, Mark had also met a man in Carson City who was largely influential in his decision to stay in the area. Franklin, a powerful, heavy-set Washoe Chief, had introduced Mark to what we would later identify as the Native American Church, an experience Mark had tried to describe to me during one of his visits back to Sausalito. He took me aside and declared, through a mist of tears, that he had found the spiritual "way" we had all been looking for.

Mark's story about Franklin was amazing. He had been a B-29 belly gunner in WW II, a post-war heroin addict in Europe and New York, and finally, an angry down-and-out wino in Sacramento. His gradual return to his people had all the elements of a Ulysses like journey and had taken just about as long. Elders among the Washoe had sought him out in Sacramento and recruited him to be a holy man in service to his people.

After many months of recovery and deep journeys of re-connection and initiation, Franklin emerged transformed. He soon became an important figure in the Native American Church, in demand to run peyote meetings all over the West, from Wyoming to Arizona.

Mark told me another amazing story about how Franklin had gone into a Carson City used car dealership, had a long conversation with the owner, an elderly Italian gentleman, and had then driven off the lot in a late model pick-up with camper unit, absolutely free of charge. Franklin, who had also met and teamed up with a beautiful Apache woman named Concha, had become an important, highly respected "Road Man," an answer to the Elder's prayers who needed decent transportation to cover his wide spread territory.

Even though Mark had already been to a couple of meetings, it was apparent that Franklin's welcoming of a small group of young Beatniks into a Saturday night peyote meeting was something of an event. Fortunately, although a few of the Washoe displayed their displeasure, most of the people simply accepted Franklin's decision without question.

I would later attend such meetings in the traditional tipi setting, but this first meeting was held inside an old two room cabin, with a good number of Washoe (from adolescents to elders) and five white kids, including myself. As my friends and I self-consciously filed into the main room of the cabin, Franklin looked up and said:

"Welcome, these are my people and we use these cans to spit in." I noticed a number of tin cans set among the circle of people. We sat on the floor around a thick piece of sheet metal upon which a small pile of hot coals had been heaped. Franklin had a small crescent of sand on the floor in front of him, upon which he would soon place a large peyote button, indicating the "meeting" had begun.

As we consumed the peyote cactus, an old man named Jimmy Summers occasionally sprinkled cedar chips on the hot coals and then delicately fanned the smoke into the faces of those around the circle. The Peyote was bitter, and sometimes hard to keep down, but the cedar smoke helped to settle an upset stomach. Jimmy Summers could maneuver a ball of smoke directly to anyone in the circle. He was referred to as the Cedar Man.

Levi Dick, who lived in the cabin, maintained the supply of hot coals which he carried in a bucket from a small wood stove in the front yard. When we had first approached the cabin, a couple of us had laughed at the odd sight of a crackling fire in a small outdoor wood stove. Later that night we would understand the pile of glowing coals as a living alter.

Levi Dick moved with a twisted limp, but in such an integrated and fascinating way he seemed to be dancing. I had never imagined that anyone so crippled could move so gracefully, but the twist of his body, with one leg shorter than the other, was the reason itself for his rhythmic, flowing movements. It was hard not to watch him as he moved about in his perpetual dance. We later learned he had been thrown from a horse when he was a boy. Levi Dick was called the Fire Man.

As mentioned earlier Chief Franklin was the Road Man. His job was to "keep the meeting on the road," to help people avoid too much wandering off into the fantasy mind. Meetings were called for the purpose of prayer, to focus energy on the community. And since these meetings were held almost every Saturday night, rain or shine, there was plenty of variety.

"That old woman over there at Woodford's, my cousin Bernice. She has had a lousy cold for some time now. I would like to pray for her." That was good enough.

"And we should pray for those guys back in Washington D.C., that they figure out what they are doing with the gov'ment."

"And those astronaut guys who are trying to go out into space, we should pray for them too, they must be pretty scared."

All through the night, a feathered staff, a rattle and a peyote drum were passed around the circle so that each man got a turn, first with staff and rattle and then with the peyote drum. The drum was made of a small, round-bottomed metal kettle, partially filled with peyote tea. The top was covered with a wet animal skin, tied onto the kettle with rawhide, which I learned was knotted in such a way that represented the Universe. A slender wooden drumstick was used to keep a steady beat, a heartbeat, which varied in tone as the liquid inside the kettle was swirled and tipped.

The man who held the feathered staff and rattle was expected to chant, to sing. So, all through the night a song was in the air. When the staff and rattle was handed to my friend, Mark, he started out making chant like indigenous tones, but then broke into English.

"My heart is so happy to be here," he sang. "Oh, thank you, thank you, thank you, thank you. With my brothers and my sisters of the Earth. Oh, thank you Great Spirit, thank you Jesus."

The Washoe people obviously approved of Mark's gift of spontaneity, which encouraged the rest of us to do the same when our turn came. And from then on, the native men in the circle began to sing not only the Peyote songs in their Washoe tongue, but spontaneous English verses as well, some of them pretty funny.

I should explain that by Native American custom the women and children formed a second circle behind the men and didn't participate with the drum and staff. Over time, however, as I attended many other Native American meetings, I saw this custom change into one circle.

Although acceptance of our presence among the people was a little strained at first, but tolerated on Franklin's say-so, as the night of drumming and singing and eating peyote went on, there was a growing sense that we really were all one people. Even the old woman across the room, who had openly glared at us the night before, gradually softened.

*   *   *

For those in the Native American Church peyote was always referred to as "medicine," a gift from God to help the people preserve the soul of their culture. It was always taken with reverence. Indeed, taking mescaline with a group of friends at a party and eating mescaline (peyote) with a group of Native Americans at a meeting were two entirely different worlds.

In the years that followed that first meeting, I would continue to be inspired by the spiritual openness of most Native Americans, particularly Franklin, Jimmy Summers and Levi Dick. Later on, however, in New Mexico and Colorado, I would meet other Native Americans who enjoyed putting us white kids through some tougher initiations.

*   *   *

Just before dawn Levi Dick brought in a fresh bucket of coals and knelt down by the piece of sheet metal. The kerosine lamps that had provided some light were extinguished. It was very dark. As the crippled old man moved his bare fingers through the hot glowing coals, with delicate purpose, the vaguely sparkling shape of a bird began to emerge.

The undulating wings, fiery claws and sharp beak that were formed beneath his fingers held us in silence, spellbound by the magical artistry of what he was doing. With a final touch, he sat back from the coals and reached for his fan of bright feathers. The fan in Levi Dick's hand fluttered like a living thing; and, in the resulting breeze, the firebird became a dazzling vision that seemed to lift off from the floor.

The Native Americans around me uttered a soft and reverent sound - "ah ho." Their voices were hushed, but oddly matter-of-fact, as though such a phenomenal sight was common in their world. We all sat in silence for a long time.

The next time Levi Dick went outside, I glanced at Franklin, who had earlier explained the pee-call protocol for leaving the meeting. He nodded, and I remembered to go counter-clockwise around the sheet metal. When I got outside, Levi Dick was just stirring some hot ashes in the stove. A burst of sparks flew up the short stove pipe and into the cold desert dawn.

I didn't know what to say. I had followed him on impulse, wanting to let him know how I felt about the incredible thing he had done with the Firebird. As I looked around in the growing light, I noticed what

I could not have seem the night before. There were three automobile corpses stacked one on top of the other in the sandy backyard of Levi Dick's cabin: a disintegrating old Model T, half buried in the sand; an old Buick with no tires and a few missing teeth in its grill above that, and topped off with a bullet nosed Studebaker, listing to one side, with rust streaks running down from its empty eye sockets.

It was a stunning sight. And I immediately knew that the way these vehicles were arranged in the desert sand had to be deliberate, an intentional work of art. There was no other junk around, nothing incidental. Except for the vehicles, the yard was perfectly clean.

As I stared at the arrangement of this strange sculpture, I began to see it as some kind of statement, and it was incredibly, deeply funny. Admittedly, I'd been eating peyote, and yet I saw what I saw. I suddenly understood it as a statement of white man's transient passage across this eternal landscape.

When I turned back to face Levi Dick, he was watching me closely. There was a knowing kindness in his face, almost as though he knew what I was thinking. As I looked into his eyes, his face began to change. The wrinkles deepened, the skin disintegrated and then disappeared. I was paralyzed. I was staring at an empty skull, except for the bright eyes that remained.

And then, the smooth pink flesh of a baby's face grew over the skull. As soon as that was in place, an older child's face took shape, then a young man's face, then an older warrior's face, then an ancient wrinkled face, then once again, a skull. And then the whole process started over. Again, and again, faster and faster, generation after generation; and I knew Levi Dick was aware of what I was seeing.

After that infinite moment, the old man's face became his own again and he reached out to lightly touch my shoulder. He looked down and gently tapped the booted toe of his shorter leg on the desert sand. Then, he said the only words that passed between us that morning.

"I live here," he said, in a soft voice that was somehow distant and yet inside my head at the same time. And with that one simple phrase,

I felt the passing of ten thousand years and something so profound came into my heart that tears welled up in my eyes. In that brief instant I would know the real tragedy of my kind, the displacement and loneliness of a lost tribe. Levi Dick's hand tightened on my shoulder.

When we went back inside, the mood in the cabin had changed dramatically. There was laughter and conversation. My friend Mark gave me a questioning look and then smiled as I sent back an amazed expression. Mark and I had been seared on either side of Franklin, an honor that Mark had arranged. So, I returned to my place on Franklin's right hand.

"I was just about to take it off the road," Franklin said, his round face beaming. As I resumed my seat next to him, Franklin's beautiful wife, Concha, was fulfilling the only female role in the ceremony, that of Earth Mother. She brought in a bucket of fresh water and a dipper for the morning Water Call and said a prayer to bless our morning meal of meat, fruit and corn. The bucket was passed around as Levi Dick gently swept the sheet metal clean into his bucket and large platters of food were brought in.

Franklin removed the large peyote button from the small crescent of sand and placed it on a miniature Navajo rug on the floor between us, along with a small rattle, an eagle feather and a slender drum stick. The meeting was officially off the road. People went back to talking and getting ready to eat. The elders were warming up to tell outrageously funny tall tales with dead pan straight faces.

As I glanced down, Franklin had just opened his medicine box, a shallow rectangle of wood about six by eighteen inches. The peyote button, feather and rattle all jumped unassisted into the box, followed by the drum stick and miniature rug. My jaw dropped. I stared at this phenomenon for a second, and then looked up at Franklin.

"Shazam," he said quietly, honoring me with a wink and a wide grin.

Juanita and Russian George

Oh yes, Juanita - I had an off and on relationship with her over many years. Two words best describe what I remember about her - generosity and volatility. My most memorable exchange with her occurred late one night after she had moved the restaurant to her ferryboat location (Juanita's Galley), and I was staying on the old ferryboat next door. She and I had what I can only describe as a "curse out."

I don't recall how it started, but that soon didn't matter. Juanita was in a rage about something, spewing freely, and I was in her line of sight. She was on the aft upper deck of her ferry and I was on the aft upper deck of the one next door. We had no more than a gulf of ten or twelve feet between us, but we both knew it would have taken a long journey, down across muddy and dangerous boardwalks, for either of us to reach the other. That fact alone allowed us to really cut loose.

Juanita could have claimed a graduate degree in the art of cursing. I did my best, but had little chance against her mastery of foul and abusive language. We knew the match was over when I started repeating myself and she was just getting warmed up. A few nights later, when we encountered one another in her place of business, we glared at one another for a moment and then broke into laughter.

* * *

I also recall a character we knew as Russian George. A small man he was, with a full and long gray beard. Winter or summer, no matter, he always wore an old overcoat that reached almost to the ground. It was quite a sight to see his overcoat floating along under his long gray beard with no apparent evidence of legs or feet.

During my earliest days in Sausalito, I lived in an old hotel on Bridgeway in a room next to Russian George. Night after night I would hear an odd rustling, crinkling sound coming from his room. It sometimes kept me awake. One morning as I was passing his open door on my way to the third-floor community bathroom down the hall, I looked in at an amazing sight. Against the far wall of his room was a pile of wrinkled paper bags. I guessed he must entertain himself by opening those bags to see what he had put inside and then closing them in order to forget. I had been warned never to leave anything in the bathroom or Russian George would grab it.

It was said he had been a friend of Jack London's, but I never knew if that was true. He spoke a strange language all his own and few people could understand a word he said. All I got was something that sounded like; "wijay wijaw wijay wijaw." Until early one morning, when I was returning to my room from a party where I had consumed a ration of LSD, I ran into him in the hallway and perfectly understood every word he said. We had a brilliant philosophical conversation, but, unfortunately, I also soon *forgot* every word he said.

*   *   *

Juanita and Russian George were like signposts on my youthful journey through a time and place that was still heavy with evidence of a vanishing world; a world united with the clarity of a common cause; a world rich with characters who defined themselves well before a pause in history made their stories stand still.

I walked down the streets of a small town before it became a tourist attraction and enjoyed the purity of its transition from a WW II ship building industry to an enclave of artists and free thinkers. It was also a time of revival, with folk music from the thirties, old voices of rebellion in service to an awakened post-war hunger for a new cause. A new day was breaking against a solid background of classical music, jazz, poetry, literature and chess.

I remember the occasional comfort of Sally Stanford's plush Valhalla, a soft and elegant view of San Francisco Bay. I remember squeezing into the Glad Hand to hear local stories for the first time. I remember sitting in the Kettle Delicatessen engaged in arguments about freedom versus determinism. I remember when the Tides Bookstore opened, and the No Name Bar; I was there. I remember bouncing across the bay in a small fishing boat to Sam's in Tiburon, and returning home with a boatload of drunken, singing sailors who were barely able to find the dock. I remember the fearless wonder of endless energy for whatever came next, how good it felt to live in the flow of the unknown. I am grateful to have been a part of that time and place and cherish the memories.

Mixing Clay

It seems impossible now there were ever so few people living in Sausalito. It was the mid nineteen-fifties. I could walk the entire length of downtown Bridgeway, from Sally Stanford's Valhalla to where Caledonia Street cuts in, and only run into a few locals. I believe some of us were well aware of how lucky we were to be there at that time. I know I was. For a few of those years before it was "discovered," this little fishing village on San Francisco Bay, and the abandoned shipyard waterfront (all the way down to Gate Five), was my most interesting and happy home.

One of my first jobs around town was at Heath Ceramics, a small factory on the top floor of what later became the Village Fair, across Bridgeway from the Municipal Marina. Broad cement steps went up the hillside next to the building, past a small wooden porch and a back door that was our third story work entrance.

Heath Ceramics employed around twenty-five people, some of whom had been with the company almost since its beginning. My understanding was that Brian had at one time been a social worker, was a mechanical engineer, gifted at designing tools; and, at running the company. His wife, Edith, was responsible for the designs and glazes that made their heavy stoneware so marketable. Business was good.

As Brian's most recent employee, I started with the job that many of those in the shop had held before me – mixing clay. With the aid of an electric chain hoist, I would lift sacks of powdered clay up a ladder and into a huge wooden vat, with a prescribed amount of water. After a large propellor at the bottom of the vat had finished the mixing, I would pipe the thick liquid into a series of presses and hope I had done an adequate job of cleaning the canvas gaskets between the pressure plates. A leak of pressurized slurry was a mess worth avoiding.

As the weeks went by, I learned that Heath Ceramics had collected quite a group of employees. As I got faster at mixing clay, I found time to start learning how to stack the kilns. This brought me into contact with more of my co-workers. It seemed there were some pretty well educated drop-outs in the crew, represented by more than a few graduate degrees. At least that's what I heard from a tall, thin fellow with an MPA. Heath Ceramics had attracted a unique group, all in some way rebels, or outcasts, from the mainstream.

I hadn't been there long enough to attend any of the employee gatherings I'd heard about, and I wasn't sure I would want to. Apparently, one of the benefits Brian offered, as well as profit sharing and a casually supportive work environment, were occasional social gatherings hosted by the company. My new MPA friend told me that these parties were intended as a place where employees could work out their differences – shop related conflicts or other problems.

*   *   *

I had been there almost two months when "IT" hit me. I was standing on the ladder by the mixing tank, staring out the large frame of small casement windows toward the Municipal Marina across the street. I was hypnotized by the gently swaying masts, the faint sound of lightly blown rigging, and the bright blue water of the bay. Suddenly, the idea of being inside that building made no sense at all. It was a beautiful Spring Day and I was inside sniffing powdered clay. I climbed down the ladder, took off my apron, and went to knock on the door of Brian's office.

"I'm sorry, Brian," I said. "I can't do this anymore." He looked up from his desk as though I had just said something profoundly interesting. But before he had time to compose a response, I was headed for the back door.

"Wait a minute, Ray. Let's talk about this." He followed me out the door and down the cement stairs. When I reached the sidewalk, I turned to him.

"I'm sorry, I really can't talk about it, or explain it, Brian," I said. "I just have to quit now." Regardless of that statement, he fell in step with me as I continued on down the sidewalk.

"Please, listen to me," he said. "Think about what you're doing."

"I know what I'm doing," I replied.

"But what about commitment?" he persisted. "You could at least give me some notice." There was a cautious mixture of hurt and anger in his voice.

"C'mon Brian," I said. "I'm not leaving you in any real bind. Half the people in the shop know more about mixing clay than I do, and we both know there's some down time between rounds."

"But it's your responsibility," he said. He was beginning to annoy me.

"No, it isn't." I responded. "It's your business, and your responsibility." He remained silent for several paces, still keeping me company.

"But why are you doing this?" I could tell it was an honest question, but there was also an edge of accusation in his voice.

"Look around," I said." It's a beautiful day and I'd rather not be at work. Isn't that reason enough?" We had walked almost to the corner of Princess Lane, where I had an upstairs room. As he began to follow me up the stairs, I was torn by the fact that he really dud seem to care; and, that I really couldn't change my mind.

"Listen," he said. "You've just got a case of spring fever. You'll regret this later. Come on back and mix one more pressing and I'll let you off early."

"I'm already off," I said. "And I won't be back tomorrow." I could sense he was getting closer to giving up on me, but his kindness made me feel guilty.

"Look Brian, I can't explain it. It's just something I have to do. I'm sorry if you don't understand. I really do appreciate that you gave me a job when I needed one, but I don't need a job right now. My rent's paid and I got money to last a while." By this time we were standing in the short hallway in front of my door.

"But what's to become of you?" The frustration in his voice had taken on a caring, parental quality. "What about your future?"

"Well," I said. "First, I'm gonna get cleaned up; then I'm gonna drop by the Chinese market for some raisin bread and cream cheese; and then, I'm gonna climb up to my favorite little bench overlooking the bay and write some poetry.

BLOW THE MAN DOWN

About every six months, Don Fowler's good looking 40-foot ketch would show up to provide a picturesque addition to the Sausalito waterfront. So long as he didn't try to make his anchorage permanent, across from downtown Bridgeway and the old Glad Hand wharf, the city left him alone. And, at about the same time some official might get the idea to ask how long he planned to stay; he was gone.

Don, a stocky and muscular ex-Navy Commander, was a picture-perfect match for his role of sea-faring adventurer. He was ruggedly handsome, could probably have his pick of available women around town, but had a habit of hanging out with less attractive women and making them feel like Queens.

As I look back, I also realize he had a habit of selecting male friends whose egos would benefit just from being seen in his company. The first time I rode in the little dingy out to his boat I was surprised by his interest in me. I was much younger, and if it were not for his gift at drawing out conversation, I'm not sure we'd have had much to talk about.

Aside from the local social scene, Don's time on shore was mostly about taking on supplies, which mainly consisted of large cans of Bugler tobacco and as many jars of beef stew as he could put up. Canning stew, with a pressure cooker on his small coal burning stove, was one way he could measure the days he would be out at sea.

As with other older people who have influenced my life, I wish I'd been older myself at the time. In spite of his usually conversant and jovial manner, I never did quite understand what it was that motivated Don to spend months at a time alone at sea. I had seen a locker full of books on his boat, and word got around he was a writer, but he never mentioned it and I didn't ask. At times there was a fleeting, dark cloud about him, and I got the feeling there was something in his past that he never talked about, something tragic.

On one of his shore leaves, Don asked if I'd like to sail down the coast with him, maybe to Mexico. I was floored with excitement. You bet. The idea of being at sea on a sail boat was like a dream come true. The night before we were to leave, our friends threw a big Bon Voyage party. And, as was usually the case with parties around Sausalito, people showed up whom nobody knew, but all were welcome. Don drank quite a bit, which surprised me; he usually didn't drink very much. He even invited a couple of guys passing through from France, whose heavy accents made them not so easy to understand, to come along on our trip. This surprised me even more. Don was usually far more careful about people he allowed on his boat. They claimed to be experienced sailors.

Later that same night, the four of us somehow managed to get to the boat in the little dingy without falling in. I had some trepidation about a group of drunks trying to sail out the gate at night, but Don was clear about being Captain of the ship and he wanted to weigh anchor. So, anchors away.

It was choppy under the bridge and pretty windy inside the gate – conditions were rough. Don ordered us to lower and secure the aft (mizzen) sheet, which was flapping wildly as it came down. The two French guys thought they would help by trying to completely unhook the sail from its track on the mizzen-mast, an act that made no sense and revealed their lack of experience. When Don saw what they were doing, he swore at them from the tiller.

"You goddam idiots," he yelled. "Get your asses below and stay out of the way." The two idiots were obviously confused, but I helped them to understand and they did as they were told. After we had cleared the gate and were a little further out, Don asked me to take the tiller and went below. I could understand his anger, but I had also noted that the alcohol had made him into a different person.

I felt sorry for the two Frenchmen. They obviously didn't speak English very well and I wondered if they had really understood what they were getting into. I listened as Don lectured them about honesty, trust and seamanship. And, after a few minutes, things became quiet. Before long Don stuck his head out of the cabin hatch.

"I got those two settled," he said. "But they'll be put ashore tomorrow." He paused for a minute. "They were a big mistake." I couldn't be certain, but I had the feeling he might be apologizing to me.

"You okay to handle it for a while?" he asked. He was more sober now, as though his tirade with the two Frenchmen had burnt out the last of the alcohol and all that was left was a tired sadness.

"Sure," I responded. "This is great, I mean..." I could see by the dim lantern light that he almost managed a smile before ducking back into the cabin.

There were four bunks forward and another in the main cabin, so at least it wasn't crowded below. But at that moment I was so high on the experience of sailing, I quickly forgot about the others. I continued westward for much longer than Don had told me, until I found a strong and steady north wind, and then fell off to the south on a broad reach.

I was in heaven. A wind like that doesn't happen on land. I was almost standing on the cockpit gunnel and sometimes taking a little water over the starboard deck. The boat was alive and I was alive with it, like we were joined into one seagoing creature. There was a small moon high overhead, a few clouds, stars like I had never seen them, and a stunning phosphorescent wake that gave evidence to slicing speed. I don't know how long it lasted. The only interruption was when one of the Frenchmen came topside with an obvious need and I directed him to heave over the stern. He heaved and moaned, looked around for a minute, and went below again.

The wind died down considerably before dawn, and, as the sky brightened, I realized I had taken us far from the sight of land. When Don came up and handed me a mug of coffee, he looked around and swore under his breath. I knew he had wanted me to keep a watch for lighthouses, and at least to keep the coastline on our horizon. I watched his face, expecting him to blow up at me, but he just stared out at the horizon. His eyes reflected the distance, they were the same color as the sea.

After going forward to blow out the running lights, he came back humming to himself. He took over the tiller, drew in the boom to head east, and, in a robust baritone voice, broke into a sea chanty.

"Come all ye young sailors, who follow the sea,
Yo Ho, blow the man down,
please pay attention and listen to me,
give us some time to blow the man down."

When the two French guys came hesitantly up through the hatch, Don acted out the perfect Long John Silver. I had never seen him like this.

"Ahoy and avast May-tees, did ya get some o' me special blend. 'Eres a pot on th' stove." The vagabond duo looked at one another and then back to Don, a faint smile beginning to play on both their faces. Don kept up a very entertaining persona, and, hangovers notwithstanding, it wasn't long before we were all caught up in his mood. After a while we sighted the shoreline and gradually recognized the terrain around Santa Cruz.

We went in with the little Diesel engine and found a temporary dock. Don had kept up the Long John Silver act a bit too long. It had become irritating. But when we were all finally standing on the dock, he suddenly dropped the act. With a solemn handshake, he spoke to both the French guys.

"Under different circumstances," he said. "You guys would be dead. I don't see how you've made it this far." Then he turned to me.

"I'm sorry, Ray," he said. And I could tell he truly was. "We'll try this again sometime, just you and me, but right now I need to be alone."

We silently watched from the dock as he sailed away.

ROSE TEA

It was a dumb thing to do, but I didn't realize that until it was too late. I had driven my pick-up down a grassy slope and couldn't get back up. The wheels would just spin out in the slick grass. I stood on the back bumper while my date got behind the wheel, but no luck.

I had been so proud and excited about my new, used truck, a 49 three-quarter-ton Chevy, I couldn't wait to go out and do trucky things. My new friend, Carla, and I had driven out to the coast from Sausalito and up along one of my favorite stretches of Highway One, from Stinson Beach to the town of Point Reyes; and then over to the Inverness Peninsula.

My lust for adventure took us to exploring up dirt roads, further and further, until, I put her in granny gear and went a little too far into the countryside. And now, here we were, miles from the nearest phone and it was late in the afternoon.

There was a chill in the air and a hint of fog was beginning to drift in from the ocean. I felt embarrassment at getting us stuck, and, as my manly pride began to dream up some lame apology, I noticed that the pretty girl I had whisked away from the comfort of Sausalito was actually enjoying our situation.

The slope of the hillside continued on down to a creek some distance below. I looked around for an alternative route to try, but there was no way out but back up the way we had come. We took a time out to sit on the tailgate and appreciate what a beautiful spot we were stuck in. The late afternoon landscape around us was a gift of natural beauty, so perfectly arranged – every bush, every tree, every bump and blade of grass – one couldn't help but feel the presence of spirit, almost as though the landscape itself was conscious.

Then, just as we were closing up the truck and gathering ourselves for the hike back to civilization, we were startled by a voice that called out to us.

"Hello, hello, how nice to see you." The voice was a cheerful falsetto. And I thought I detected an Irish accent. The woman waved as she came out of a small grove of trees nearby. She wore khaki pants, hiking boots, and a large, floppy hat. She appeared to be around five feet tall and on the slender side.

"We got stuck," Carla called, waving back to her. As the woman came closer, I could see she was carrying a handful of green, leafy plants.

"Not to worry, Darlins'," she said, her voice lower and definitely Irish. "I'll call my garage in th' mornin'. They'll come give you a tow. That way I can get some bleedin' use out of my Triple A insurance card."

It was difficult to tell how old she was. Her face was slightly wrinkled and some wisps of gray hair were visible beneath her hat, but her eyes and her energy were so young, and there was a warmth about her that was irresistible.

"My house is just a-wee walk away," she said. "So, we'll have some tea. An' I've already gathered these nutritious greens for dinner," she lifted the handful, "an' I have a lovely guest room downstairs. You do sleep together, don't ya?"

This unexpected question had a surprisingly pleasant impact. Carla and I exchanged quick glances. We had known one another for only a short time, but a definite attraction between us had just in that moment been confirmed.

"We wouldn't want to impose," I said, insincerely.

"We should at least try to get back," Carla said. But there was just the right amount of ambivalence in her voice. I think I might have blushed a little.

"It would be a truly great pleasure," the woman laughed. "I'm Rose." Exchanging the greens to her left hand, she brushed her right hand across her khaki pants and reached toward us. She didn't shake hands so much as hold hands. I had never met anyone more friendly.

As we walked to her house, she asked personal questions about us, and our families, and she made us laugh. There was something remarkably "off the wall" about her, a combination of humor and imagination that was perfectly Irish, elfin like. But sometimes she seemed a little out of control. A couple of times she laughed so hard we had to stop so that she could catch her breath.

Her storybook cottage was on a wooded hillside not far away, surrounded by a rainbow of rose bushes. The heavy stonework foundation supported a beautifully crafted, half-timbered home with a thickly shingled roof. I noticed a dirt driveway and a dusty old Mercedes on the other side as we approached from the woods. We walked down a pathway lined with rose bushes and into the kitchen. There was a beautiful old wood stove, and lots of antique cooking utensils, but the kitchen was clean and comfortable.

"Sit down, Darlins," Rose chirped. "I'll put on th' tea water. An', oh yes, tele th' garage." She stirred warm ashes in the stove, added some kindling, and set on a heavy iron kettle.

Carla and I sat down at a stout rectangle of table and looked around the small country kitchen like a couple of children visiting Auntie Rose. I could tell she was enjoying our adventure as much as I was. She took off her pretty knit cap and loosened her auburn hair. I watched as she engaged in conversation with Rose. I liked the way she was so relaxed and equal to the older woman. I was already impressed with her intelligence and good looks, but as I watched her, she was rapidly becoming my greatest desire. I could feel myself getting ready for her as my lustful mind began to forecast sensual fantasies.

Then, suddenly, I felt like such a jerk. While my two companions were innocently visiting, I was sitting there licking my lips like a lascivious lobo. The old joke about "Gee Honey, we must'uv run outta gas" flashed through my mind. I didn't like the feeling of seeing myself in that category. When Rose left the room to make a call to the garage, I had to ask Carla the question.

"Are you really comfortable with our spending the night here?" I asked, feeling suddenly awkward. She was silent for a moment. I could tell she appreciated the question. Then she nodded.

"Yes, I think so," she said, reaching her hand toward mine across the table. "But that's partly up to you." I took her hand and sank into her gray-green eyes. There was comfort in our touch, and sweet promise.

"I talked to th' driver, Ben, at th' garage in Point Reyes," Rose interrupted. "He said they couldn't have come until after dark anyway. They'll call us in the mornin'." She seemed delighted with the whole arrangement.

Rose showed us around her little property, and then to the downstairs guest room, a comfortable little cavern with its own small fireplace, an outside door and one small window. The high double bed was covered with a beautiful, handmade quilt. It was perfect, a storybook bedroom. Carla and I were inspired. We went back upstairs and continued our gentle foreplay, an occasional soft touch, a smiling glance. There could be no doubt we were working up to a wonderful night.

"Tea's ready," Rose called. We joined her at the kitchen table. The tea was delicious. I had expected the usual flavor, like Lipton's Tea, but this was quite different. There was a scent of roses, and a sweet taste, like honeysuckle. And an aftertaste that called for more.

"Wow, this is really good," Carla exclaimed. "I've never tasted tea like this. Where did you get it?"

"A friend of mine sends it to me from the Orient," Rose grinned. "I sprinkle the used tea leaves around my rose bushes. They love it. Now drink up, Children, there's plenty more."

As we drank and chatted, I slowly began to notice some strange and powerful effects. I was looking across the kitchen and out the window. It had become awfully bright outside. In fact, everything seemed to glow with a light of its own. I watched with amazement as one of the rose bushes was transformed into the brightly glowing, naked figure of a beautiful woman, dancing sensuously across the yard. She was followed by another rose bush that had become a painted harlequin, playing its penis with a bow, like a fiddle. There was no mistaking the Irish lilt to the music. And there was no mistaking that I was out-of-my-mind hallucinating. I shook my head.

Carla had her head down on the table. I couldn't tell if she was laughing or crying. Her hair was radiating waves of violet light. I looked at Rose, her eyes had grown three times larger. She appeared younger, a different person. Carla lifted her head. There were tears in her eyes, but she was laughing.

"My God, Woman, what have you done to us?" She began to laugh even harder, but then became quiet as Rose reached across the table and took her hand.

"Dammit, Rose," I exclaimed, suppressing a giggle. "You should have told us what we were drinking."

"It's a kind of aphrodisiac," she responded, softly. The bright eyes of her loving attention were clearly focused on us both.

LOST WHEELS
AND THE FOUR HORSEMEN

June 29 – My bicycle was stolen from in front of the public library yesterday, in the middle of the afternoon. It had been secured with a sturdy lock and cable, but no matter. When I came outside and walked to the bike rack, I just stood there, in disbelief. What a shock. The horse I rode in on was gone. It was a long walk home.

Now I'm going through an inevitable period of mourning, you know, like how it feels when a dog dies and you don't want to get another one right away. I keep remembering every detail of my almost daily involvement with that bicycle: the broken tip at the end of the left brake handle, the little switch that engaged the Zap motor I had installed; the gentle sound of its bell, the seat, reflectors, fenders, frame, tires and spokes – all the details of an active relationship made much more intense by its sudden absence.

This morning I walked over to the police station to turn in my stolen bike report. As I passed downtown and headed east on the deserted sidewalk next to Sonoma Avenue, I noticed how quiet and somber the world seemed; except, of course, for those oddly arrogant, big shiny beetles whizzing by on the street, intent in their isolation - their little bubbles of privacy on wheels. I was a lone pedestrian.

Since I had last noticed, the police station had moved from Santa Rosa Avenue up to Brookwood, with more Civic Center in between. It was a longer walk than I had expected. And, since it was Saturday, the sun beat down on the silent monoliths of a city government at rest. The wide stretches of empty concrete seemed as vast as an African desert. It was hot and I was grateful for an occasional breeze.

There was no joy on the streets. As I stopped at a glaring, deserted corner to wait for the signal light, I heard an eerie sound, like a distant trumpet, and something akin to a battle cry. I looked in every direction. There was an acrid odor hanging in the air, a thickness of foul-smelling smoke. I closed my eyes. There was a feeling of pressure in the air. I felt a muffled, booming vibration beneath my feet. Through the haze of my grief, I saw four ragged horsemen sitting on the lawn in front of the Civic Center. They sat in silence, gaunt and tall skeletal figures atop their battle-weary steeds. They slowly looked around, coldly bathing the walls of Santa Rosa with unholy indifference. Then, they nodded to one another and disappeared.

Damn, I'd had that bike for eleven years.

GO FLY A KITE

The mysteries around memory have been debated for a long time. My current reading on the subject makes the crucial point that memory is a living thing, always changing, because we ourselves are always changing. Freud told us that we "look at the past through the lens of the present." And, although there are exceptional cases of photographic recall, oddities of calendar calculation and mathematical memory, for most all of us there are no accurate, fixed memories, waiting in storage for our exact recollection. The best we can do is a reconstruction.

The neurons in our brains that fired during the initial experience will only be approximately rekindled, and, as indicated by Sigmund, only in a current context. And, the odds are that the memory has already been altered by previous reconstructions. Nevertheless, the things we remember most likely did happen, although not always, necessarily, exactly as we remember them.

The following experience took place during a rather interesting, but sometimes frightening, period of my life – a time of risky behavior and psychic exploration. There was power, there was magic, but sometimes it was difficult to tell how much of what was in the world and how much of what was in me. My internal and external realities sometimes tended to overlap. I understand now that only infants and psychotics are supposed to enjoy this condition; so, I guess I was somewhere in between the two at the time.

*   *   *

I was staying in Big Sur with my friend, Sarah, and her five-year-old son, Isaac. The house was located on a windy hillside high above the ocean. The rugged coastline was a constantly changing, dramatically beautiful, living post card; forever flexing its aesthetic muscle against the infinite background of ocean and sky.

Sarah was a good and caring person, deep into the benefits of health food, nutrition and yoga. She was financially independent (family wealth) and fancied herself a patron of the arts, particularly of the wildly inspired young "artists" she occasionally adopted.

During one of my many art projects, I had accumulated a great deal of calligraphy. Sitting on a low four-legged bench, unrolling a sixteen-inch-wide roll of paper beneath me, I experimented with closing my eyes and allowing my hand, holding a wet brush, to be guided by my imagination as it danced above the paper.

My hand often seemed to move on its own, in a rapid flight above the paper. Then, I would open my eyes to view what had happened. Sometimes I would add a stroke or two, accentuating the gestalt of a suggested form; sometimes the gift was already done; or, it was nothing. Image after image unrolled beneath the bench and gathered on the floor behind me.

On one of our trips to town, Isaac and I sat in the back seat of Sarah's car and fantasized about building a really big kite out of all this calligraphy. We would glue the rolls together, side by side, making a huge sheet of paper. Sarah was in cheerful agreement. And since it would obviously be a rather large kite, I secured some thick aluminum rods and steel wire to make the cross frame. I also secured some deep-sea fishing tackle, with a large reel and high-test fishing line.

Indeed, it did turn out to be a giant kite. I followed my intuition into a construction that was at least seven feet high, stabilized with taut steel wire and covered with a skin of calligraphy. Isaac was quite helpful. In fact, he was an amazing kid. He was extremely patient, and had a precocious grasp of how things worked. There was something about him that seemed much older than five years.

After we had covered the frame with calligraphy, I sprayed it with lacquer, which did an incredible number on the relationship between the figures and the background. A deeper dimension emerged. The kite took on an even more awesome presence.

Sarah had gone to visit a girlfriend in Carmel when Isaac and I took the kite out onto the hillside for a test. There was a fairly strong wind, and as I tied on some strips of clothing I had brought along for tail balance, Isaac was hanging onto the bottom of the kite.

A sudden burst of wind, at just the right angle, and whoosh, he was airborne, for just a few seconds. I grabbed the fishing line. The rod was anchored to a heavy stake I had driven into the ground. I quickly pulled him down. He was exhilarated out of his mind.

"Let's do that again," he shouted. His excitement was contagious. As insane as I now know it was, the idea of flying Isaac as the tail of the kite was so powerful, so fascinating, I found myself acting without thinking. I used a pair of jeans from the clothing bag I had brought from the house, with the pant legs carefully tied around the wire bridle at the bottom of the kite. Then I tied Isaac into the pant legs while he was standing in the crotch of the jeans. He looked secure.

The wind was strong and steady. A careful lift and I watched in wonder as Isaac's feet left the ground and he started to drift away. I sat down and straddled the butt of the fishing pole and the wooden stake, hanging on as Isaac climbed steadily, dangling from the bottom of the kite, higher and higher above the hillside. I could feel the powerful pull of the kite on the fishing pole. I was entranced.

But then, suddenly, I was terrified. This was crazy. He wasn't that secure. His weight could pull the wire from the frame. In a panic I started to reel him in, but I hadn't reckoned on the force of the wind and the unknown aerodynamics with which I was dealing. There was a sudden strong gust and a strain on the line that yanked the stake right out of the ground. I almost lost my grip on the pole. I grabbed onto the line itself and wrapped it around the heavy sleeve on my right arm, hopelessly trying to stand my ground.

I was dragged across the hillside for about thirty feet before becoming airborne myself. I looked up the line to see Isaac now swinging just beneath the middle of the kite. The way I had tied the jeans had slipped up to the center of the bridle. The kite had become something that was not so well known at the time – a hang glider.

As the ground fell away, I thought at first we were rising, but then I realized we were just being carried away from the hillside, blown at a southerly angle toward the ocean. The lift of the kite was just enough to keep us suspended in a kind of horizontal fall. We crossed over Highway One, with just enough height. The fishing pole, trailing beneath me, barely brushed the top of a telephone pole. I struggled to reach my pocket knife with my left hand, managed to open it, and cut the fishing pole loose. It disappeared, along with my knife, into the landscape below.

A few seconds later and we were descending along a rugged cliff toward the beach far below. The kite was staying above me, but like a rapidly descending glider. I tried not to panic. A multitude of thoughts occurred to me all at once; but fortunately, my body took over. Some part of me was able to stop time and view the whole scene in a strangely calm and objective way. Data collected, calculations made, reflexes anticipated; all without a conscious thought.

A number of rocks jutted out from the steep mountain-side, one of which was rapidly coming up beneath me. I knew we might suffer serious injury if I hit anything squarely, so I had to ricochet off the mountainside just right. All the while I could vaguely hear Isaac's wild squeals of excitement from up the fishing line.

It was a short ride to that first jutting boulder, which I touched and glanced off with a spring of my knees. We gained just the right trajectory for the next "ricochet" further down. At the next two landings I managed to stop just long enough to resist the wind and raise the kite just a little. Then, I fell into the loose earth of a steeply inclined bank and managed to slow my decent all the way down to the beach.

I dug my heels into the sand and brought the kite down. There was far less wind here at sea level. As soon as the kite was flat, I ran toward it. I moved the kite aside and there was Isaac, spread eagled on the wet sand, still tied to the jeans. He was staring straight up into the sky. Oh my God, was he unconscious, was he dead?

"Good job," he smiled, as I knelt down beside him. "But I don't think we should tell my mom."

*   *   *

I stayed in touch with Sarah over the years, but lost contact with Isaac until we met again at Sarah's memorial. She had succumbed to cancer. Isaac's education had led him to archeology and travel, but then he had discovered his real passion and became a high school teacher. His choices were a tribute to his mother, who had taught him the value of finding his own way. After the funeral, at a reception in the family mansion in Mill Valley, Isaac and I wound up alone on an upstairs veranda, reminiscing about his childhood in Big Sur.

"Remember that time on the huge kite," he said, "when you flew me all the way down to the beach?" I started to laugh, but he appeared to be perfectly serious.

"But that never really happened," I said, and immediately regretted opening my mouth.

"Yes, it did," he demanded. "You were there. I remember." He seemed to be angry, even a little desperate. I felt sorry to have triggered his upset, but couldn't stop my mouth long enough to think.

"It's true we flew a big kite," I said, still not sure he wasn't kidding. "But flying down to the beach was a fantasy we dreamed up while sitting on the hillside – after the line broke and the kite drifted away toward the ocean."

He looked at me as though I had stabbed him. I painfully realized that I had just taken away a piece of his identity, his personal myth. He could never again hold that story in the same way. Without a word he just walked away. And I haven't seen him since.

Isaac, wherever you are. I was just kidding. It really did happen.

MURIEL

Waltz Gardens was a fuchsia nursery situated behind a large private home on a back street between Kentfield and San Anselmo. The neighborhood had an old and elegant Marin County feeling. Quiet cultural ghosts lived in the architecture of a world gone by.

My need for pocket money had inspired me to answer an ad posted on the employment bulletin board at Marin Junior College. But, when I first saw Muriel Waltz, whose elderly parents lived with her in the large house, I wondered if I would last.

Before she came into view, I could hear the sound of her dragging right foot as she scraped through the loose gravel in the large back yard. Her body was twisted by cerebral palsy, her face was distorted, her mouth was pulled over to one side, she had difficulty talking. And aside from the dragging limp, her right elbow bent sharply upward to support an apparently useless, dangling right hand. She was often twitching and shaking. I wasn't quite sure how to handle the sight of her.

At first her white-haired mother was around to help me understand Muriel's pronunciation, but then I was left on my own. It was difficult to deal with her and I wasn't at all sure I wanted to stay. Then, something quite amazing happened.

One day after I had completed one of my chores and was walking past the greenhouse, I glanced through a clear spot in a pane of glass and came to a sudden stop. The woman sitting at the small wooden table inside was definitely Muriel; but not Muriel. This woman wasn't shaking, or at all twisted and distorted. In fact, the serene calmness of her soft, even features was stunning; she was utterly beautiful. There was an aura of light around her, a pure angelic quality that made me feel as though I was spying on something sacred, and private.

The two flowering creatures on the table in front of her were vibrantly alive, but perfectly still, as though breathlessly awaiting her touch. She was engaged with such total concentration I could feel the energy of her focus. I soon realized that I was witnessing the delicate marriage of arranged pollination.

She was not only a rapt participant, but a purposeful creator, facilitating the inception of new life. The needle thin instruments in her now steady hands were manipulated with surgical skill, and with all the caring passion of a faithful lover. I later learned that Muriel Waltz was well known in the fuchsia world for the rich varieties she had developed.

That sacred moment would completely change my way of being at Waltz Gardens. I couldn't wait to get to work in the afternoon after class. I found excuses to talk to her, to be around her. And I understood every word of our conversation. She was well informed on a wide range of topics. Her thoughts were complex and interesting. The physical distortion of her disease no longer mattered. That mistaken appearance was now transparent. All I could see was the magically beautiful woman I had seen through the pane of glass. I had the most profound crush on her.

It was devastating when her mother died and Muriel closed the nursery for an indefinite period. It was not until the last day we worked together that our eyes met in a way that I knew she understood what had happened to me. The naked honesty that was shared in that brief glance was one of the most intensely intimate and erotic experiences of my young life.

THE POET OF MOUNT TAM

I heard of Ron's death well over a year ago, when Jim Hansen called from Santa Fe to tell me about it. I hadn't heard from Jim, or Ron, in a long time. They were both a part of my early Marin County history, from the mid-fifties to the mid-sixties, and since they both had settled in New Mexico, I hadn't seen either of them since my last visit to Santa Fe in the late nineties.

Once again, I mused over how the news of an old friend's death can bring that person so much to life. For days after I heard about the discovery of Ron's body (natural causes assumed), his presence was stronger than it had been in years; almost as though he had come to visit. I kept going over memories of the times we had spent together. I especially recalled the day right after his father had committed suicide, when Ron and I had gone to the small house in Tam Valley to look for a suit for his father's burial.

The house was empty. Ron's mother had gone to stay with friends. Ron had moved out some years before. He averted his eyes from the large blood stain on the floor at the far side of the double bed, where his father had bled out after slashing his wrist. But I deliberately stared at the stain, recording every detail of it as though I could somehow carry the painful memory of that image for my friend.

Later that day we drove up Mount Tam to sit and talk about the mystery of death, about where his father had gone, about where we will all go in due time. Ron began to talk about the tragedy of his parent's relationship, about how his father had accidentally put out one of his mother's eyes during a fight. And how she had never thereafter failed to make strategic use of the incident. I listened as Ron tearfully blamed his mother.

"I can't stand to be around her," he softly cried. "I can't even share my grief with her right now." It was a long day, that day so many years ago. But I would relive every detail of it in loving memory of my friend.

Jimmy sent me a fairly recent photo of Ron, along with a couple of books of Ron's poetry, the publication of which I hadn't known about. There, in a somewhat unfamiliar older face, above a full grey beard, were those same intensely haunted eyes. Even as a youth Ron had carried a lot of sad history in his eyes, not only in regard to his parents, but something more, something on a far larger scale. It was as though he knew some dreadful secret about life that he chose not to share with the rest of us, except by dark innuendo in his poetry. When I had first met him, a thin boy of eighteen in the black turtleneck that was so often a part of his costume, he fit perfectly into the Beatnik model of a lean and hungry, suffering young poet.

Ron and I, and another young man named Joey (without whom my story would not be complete), were part of the Beatnik Sausalito-North Beach scene, with occasional trips to the extended community network in Monterey and Big Sur. The three of us poetic musketeers spent a lot of time together, which suddenly changed when Joey and I moved to Monterey and Ron stayed behind. Eventually, as was the case with a number of us, Ron's move to New Mexico probably had something to do with both the rising cost of living in Marin and the ever-increasing influx of superficiality into our beloved Sausalito.

One of the jobs I took around town, to which I returned a few times over the years, was working the counter at the Kettle Delicatessen, on the corner of Bridgeway and Princess Lane. From time to time, I would help feed a few hungry friends, especially a couple of poor houseboat families with children. It was a while before I learned that Joey actually lived in an elaborate mansion up the hill. No more free sandwiches for him.

Joey had been adopted into a wealthy family with parents who were much older than his biological parents might have been. He was haunted by the fact that all records were sealed and he would never know who his biological parents were. His literary and musical education (he played the piano quite well) had been gained in expensive private schools back East. In fact, both Joey and Ron were well versed in the arts and knew much more about poetry and classical music than I did; but we were nonetheless well matched in many crazy and creative ways.

So, I actually had much more contact with Joey over the years, a relationship that ended when I quit drinking and he didn't. In fact, Joey drank himself to an early death several years ago, still waiting for his aged parents to pass on and leave him a fortune. For all the time I knew him, Joey simply assumed he would someday enjoy a wealthy lifestyle. He lived off that potential in a way that he never had to outgrow. Lucky me, I guess. I was the oldest and outlived them both. Now those memories hang like dusty costumes in a long-forgotten corner of the closet. The three musketeers of a bygone era are safely tucked away somewhere beyond time.

"Promise me something," Ron said as we sat on Mount Tamalpais that day. "Promise me that if I go before you do, you'll see to it my ashes are spread over this mountain."

"From an airplane," I laughed, but then gently laid my hand on his shoulder. "You'll be around a lot longer than me," I said. Anyone who knew Ron well also knew of his wish to have his ashes spread on Mount Tamalpais. He grew up with the dream of someday becoming known as the Poet of Mount Tam. Jimmy and I set a date for him to come out from Santa Fe with Ron's ashes, but then I got another call.

"Do you know of any relatives out there?" Jimmy asked. "The authorities here say they have to hold Ron's ashes for a year, just in case."

"He probably won't mind waiting another year," I said. "And yeah, I'll try to find out if he has any relatives around Marin County. But I don't think so."

"We believe he had a daughter," Jimmy said. "But no one seems to know where she might be." I remembered that Ron had been briefly married, but it didn't last. When she became pregnant, she had returned to her parents' home and Ron had added another tragedy to his life.

I did a typical search for relatives, and his daughter, but to no avail. Ron was apparently alone in this life. But Jimmy and I would see to it that he wasn't alone in his death. I was honored by Jimmy's request that we share the fulfillment of Ron's final wish. We would faithfully bring the Poet of Mount Tam back home to his final resting place. There are some things in life you do because you recognize the place where time touches eternity and soon enough it will be your turn.

As was predicted it was about a year before Jimmy called and told me he was on his way. He would be staying at his family home in Sausalito, where his ninety-five-year-old mother and his sister still lived. Along with Joey and a couple of others, Jimmy was yet another local boy I had met when I first came to live in Sausalito. His father was an MD who provided a comfortable living in their stately home with a beautiful view of Angel Island. Jimmy was one of four children, with two brothers and the sister who had become a registered nurse and now took care of Mom. Years before I had wanted a lot more to do with that lovely sister, but she'd had my number at first glance and it wasn't on her list.

"How was your flight," I asked, when Jimmy got in touch.

"Okay," he chuckled. "Pretty much like the last one." Even though I hadn't seen him in years, I could picture his smile. Jimmy had always smiled a lot. He had bought an interest in a tour bus line and drove tourists to see the Pueblos between Santa Fe and Taos. Before arriving at their destination, Jimmy would deliver a talk over a speaker system on the bus. He would advise the bus load of tourists, in no uncertain terms, to be respectful in their behavior toward Native Americans. When I'd last seen him in Santa Fe, Jimmy handed me one of his business cards. "HIRE POWER" was printed on the card in large letters.

We met at the houseboat of a woman Jimmy hadn't seen for a long time. Barbara was an artist, a stubborn Bohemian type and part of the communal history we all shared. Now, in her eighties, she talked about her memories of Ron.

"He once tried to court me," she said, with pride in her laughter. "But he was too young, cute, but young." Barbara was still painting and still fighting those in the establishment who wanted to get rid of the old houseboat community which hangs on still at the north end of the Sausalito waterfront. A lady friend of hers who lives in Sebastopol gave me a ride down to Sausalito and would wait for me while Jimmy and I went up the mountain to distribute Ron's ashes.

Past the Mountain Theater, on the road toward Bolinas, there's a place to pull off and park next to a trail that leads to a truly beautiful spot. There, next to a rocky outcrop and a couple of small weathered oak trees, with a wide and glorious view of the Pacific Ocean, is a place where I suspect more than one container of ashes have had a final fling. Nevertheless, Jimmy and I were carefully mindful of a few sightseers in our vicinity.

We sat for a while on a couple of flat rocks, absorbing the environment and the reason we were there. Although in our youth we had been spiritual explorers in a wonderland of LSD, Peyote and other drugs, our individual lives had left that world far behind. Jimmy and I had been clean and sober for many years. I glanced over at who he had become, this strong and dignified looking, heavyset man with long and wavy grey hair. I thought back to the foolish and dangerous times we had shared and let the wonder of our survival sink in.

Jimmy removed the little square box from a bag he carried and we prepared to bid our brother/friend farewell. I had brought my Tibetan chimes, the clear and sweet ringing tones of which seem to fit any and all occasions. I spoke directly to Ron and expressed my prayerful wish that he had finally found the blessed peace I suspected had eluded him for all his life. I called on Deity (as I understand it) and asked for love and protection for my brother's soul. Jimmy has been Bahai for a long time. He took out a small book and read a long, beautiful prayer.

We walked down to where the incline was sharper and off the trail. Jimmy offered me the little white square box, but since he had carried it for such a long way, I deferred the duty to him. He broke the seal and pulled out a clear plastic bag of ashes. As he opened the bag and flung the contents out, a gust of wind brought a good portion of the ashes back to cover us. We laughed and brushed ourselves off. As we looked at one another through a fine coat of Ron's ashes on both our sun-glasses, I sensed we both felt this was somehow just as it should be.

"I guess we're getting a goodbye hug," I said as we both laughed. It was a partly cloudy and breezy day. The wide Pacific gave back the vague images of a mottled sky. I looked at the tall grass where the bulk of Ron's ashes had gone. There was not a trace of them now. No marker, no cross or star, no physical evidence that he had ever existed. Just two old guys who had honored a promise climbing back up the mountain-side. The Poet of Mount Tam had taken his place in history now, and only a few of us would be around to know about it.

THE FEELING

Sunday morning. The sun feels warm and friendly; the air is clean and bright. I'm riding my bicycle down Wilson Street, looking toward a distant band of clouds near the horizon in the southern sky; and then it happens. IT is a sudden, profound feeling of extreme well-being, oddly alien, and just as oddly familiar, a sense of completeness. It's me but not me, like a vague memory I'm having that belongs to someone else. But the feeling is so strong and so deep inside me.

I think back to other incidents of my experience with this same particular feeling, which is always associated with scenery. I think back to that first dream, a vivid dream, of lying far forward on the bow of a sailing vessel, moving slowly between massive glacial walls, in what I can only describe as a fiord. Then, at a later time, I dreamt of a deeply green and steeply terraced valley wall, with wide wooden balconies at various levels, with hanging plants and artful mobiles floating and turning, with wind chimes softly singing. And with each of these I had this same deep, awesome feeling of belonging.

Eventually those dream feelings began returning during my waking hours as well, and always, as with the band of clouds in the southern sky, a bit of scenery has triggered the feeling. At first, I thought this feeling was only associated with the containment of high walls, whether green or icy, which would speak to a sense of security. But, as with the distant sky this morning, open and soaring like a wild, joyous spirit as it ricocheted off the cloud bank and into infinity, the feeling of boundless elation is always the same.

I remember how the poet, John O'Donohue, wrote so eloquently of his beloved Irish countryside. He introduced me to the unique and wonderful idea that certain Irish landscapes were conscious, even conscious of him being conscious of them. I think I've experienced something like this in what I would call power spots, where I sense something similar to an "awareness" in nature. I recall, mostly as a child, discovering such secret places in the woods, places that somehow felt alive.

And this brings to mind the so-called "primitive" notion of animism, of world soul, a belief that all things on earth, whether animate or inanimate, are alive, imbued with soul. This world view is still common among some native cultures, and was once held by large segments of the population in Europe. Such was a common belief, known as Christian Animism, during the Middle Ages. The concept of "soul," which we tend to think of as something contained within us, somehow within our bodies, was then conceived of as something that contains us. Soul does not dwell in us so much as we dwell in soul.

None of this, however, can really explain the feeling I'm talking about. It's somewhat like what I've heard concerning past life experiences, somehow triggered by the aesthetics of nature. To be with such a powerful sense of well-being might mean a life far beyond any struggle to survive, a life so pampered and supported that not even the slightest doubt of self-worth could intervene. Or, could this simply be the feeling of one who is secure in his or her relationship to nature, in the sense of belonging to the natural world? One of my favorite writers, Laurens van der Post, has made the following comment:

"The great need of our time is somehow to get rid of the pretense, this awful secrecy in life, where people profess to be one thing and live another. Somehow that has to be brought out in the open, so that we will stop pushing the natural part of ourselves into a corner."

I wonder if what I feel, as I ride my bicycle down Wilson Street, is this "natural part" of myself trying to get out. In spite of the forceful unity of our socializing technology, which is a poor excuse for civilization, this natural part of me still labors to breathe, even though compressed beneath the unnatural layers of our quest for comfort and convenience. Can you imagine explaining a fitness salon to a laborer in the field who works hard to gain a living from the earth? I wonder if we are not insulating ourselves out of existence. Or, as I think it was Neil Postman who said, "Entertaining ourselves to death."

And so, as I ride my bicycle down Wilson Street, looking toward that distant band of clouds in the southern sky, I wonder if this sudden feeling of joyous belonging is but a blessed glimpse through a hole in the civilizing insulation that surrounds me. For countless miles in every direction, we have rearranged and overrode any natural ecosystem that stood in the way of our culture of convenience.

But then, the natural part of me wonders why I can't just ride my bicycle down Wilson Street and enjoy "the feeling" without investigating it to death. It occurs to me that the human mind is like a babbling monkey that never shuts up, a conflicted creature of cascading associations forever ready to run with the slightest notion, ad infinitum. Perhaps, after all, it is the duty and the destiny of our species to do exactly what we are doing.

RANCHO CARMEL

I look back now with a complex of feelings about the variety and fragmentation of my youthful work history. For the most part I am proud of the abilities I found and exercised in spite of my somewhat invisible disability - visual impairment. In fact, I started wearing contact lens, just after they came out, from the time I was nineteen until I was around thirty, a decade of denial. I pretended I could see as well as anyone and I was so good at it that even those who knew better would forget my limitations.

At this point in my life, I make the joke that my "legal blindness" simply means I can't be arrested for being near-sighted. But, over the years, this congenital condition has been the source of great distress, especially in terms of the complex psychological problems to which such a physical deficit can contribute. At any rate I hardly ever had a problem finding employment, the difficulty came as a matter of trying not to be found out.

I had a number of jobs during the various times I lived and worked around the Monterey Bay Area; dishwasher, dance instructor, hospital janitor, car wash manager, liquor store clerk, and caretaker on a ranch in Carmel Valley. This story begins with the liquor store and moves on to the ranch.

* * *

The store was called the Liquor Chest and was owned by the then mayor of Monterey, Sparky Pollard. I quickly found ways to memorize the keys on the cash register and recognize bottles and prices without looking too closely. It was soon a fact that most of the information I needed to do my job was committed to memory.

Sparky was a congenial, heavy set guy who always wore a yachting cap and did in fact own a yacht. He also stocked a large selection of good wine in his store and made it a condition for getting the job that I should learn something about the varieties we carried; which I did. However, during the entire time I worked there, somewhat prepared and willing to talk about wine, the only questions I ever dealt with were of the "red wine with beef, right?" or "white wine with chicken, right?" kind of inquiry. Oh well, I did learn some things about the history of wine making in California.

I was one of five clerks who kept the place open seven days a week. Sparky was a good boss, which meant he pretty much left us alone to do our job. There were two conditions of employment that still stand out all these years later. One; it was Sparky's policy that each clerk could take one bottle of anything we wanted, once a week, no matter how expensive. And two; he kept a large amount of cash in a built-in floor safe for honoring late night and weekend personal checks for his friends. It was also part of my job to memorize the names and photographs of these gentlemen.

I don't remember the year, but the Monterey Jazz Festival was fairly new at the time. On that particular festival week-end I looked down into the floor safe, built into a concrete block in a storage room, and marveled at the one-pound coffee cans full of currency. The bills were packed into the cans on edge, so that all one saw were the wavy lines formed by the edges of all those bills. I had just put the cash box in the floor safe after a busy late-night shift, and was momentarily hypnotized by the sight of all that cash. I could see how some people might have succumbed to such a temptation, but I knew better. The only thing I ever did to feel guilty about on that job was to unlock the store once, in the middle of the night on a weekend, to get more booze for a party.

Part of my job was to occasionally make deliveries, which I did, with the aid of a pair of good binoculars. Once again, I don't remember the year, but one memorable experience happened when I was making a substantial delivery to a large modern home in Carmel Valley. I had a case of gin, a case of scotch, and a case of bourbon, all good labels. I was greeted at the kitchen door by a busy and distracted Richard Nixon, who was then involved in California politics. Some kind of political conference was apparently taking place in that house over the weekend.

Eventually, one of the other clerks noticed me checking the I.D. of a youthful looking customer with my pocket magnifying glass and must have said something to Sparky. Of course, it was a sincere and gentle lay-off, but, as with a number of employers with whom I 'd had a similar experience, somehow knowledge of my limited eyesight meant that I couldn't be trusted.

"You understand, Ray," Sparky said. "Now and then we get those people from Seaside who shoplift. And what about handling money?" Of course, it didn't seem to matter that my till had never been short. And I had already dealt with a gang of guys who tried to distract me at the counter while a couple of them did some quick shopping. I put the brakes on their plan in a hurry. I was sure nothing got out of the store that night. Nor did I bother to mention the incident to anyone.

What I did with the experience, every time I lost a job (which was honestly devastating), was to overcompensate. I pretended I had quit. I emphasized my freedom. I had saved some money, had a good running vehicle, and a choice of people to see and places to go. I was free to travel, to find new experience, to think, to wonder about what really mattered. I had recently paid my rent, but I told my landlord I might be leaving soon.

And then there was Nicki, my friend Nicki. Depending on the hours of my shifts at the Liquor Chest, I would often drop by the Palace Bar, located on the waterfront at the Monterey end of Cannery

Row. Nicki was a cocktail waitress there. She and I had developed an interesting relationship. It wasn't so much that we fell in love as we fell in friendship. There was an understanding between us that tended to finish one another's sentences, and laughed when no one else seemed to get it.

The first night I went home with her, to her comfortable little cottage in Carmel, we just lay in her bed talking until dawn.

"You wonderful man," she said. "You didn't come home with me for sex after all, you just wanted my company." Of course, that made the sex all the better in the morning.

I couldn't lie to Nicki, even though I was a little desperate to protect my presumed macho image. When I told her about my lost job and that I was thinking of leaving the area, her sadness was apparent.

"But I'm not through with you yet," she said, and managed a soft chuckle. Then, she continued in a more serious tone.

"I understand you've been hurt. But please, don't run away." When I started to object to her statement, steeped in my own denial, she just hugged me until I relaxed. She was keenly perceptive. She offered just the right amount of sympathy tempered with just the right amount of respect.

The following day, while checking the want ads in the newspaper, I was stopped by an ad for caretaker on a ranch in Carmel Valley. The position included living quarters plus a small stipend. I continued to look through the paper, but was drawn back to the Carmel Valley ad. It offered a way to "get out of town" and still be able to see Nicki.

However unrealistic it might have been for a visually impaired guy to apply for a care-taking job in the country, it only mattered to me as a challenge. My life was always locked between accepting my limitations and not trying too hard, or, forging ahead with the attitude that I could overcome any obstacle. I understand how this might seem to some like a self-centered and risky course of action, possibly even a threat to others, but I really didn't know how else to financially, or psychologically, survive.

"You should check it out," said Nicki. "I'd love to have an incestuous country cousin."

I made the call, to a number in San Francisco, and arranged to meet the owner at the ranch in Carmel Valley.

* * *

When I first met the owner of the ranch, a muscular middle-aged man with sandy hair and quick blue eyes, it was as though he reached out to shake my hand from inside a glass cage. There was an aura of protection about him, as though his life depended on keeping his distance. I eventually learned that he lived at the intersection of more than one wealthy family, and, as a consequence, periodically inherited another fortune. Poor guy. One of his inherited acquisitions had been the ranch.

Although I only saw him a few times, and briefly at that, this guy, whose name was William, made a lasting impression on me. He was soft spoken and very much in control; but, when he took me on a wild tour in the ranch jeep, he seemed determined to kill us both. It was all I could do to keep from being bounced out into the landscape. Although I never said it to his face, I nicknamed him "Volcano." There was an explosive energy about him that lurked like an imprisoned madman just below the surface.

The ranch was at the upper end of Carmel Valley, several thousand acres bordering on Los Padres National Forest. Volcano and his family (wife and two children) only visited the place a few times a year. But, during deer hunting season, a number of his business associates stayed there.

The core of the place was a large compound. There was a recently constructed motel like row of guest rooms, where the deer hunting friends would come to get drunk and play cards and shoot high powered rifles. I did in fact discover some bullet holes around the place, which didn't make me feel too comfortable about the possibility of being there during deer hunting season.

There was the main house, a beautiful old four-bedroom structure surrounded by a wide veranda. There was a large, well-constructed old barn in which I found an amazing collection of antique farm equipment; a kind of industrial art museum where I would sometimes go to meditate. It was fascinating to see the soulful love affair mankind had enjoyed with early farm equipment, the filigree and embellished iron sculpture of mowing and reaping that was still so alive in a musty old barn. I wondered who had so carefully put together such a collection, but never found out.

There was a tack room and smaller barn with four stalls and an equal number of horses. Fortunately, since my experience with such animals was quite limited, a Carmel Valley cowboy named Fred, who lived a little way down the road, mostly took care of them. Finally, there was the old adobe (my place if I got the job), one of the very first buildings in the entire valley. It was set near the road in a small grove of trees, cool in summer and reputedly easy to heat in winter. I loved that old place. I don't know how many (if any) others had applied for the position, but William the Volcano indicated he would like for me to stay on.

The duration of my residence at the ranch was a healing and rewarding time, made all the more so because of my relationship with Nicki. This was for me a rare relationship. My usual tendency with an intimate partner had amounted to a pattern of insecurity, possessiveness and mistrust, but somehow Nicki was more than a "woman" to me. She was first and foremost a good friend. That doesn't mean our time together was without passion, quite the contrary; but, because she was so self-possessed and we connected in such an authentic way, I was able to let go of my usual expectations.

After I got settled into the old adobe, with its large screened in porch and cave quiet rooms, I set about exploring the wide-ranging topography of the ranch and learning some things from Cowboy Fred. He really did look the part; muscular build, curly black hair, always joking. He and his lovely wife made a good living renting horses, giving riding lessons and guiding horseback trips into Los Padres. Fred sometimes worked hunting trips with a local legend I only knew as Lambert, a tough, work hardened old timer who never stopped smiling.

Further up the valley and deeper into the wilderness, where the rough dirt roads got even rougher, was the Lambert Ranch; a collection of weathered buildings that looked as though they might have sprouted up out of the earth itself. Old man Lambert was reputed to know a great deal about the habits and movements of the wild boar in Los Padres, transplanted from Europe some years before. Hunters from all over the world occasionally came to his ranch. Fred told me a story of how Lambert had tested a couple of archers who came looking for a trophy.

"I always carry my own rifle," Lambert had told them. "But, for safety's sake, I wanna make damned sure you boys know what you're doin' with them bows." He looked around the yard for a target. "See them chickens over there?" he asked, indicating a few loose hens some distance across his yard. "How about dinner?"

Fred claimed that one of the men quickly raised his bow and took the head off one of the chickens, but I wasn't so sure I could believe that. Nevertheless, both archers did display the kind of expertise that gave Lambert confidence, the kind of skill that just might put an arrow into the snout of an angry, oncoming pig. I was so impressed and challenged by Fred's story, I wound up buying myself a pretty good bow and some blunt arrows.

Near the ranch compound where I lived there was a large fenced in field which became my target range. I took a chunk from a bale of hay, a little bit larger than a chicken, and placed it out in the field. I would walk around the periphery of the field, at different distances from the target, and try to put an arrow into my straw chicken. I was fascinated with the practice of archery. There was a sensory elegance to it, a way of using my intuition and my body that didn't depend so much on my eyesight. It was a continuous act; raising the bow, pulling the string, looking at the target, and then knowing just when everything came together at exactly the right instant to let go.

It was during my bow and arrow target practice in that field when I discovered the path that went nowhere. It started at a rough pole fence on the most wooded side of the field, went out onto a small rise near the center of the field, and then stopped. It made no sense. The path was worn through the grass to bare earth, and then, for no apparent reason, it simply ended. Spooky. When I finally discovered the solution to this mystery, it was so unexpected, so uncanny, I felt transported to some kind of "twilight zone." As a matter of fact, it was around twilight when it happened.

There are two times of day when I can see best; dawn and dusk, so I frequently took an end of the day walk around different parts of the ranch. On that particular day the hush of approaching evening was exquisitely soft and magical, like the whole world was holding its breath, in awe of itself. It was so quiet, so still, I felt the usual boundaries of my life dissolve into the soft earth around me.

I was standing by the fence next to the field, as silent and still as a fencepost, when suddenly two deer appeared behind the low pole fence where the mysterious path began, maybe twenty or thirty yards from where I stood.

They were a couple, a buck and a doe. Then, with the incredible ease which only such creatures possess, the buck lifted straight up and over the fence, and onto the path. His partner stayed in place, watchful.

The buck slowly strolled out along the path to where it ended and stood there, motionless, looking down the valley toward the fading light of sunset. There was something so mysterious and elegant in that moment, so full of grace, I felt that all of creation had called a truce. There would be time for the rule of survival after the sun went down. But for now, we were sharing an instant of timeless balance, an instant when all was right with a universe in contemplation. The buck stood there for an eternity. The doe didn't move and I didn't move. Then, as gathering darkness signaled a change of shift in the wilderness night, the buck turned and retraced his steps to the waiting doe. Once again, he lifted like a spring over the fence and they silently disappeared into the woods. As darkness surrounded me, I stood there for a long time, filled with a deep sense of wonder, and gratitude.

I have carried that memory with me like a precious jewel, somewhat afraid to share it, this being the first time in writing. Like the poet, Rilke, I believe there are subtle and mysterious energies in the natural world that have; "due to our daily defensiveness been so entirely eliminated from human life that the senses with which we might have been able to grasp them have atrophied."

That summer in Carmel Valley, as I retreated deeper into the unrealized layers of my own belonging to the beauty and mystery of nature, I began to better understand the distance of man's culture from the sublime scheme of things.

Anyway, I didn't try to spot the deer again, in part because Nicki and I soon found me a dog. We got him at the pound in Monterey, a skinny, homeless and nameless, mostly Irish Setter. When he stuck out his left paw in response to my handshake gesture, I immediately named him Lefty.

My new dog and I enjoyed taking long walks in the woods, or down the winding country road that ran past the ranch. And sometimes we enjoyed chasing wild chickens. A Mexican family who had previously occupied the old adobe had left their chickens to fend for themselves. Unlike Lambert's domestic birds, these chickens had gone completely wild; they were amazing. When I first tried to catch one of them, I was bewildered by its behavior. These chickens had learned how to fly, albeit not too high and for short distances, but they could take off and fly. Mostly they hung out in the limbs of a nearby tree.

I won't pretend it was intentional, but I actually did bring one of them down with a blunt arrow. Nicki was visiting and I was showing off. I knew it was a lucky shot, but she insisted it wasn't. Then, to our amazement, the wounded chicken got up and managed to get back up to the tree. Our laughter was mixed with a desire to help a creature we couldn't reach.

Nicki came out at least once a week to spend the night, sometimes showing up in the early morning from her job at the Palace Bar. On one occasion she came along to witness one of my musical echo trips with Lefty. I had a little C Melody saxophone that I would now and then take to my favorite echo place, a low ridge near a canyon wall. What I had done before Lefty came into my life was to quickly blow a phrase and then quickly join in with its echo, creating a very brief duet.

At first I thought the pitch of the sax was painful to Lefty's ears, and that's why he was howling. But I soon learned, through trial and error, that he was singing. What a wild and wonderful music we made.

At another time when a military jet aircraft was flying low along the coast, miles away at the mouth of the valley, its distant engine noise triggered overtone frequencies that echoed from the mountains to fill the sky with magnificent organ music. Even a war machine could bring joy to my ears in that wilderness setting.

Before I had moved onto the ranch, I made one trip up to Petaluma where my mother and step-father lived. Their place, with converted old chicken houses on the property, provided rent free family storage. One of the things I brought back to Carmel Valley was a 410 gauge/22 caliber over-and-under shotgun/rifle. I had started the habit of taking early morning walks down the road with Lefty, and one morning I took this combination shotgun-rifle along with me, like, you know, to carry it in the crook of my arm like a typical country squire.

After a while I realized I had not fired this piece except just after I had first acquired it. So, for no damned good reason, I inserted a 410 shell, lifted the barrel, pointed into a nearby bank and pulled the trigger. BAM! What a noise. I felt like I had just let out a loud fart in church. The rustling of small creatures and vibrant birdsong of a moment before was gone. Silence. I sensed that every critter for a mile around had stopped whatever it was doing and looked in my direction. Poor Lefty actually seemed to be embarrassed. I hadn't even shot AT anything. We all stood frozen for a long moment before going back to the business of life. That was the last time I pulled the trigger on that particular firearm.

On one of our morning walks down the road, as I was passing a wide wooden gate I had passed before, there was a little old woman pulling the contents from a mailbox at one end of the gate. The mailbox was mounted on a post, as usual, but she was able to swivel it around toward her, from the inside of the gate, so she didn't have to open the heavy gate and go around into the road. Lefty ran ahead to stick his nose through the fence to receive a gentle pat on the head.

"That's really a neat mailbox," I commented. Her body was bent and thin, but when she looked up from petting Lefty, her eyes were as bright as those of a child.

"My husband's a fixer," she said. "He even fixes things that ain't broke." She laughed at her own words, a soft and pleasant laugh, and then bent down to pet Lefty some more. "And this is a really good doggie," she continued. "Our dear old Sally died a few months back and we just haven't...." Her voice trailed off, but I got the message. I correctly assumed that Sally had been their dog.

Neither she nor I could know in that moment that Lefty had just found a new home. In a matter of days, Nicki's father would die in New York and she would return there. Shortly after that I would give notice to William the Volcano that I needed to move on. Meanwhile, I got to know Mabel and Roger, both in their late seventies, who had retired to their summer cottage years before. As Mabel, Lefty and I walked the short distance back to her neat little home, a tall and thin old man emerged from the woods on the far side of the house. In the short time that remained for me in Carmel Valley, I would come to know and respect this man for his wealth of knowledge and his gentle soul. Now, as he appeared from the woods, holding an old fashioned two-handed mowing scythe, his bride of many years let out a long and loving sigh.

"He's such a handsome man," she whispered. "He looks just like his daddy."

LEARNING IN MONTEREY

Monterey was a second home to me; second to Marin County. I went to live there for the first time as an Artie Morie dance instructor. I had been working in the San Francisco studio, on Sutter Street, when I heard about the need for a male dance instructor in Monterey. I was going through a break-up with one of my co-workers at the time and being in the same studio with her was difficult. The change of scene made sense. I went for it.

My new boss, a short and bulbous, dynamic bleached blonde, lived in Carmel and drove around in a new Lincoln convertible with two huge, slobbering Great Danes in the back seat. Riding with her was a nightmare. The dogs obeyed her when she was looking at them; but, when her attention was elsewhere, they nudged my neck and ears unmercifully with their wet snouts. I stayed in the guest cottage behind her quaint Carmel home as briefly as possible.

I soon found a place in Pacific Grove, right across the street from Monterey Bay. It had been a bakery at one time, at the waterfront intersection of Ocean Ave and Pacific Grove. Across from my large, store front picture window was a low sea wall and a postcard view of the rock formation known as Lover's Point.

Inside the bakery turned duplex, high walls and ceilings had been carefully covered with thick paper egg crate inserts, the latest thing in decorative insulation. My neighbor was a lesbian violinist who did large abstract paintings between fits of passionate fiddling. Living there, with the occasional sounds of a wailing violin, was "Bohemian" as hell, although we did have a little conflict over her late-night inspirations.

My new landlady was also an artist, a seascape painter, and a beautifully petite mixture of Russian and Chinese. Regardless of our age difference, I was strongly attracted to her. And being the bold young fool I was, I politely hit on her. She was a very caring lady and gentle in her response that she wasn't into "experimenting."

During my time at the Artie Morie Studio in San Francisco, I had been able to focus more on dancing than on selling. But in Monterey, the dancing was secondary, which mostly amounted to guiding elderly women around the dance floor who had been sold expensive, long term contracts. I felt cheapened by the experience and it became harder and harder to accept what I was doing.

My new employer (Dorothy) was masterful at emotional selling and a powerful mentor. We had a routine that I knew was wrong, but I tried to adjust to it for the sake of money. I would bring a customer into her office and present my proposed lesson plan for approval. She would watch us dance for a few minutes, and then deny my lesson plan, saying that it was too advanced for my student. I would argue with her. She would carefully express her doubts about the customer's ability and I would pretend to become angry.

The degree to which our act would go to get a contract signature depended upon the individual we were dealing with and how much the studio had grossed so far that month. As a final ploy, I would slam the lesson plan down on Dorothy's desk and threaten to quit. She would grudgingly give in and the poor deluded customer would usually sign on the dotted line.

I knew this kind of pressure was wrong, but I soon found out that Dorothy was training me to become studio manager. I would even receive a percentage of the studio's net income. With five other instructors working, that could amount to a good living. I overcame my ethical pain for a while with excuses I'd heard like "everyone does it... and, after all, its only business." But my denial could not hold up.

On one particular memorable morning, I looked at myself in the mirror and reflected on a telephone conversation I'd had the day before. A Fort Ord Army training officer had called to inquire about an expensive contract I had convinced his young wife (who was over 21) to sign while he was away on assignment. He was looking for a way out of the contract.

"It's out of my hands," I said. "You'll have to deal with the Artie Morie Credit Bureau in Kansas City. The phone number is on your statement"

"Just let me ask you one fucking question," he was livid. "Do you actually think this is fucking right?" His voice was like a bayonet to my conscience. No, it wasn't right.

On that final day, when I saw the cynical young con man looking back at me from my bathroom mirror, I knew I had to quit.

*   *   *

My next job, right out of the newspaper want ads, was one of the shortest periods of employment I ever had. The job was at a Monterey car wash. The racist owner needed a "manager" to deal with the public, and, to play boss with an all-black crew of attendants. It was obvious to this crew that I knew diddly about managing a car wash. And, in spite of my efforts at friendliness, I could feel the resentment that followed me around. We all knew that any one of them was far more qualified to run the car wash line than I was.

Part of my job was overseeing the interior detailing at the end of the line, done by a couple of black girls. One day, unknown to me and the two girls, someone at the front of the line had not noticed a large mongrel dog in the back seat of the car, probably asleep at the time. When the smaller of the two girls opened the car door, the dog growled and started to lunge at her. The speed with which she reached her back pocket and had an open straight-edged razor in her hand would have put Billy the Kid to shame.

The dog hesitated and, acting instinctively, I got between them, a little faster than I could think. The girl was obviously prepared to cut the dog's throat. I shouted the animal back into the car and closed the door. I turned and looked into the black girl's eyes. The razor was still in her hand. In deference to that crew (so I told myself) I left that job the same day.

*   *   *

My next job, clerking in a liquor store, was a great relief; and, it had some surprising benefits. The store's owner invited us clerks to take one bottle of anything we wanted, no matter how expensive, once a week on Friday. It didn't need to be stated, however, that to do so at any other time would mean instant termination.

It was definitely an expensive bottle of wine that went home with me to a goodbye dinner with my Russian-Chinese landlady, Rosalie. She had sold the old bakery, plus a couple of other properties in Pacific Grove, and was taking a trip back to China to visit family. She assured me that my tenancy in the bakery was secure with the new owner.

After dinner and a few glasses of wine, plus a moonlit walk along the seashore, we came closer to "experimenting" than ever; but wound up laughing a lot instead. It was clear from the start that we really did like one another. I still treasure the memory of that wise and beautiful woman.

*   *   *

I gradually discovered that the Monterey Bay Area was a many layered cake of sub-cultures: from the fishermen along the Monterey waterfront to the farmers in Carmel Valley, from the fundamentalists in Pacific Grove to the artists in Carmel and Big Sur, not to mention the wealthy property owners of Pebble Beach and the poor population in Seaside. As with many of my fellow travelers during those restless, changing times, I would skip across the surface of these layers like a slippery flat stone that was bound to keep moving.

WE THREE

She played the piano bar in the Hotel San Carlos, where I often went after work. How old she was I couldn't tell, but I would guess now she was in her early forties. At barely twenty something myself, it was difficult for me to determine another's age, especially Kathleen. All I could tell for sure was that she belonged in that oddly alluring category of attractive "older woman," certainly not off limits to my healthy young libido.

My job, at the Artie Morie Dance Studio in Monterey, California, was right across the street from the rear entrance to the hotel. I usually left work after my last dance lesson, the nine to ten o'clock hour, and walked across the street for a drink. I hated my job, and was struggling to justify staying with it. The money was good, but the emotionally manipulative selling of expensive dance lessons to lonely souls with little talent bothered me to the core. Nevertheless, I liked dressing up and I loved to dance; so, the hook was in.

Kathleen played the old tunes I knew from childhood, the beautiful and sad war tunes of the early forties, as well as the zany tunes of that same period. She had a beautiful singing voice, but mostly played, only singing occasionally.

She was indeed attractive, but in a complicated kind of way. The more I saw her the more attractive she became, but I couldn't tell exactly why. The twinkle in her unusual amber eyes could be taken as sexy, but I eventually learned it was more about her humor and intelligence.

There was an inviting openness about her, a capacity for engaging on a wide range of topics, but still, there was an elusive and mysterious depth about her. She had a way of looking at you as though debating whether or not to share some important information.

The cocktail dresses she wore revealed a slightly thin but well proportioned, desirable figure. Her short, curly brown hair sometimes gave her a serious business-like appearance, until she cracked open that charming, challenging smile.

"Can I buy you a drink?" I asked, just after I first met her, carefully projecting my casual dance instructor confidence. At that moment I was the only customer on the other side of the piano bar. She smiled and looked briefly over her shoulder toward the gray-haired bartender.

"You could," she turned back to me. "But it would be a waste of money. If he knows it's for me, he'll hardly put any booze in it. Watered down drinks are part of my job." At first, I was thrown off by her blunt, matter-of-fact honesty, but then I felt complimented by her confidentiality.

"So, what if I get another one for myself and give it to you?" I ventured. "Or, better yet, what if I get two of the same thing? He won't know the difference."

"I like your style," she said. Her soft chuckle was warmth itself. "Do you like Manhattan's?"

"Sure," I responded, trying to remember what went into a Manhattan.

I looked forward to seeing her on those nights when I had the late lessons, and soon enjoyed the company of yet another new acquaintance, a guy who showed up at about the same time I did. The three of us easily engaged and quickly became a regular chat group. I was amazed at Kathleen's ability to focus on a conversation and still play so beautifully, without missing a beat. Sometimes the three of us would harmonize the lyrics of an old tune, amazing ourselves at how good we sounded.

"Where's newspaper man?" I asked. "He's usually here by now?"

"Gary," she spoke his name. "He'll show up. Sometimes he's a little late putting the paper to bed."

Gary was a blonde haired, freckled faced, middle aged guy with a slight paunch who always wore a blue suit and was immediately likeable. He worked as part time reporter and typesetter on the local newspaper, was well educated and something of an intellectual. He and Kathleen seemed to have a lot in common and it was soon apparent that he was totally taken with her. But, although she was genuinely friendly, she didn't respond to him with any particular encouragement. Her warm regard was openly and equally expressed toward us both. Regardless of her ability to professionally respond to the requests and attention of other customers, we knew we were special to her.

Gary and I hit it off from the start. However, even though there was a feeling of kinship between us, I would still catch an occasional glance from him that wondered if I was some kind of competition. From my point of view, such a notion was not very realistic. The age difference between the two of them and myself was apparent. In fact, some of their conversations simply went over my head. It was quite clear they shared the baseline knowledge of a preceding generation.

I sometimes wondered what business I had around their relationship, and yet, I vaguely understood I was somehow an important part of it, some kind of safety valve, a third element that kept things from becoming too intense, which Kathleen depended upon. I didn't understand this complicated dynamic very well until some time later. If I had, I might have felt used and not stuck around.

There were obviously some nights when I didn't work late and Gary would come see Kathleen by himself. But, although I knew she liked him a lot, I also knew she carefully maintained a platonic relationship with him. Even so, the first time she invited both Gary and me up to her room, I went through some difficult and stupid changes.

It suddenly occurred to me that maybe I had her figured all wrong. The idea that she might actually be interested in some kind of a menage-a-trois was disturbing, a confusing combination of excitement and distaste. There was no way I could be sexually explicit around another man, and if that was her plan, I knew I could not be a part of it. But I would soon feel ashamed of such thinking.

Her invitation had been straight forward and without innuendo. Gary was telling us about his former life in Jackson Hole, Wyoming, where he'd been raised, and it was suddenly twelve thirty; quitting time for Kathleen. Ordinarily we would have parted company, but this night was different. And there was something different about Kathleen. At times she had seemed distracted by her own thoughts.

"Maybe we could continue this conversation up at my place," she said, catching us both off guard. "I have a room a couple of blocks from here. It isn't exactly the San Carlos, but you guys are welcome" We'd all had more than a couple of drinks and were awash in the glow of our own good company, a kind of communication high, a state of exciting anticipation over the next interesting thing we each had to say.

We left the hotel, still listening to Gary's recollections, and walked the short distance to an old and stately rooming house. It was November, foggy and cold. Gary and I walked close on either side of Kathleen. He ventured an arm over her shoulders, which she didn't seem to mind. All three of us wore overcoats and as we walked under a friendly streetlight we laughed at the monolithic, three headed shadow we cast on the sidewalk. Kathleen broke into song, altering the lyrics of an old tune.

"We three, we're not a crowd, but we are such good com-pa-ny; there's Gary, there's Rabon, and me." As we were leaving the hotel, I realized I had hardly ever seen Kathleen on her feet. And then I couldn't help but notice the subtle swinging motion of her hips. She moved like a dancer; her body held a music of its own. I was darkly excited and conflicted at my thoughts.

Kathleen's room was on the second floor. She motioned us to be quiet as we climbed the carpeted stairs up to a dim lit hallway. I had an impression of three tipsy teenagers sneaking in after curfew. The room was plain and simple, with not much to suggest it was home. A double bed, a few books on the night stand; a dresser, a small table and straight-backed chair, and two easy chairs. Kathleen asked us to make ourselves at home and excused herself to her bathroom.

It was strange. Gary and I couldn't quite look one another in the eye. There was an awkward silence. I think we were both wishing the other guy wasn't there.

"Wow, she reads Faulkner," Gary picked up one of the books by the bed. "'Requiem for A Nun'" He glanced in my direction. "You ever read this?" I was uncomfortable with the slight tone of challenge I felt in his question.

"I don't think so," I said, feeling less than sophisticated. He continued to look at the book until Kathleen came out of the bathroom. I don't know exactly what I expected, but I was definitely relieved to see a long robe that completely covered her body.

"Thanks," she smiled. "I needed to get out of my work clothes." She then arranged herself in one of the big easy chairs, drawing her shapely feet up onto the seat and under her robe.

"Sit down, you guys," she said. "Take off your coats and stay a while. You can throw them on the bed. The only thing I can offer you is some wine, there on the dresser, but only one glass. You guys won't mind drinking from the bottle." She seemed nervous, not exactly the self-possessed woman to whom I had become accustomed. Was she leading up to something? Was she working up her nerve?

"And I have this," Gary ventured, as he pulled a small flask from his coat. "Medicinal brandy." Gary took the other easy chair, still holding the book from the night stand in one hand, and I pulled the straight chair around to face them both. Kathleen noticed the book in Gary's hand and let out a deep sigh.

"The past is never dead," she quoted. "It's not even past." I later learned this was a quote from Gavin Stevens, one of the characters in Faulkner's play.

"I'm so glad you guys are here," she continued. There was a different tone in her voice. She seemed oddly subdued. "I really do appreciate your company," she hesitated. "Especially today." There was another long pause.

"Why especially today?" Gary asked. Then I noticed the glistening tears that had begun to form in her eyes. Gary started to get up and move closer to comfort her, but she held out her hand to stop him and he sat back down.

"A year ago today," she said, so quietly. "My little boy, Jacob, was killed in an auto accident." Silence. In all our conversations, she had never mentioned anything like this. I didn't know what to say and obviously Gary didn't either. But, after a long moment of staring at Kathleen's quiet tears, I managed to speak.

"I am so sorry," I said. "What can we do?"

"Just listen, I guess," she whispered. "It helps to talk about it." We learned that she and her husband, also a musician, had separated after the accident. He had been driving drunk, in spite of her objections, and then she couldn't forget or forgive. The two of them had suffered only minor injuries, but the little boy, asleep in the back seat, had been thrown in such a way that caused internal injuries and his neck was broken.

After a few months of suffering, she had left Los Angeles, traveling from place to place, finally winding up in Monterey. Gary and I listened in silence as she laid out the story that had so drastically changed her life. The wine and brandy were gradually consumed, but there was no drunkenness. The three of us just drew closer. It was nearly dawn by the time she gave us each a quick hug and said goodbye.

During the next few weeks, Gary and I accompanied Kathleen home several times. The bond between us grew deeper as we each told stories about our lives, practicing what I would experience years later as "check in." We had become family, and somehow, more than family.

Gary struggled over his relationship with his father, who was back in Jackson Hole. He couldn't remember a time when the man had ever said "I love you." Gary had spent years of his life trying to prove himself to someone who forever remained unavailable. He shared the painful letters he had written to his father but never sent. The three of us worked on composing just one letter that he finally did send.

My turn came when Kathleen noticed how I pretended to read rather than hold one of Gary's letters up close. In spite of my contact lens, a product that hadn't been around for very long, she intuitively picked up on my habit of playing blind-man's-bluff. It was such a relief to finally unload my pent-up shame and defensiveness around not being able to see as well as others. I don't think I had ever felt safe enough to do that with anyone before.

Our three-way relationship lasted for a little while and then came the day when Gary didn't show up any more. Kathleen understood why better than I did, but I already knew how much it hurt him that he couldn't have the relationship with her he wanted.

"I do love him," she said to me. "But I just can't give him what he wants." I never saw Gary or the inside of Kathleen's room again, and before very long, she too had moved on.

WHY ME

It was early in the decade of the sixties. Coffee houses played classical music and the game of chess was in. Folk music was fading, Rock n Roll was gaining volume, but good jazz was a constant. It was a time of change, of trying new things, even new ways of doing college. Emersion College, in Pacific Grove, was something new.

Based on an experimental idea, it was funded by a wealthy young entrepreneur from San Francisco. He leased a beautiful old three-story mansion in a lovely setting and attracted quite a group of characters, including a poet friend of mine from Sausalito.

The idea behind the school was that one had to be both teacher and student. No credentials or degrees required, just a knowledgeable passion for your subject and a willingness to learn from others. I guess I cheated, although no one seemed to mind. My main interest was in the fencing class that was held in the spacious old attic. Ben, a fencing enthusiast from Seattle, had enough knowledge, skill and equipment for a small group of us young Renaissance types to get downright medieval.

Another favorite haunt I enjoyed was The Palace Bar, situated on the waterfront at the edge of Cannery Row, next to the Steinbeck Theater. A few different cultures came to an intersection there and found common ground. The bar was furnished with a pool table, a dart board, a few chess sets, and an upright piano.

A couple of 'lovely to look at' cocktail waitresses showed up on busy nights. Jazz musician soldiers from Fort Ord, along with local musicians, formed spontaneous combos. Students and teachers from the Army Language School mingled with local artists and an otherwise interesting assortment of locals.

It was mid-week, one of my days off, and not yet noon. I'd already done a couple of days off chores and stopped by the Palace Bar, where I could usually find a game of pool. Dennis, a photographer I'd come to know was there and ready. While we were playing, I noticed a guy at the bar who was so drunk he could barely keep from sliding off the barstool. I finished my game and, on impulse, went over to check on him. While I was standing there, he started sliding again and I managed to brace him before he fell.

The bartender indicated that he was getting ready to either call the guy a taxi, or, if necessary, the police. I was moved to intercede. Regardless of his drunkenness, the man had a warm smile and felt to me like a decent guy who was a lot more drunk than he wanted to be.

The few beers I'd already had probably contributed to my inspiration, but I knew exactly the right thing to do. I helped him out of the bar and into my car and headed for my latest rental, a little two room cabin up the hill in New Monterey. As soon as we got inside, he passed out on my bed. Good, he could sleep it off.

A little later on, after I'd made a trip to the market and puttered around the small kitchen slash dining room for a while, my guest showed signs of waking up. We came to a consensus on hungry and I heated some spaghetti I'd made the night before and finished off a bottle of wine.

We ate and drank. I opened another bottle; we drank some more. I was beginning to catch up with him. I told him about Emersion College and we agreed to take a ride over there. He was excited by the idea of a fencing class in the attic.

I wonder now what I might have heard if I'd known who he was. And I still wonder, and always will: why me? Sure, I wish I could accurately recall every word of our conversation, but I can't. We were drunk. And I don't want to put words in his mouth. That would be disrespectful.

Although, I do recall a few things he said. He definitely told me his name was John, that he was a writer, and that his financial affairs were managed by a relative. I remember looking at his dirty pants and worn boots and doubting that he had much in the way of finances to manage. But I liked his intelligent, curious nature and figured he was probably just going through a hard time and being boastful.

It wasn't until we had climbed the broad wooden steps and were at the front door of Emerson College that I found out who I had been with all day. It was summer, several people were in the large front parlor, with open windows looking out onto the wide veranda of a front porch.

"John Steinbeck is here." I heard the message repeated throughout the house. I will never forget the look that passed between the two of us. So much was acknowledged in that brief glance. I couldn't be certain that he had known, before that moment, that I hadn't realized who he was. Now, we both knew. There was no going back. We silently said goodbye as we walked through the large front door and entered the hallway together.

I have often wondered about my encounter with this amazing writer. I also wonder about what it must have been like for him, to be in the Palace Bar and not be recognized, even though the building next door is named after you. How he must have felt about the semi-museum Cannery Row had become because of him.

His visit to Emerson College was made brief when my friend, David (who lived there), and I rescued him from his apparent discomfort with too many questions. When we entered another bar, at his direction, on Alvarado Street in Monterey, he was immediately recognized and carried off by a group that obviously knew him much better than we did. I still feel a sense of pride in the historical perspective and class that David and I displayed as we didn't try to say goodbye to John Steinbeck, but with a smile and a shrug, took our leave of the bar.

Later that day I considered that maybe I should preserve the house slippers the famous man had worn, but put them on instead.

CORN FLAKES

We had been driving for a long time, on our way from Marin County down to Big Sur. The pipe had been passed around several times and we were all somewhere between earth and deep space. Billy, sitting next to me in the back seat, was actually managing to blow chords on his cornet. His black cheeks bulged as he tightened his lips to produce overtones. Rick was driving, and engaged with David, who was also in the front seat, in creating vocal harmonies that mingled with Billy's overtones. My own voice found high melodic phrases that drifted and blended between them.

The phenomena of our music were all around us; in the car, outside the car, in the sound of the motor, the tires on the highway, the streams of turbulent air being sucked past the windows, in the ocean, in the mountains, in the stars. We sang new songs and tarried just long enough to remain pure. And, by the time our music had come to a natural close, Rick had pulled up in front of an all-night, roadside café a few miles north of Santa Cruz. It was just breaking dawn.

We sat for a silent moment and then the four of us automatically got out of the car and filed into the restaurant. There were no more than a couple of customers at the counter. Without any conversation we took a table along the wall. The waitress smiled and placed a colorful menu in front of each of us. I'm not sure which one of us mumbled "Thank you."

We sat staring at the menus for a long time, carefully reading every word, over and over again. After a while the waitress came back and stood impatiently tapping her pencil on her receipt pad. She must have wondered what was up with this silent quartet somewhere between earth and deep space. I suddenly got the feeling we had been sitting there for several hours, and, it was clear that someone had to break the silence. With mounting tension, I looked up at the waitress and managed to blurt.

"We'll have four bowls of Kellog's Corn Flakes." Unable to hold back a powerful upsurge of laughter, I jumped up and almost ran for the front door. My companions were right behind me.

GOING DOWN

There was a dance in San Francisco, on the tenth floor of the Mart Building, on Market Street. It was featured as part of a convention, a private corporate affair. So, more important to us than whose band was playing or who was hosting the party, was whether or not we could get in without invitations. My friend Jess was seriously dedicated to gate crashing. You might even say he was addicted. But at least he showed a little class in the way he arranged to get his fix. He would go through the newspaper, looking for challenges, and then invite a witness. Jess was a performer; he had to have a witness.

The very first time I saw Jess, in a neighborhood bar near the Marina, he was seated at one of those wide, mega-selection juke boxes playing the buttons as though they were piano keys. His posture was that of a chimp, or a gorilla, and with brows knit together, tongue pushed forward in his lower lip, he created the perfect image of a primate playing the piano. As ridiculous as this may sound, the hilarious show he put on, combining his movements and facial expressions with the music, was clearly the work of some kind of genius.

Even so, not every challenge we went on was successful. The large Italian family wedding at Fugazi Hall a few weeks earlier had been strictly a "family" affair and Jess had only succeeded at getting us kicked out. He was an excellent mime, and sometimes, especially when he was nervous, he would impulsively begin to mime the person with whom he was dealing. When he began to mimic the hand motions of the large, hairy doorman, I knew it was all over. We were lucky we didn't get seriously thumped.

Nevertheless, his record for successful entries far outweighed his failures, and so, on this particular Saturday evening a few weeks later, I was once again ready to follow his lead into another adventure. When the matronly woman at the door of the tenth-floor ballroom asked which company we represented, Jess smoothly explained that we were secretly auditioning the band, for a possibly important job. He was so convincing in his role as the hip young music executive (even producing a phony business card) it would have seemed unreasonable not to believe him.

If it became necessary, I was prepared to play the role of associate, but usually I just enjoyed the show. Unfortunately, on this particular occasion, our success was offset by the fact that the band wasn't all that great and the females were either firmly attached or much older. We hung around anyway, for the free drinks and food, and managed to get pretty loaded. After a few drinks, Jess became typically excited as he told me about one of his latest schemes, to take a suit of armor from a snobbish hotel lobby on Sutter Street in broad daylight.

"We'll wear white coveralls," he said. "There's a guy on the desk in the late afternoons who's a pushover. We just give him something to sign and tell him we're picking up the suit of armor for a professional cleaning." We talked and drank and near the end of the evening, when the food was long gone and the music was getting worse; a number of us decided to leave the party all at the same time.

There were fourteen of us, mostly drunk and disorderly, who managed to crowd into the elevator. Then, it was only a matter of seconds after we started moving that we came to a shuddering halt. We were stuck. But most of the passengers just kept on laughing and talking. It took a long moment before the message began to sink in.

"What th' hell. Did somebody push th' wrong button?"

"You should push the emergency button."

"Is there a phone? Some elevators have emergency phones (hiccup)."

"I've pushed every goddam button here. You wanna come try, Dickhead."

"No need to get nasty."

"So, what-ur-we gonna do?"

"Christine," sighed one young man. "Just in case. Will you marry me?" Christine giggled as the young man grabbed her in a way that would definitely lead to an early honeymoon. A middle-aged platinum blonde clutched the arm of her elderly husband and dramatically announced;

"At least we'll go together, Darling."

"It's about time," he replied. "I don't think I could take another tango."

"Oh my god," someone moaned. "I think I smell smoke."

"Feel the floor, is the floor getting hot?"

My reaction time was befuddled because everything was so damned funny. Jess and I were just grinning at each other like a couple of idiot kids at a carnival, ready and willing to experience whatever came next. But the mood in the elevator quickly shifted from drunken humor to the hard edge of panic. The elevator seemed to shrink around us as the pressure increased.

"STOP!" One voice suddenly resounded above the rest. There was an instant of silence. The tallest person in the elevator, a weathered middle-aged man wearing a cowboy hat, had spoken. He was at least a head taller than most of us and seemed accustomed to telling people what to do.

"Ya'll calm down." His southern drawl was soothing, but his tone was also commanding. "We gotta wuk togetha heah." His voice seemed to dissipate the growing panic. "Fust let's see if we can get th doahs open." He pointed upward. "And th' trap doah too." From the corner or my eye, I could see Jess's lips moving as he mentally mouthed the cowboy's words.

We were packed in tight. And since Jess and I were standing directly under the trap door, we went into action. I made a stirrup with my hands to give him a leg up and he managed to knock the trap door loose and climb out onto the roof of the elevator. A couple of other guys pried the main door open a crack, but there was nothing on the other side but a wall of concrete.

"Theah's a doah in th' wahl up heah," Jess called down from the roof, not sounding at all like Jess. "Hits no moren a couplah feet abuv th' top ah th' elevatah."

He could have been the cowboy's younger brother.

"Way ta go, Old Son," the cowboy called up to Jess, who drunkenly smiled down in appreciation of his own cleverness. The elevator erupted with questions.

"Can you get th' door open?"

"What th' hell floor are we on?"

"Is anything broken up there?"

"Sahn up heah says aeith floah," Jess responded. "Nothin's broken. Cable's holdin',' this thang looks solid. An' so does this doah. Ah'll need some hep." He reached down to grab my hand and with the help of a push from below, pulled me up onto the roof as well. Jess and I had been doing some pretty serious drinking, but in that moment we were both critically aware that the top of an elevator, eight stories up, was no place to stagger. We were deliberately slow and all the more careful because we knew we were drunk.

The shaft was a double wide, with room enough for two elevators to pass, but all the cables were quiet. My experience of the depth beneath the large dangling box was visceral. I was wary not to look over the edge. We managed to reach a lever and force the sliding metal door open that was slightly above the elevator, exposing a dim-lit eighth story hallway. With a little care, the trip from the trap door and up into the hall was not a difficult one. But just how well the drunks in the elevator would handle it remained to be seen.

"Alright," I called down through the trap door. "We've got a way out up here." Jess climbed into the hall to look around and I knelt down by the trap door, ready to pull people out. But then there was a commotion in the elevator. Voices began to rise.

"No way, Pal," said a rough male voice. "You're not gonna stay down here and look up my girlfriend's skirt. I say the guys go up first."

"With all due respect, young man," said an older, slightly whining voice. "I don't give a damn about your girlfriend's behind. I'm an attorney and I'm not leaving this elevator until the police get hare to make out a report."

A husky female voice interrupted.

"Ain't there some rule about women and children first. I don't give a damn who sees my ass."

"That's only if you're abandoning ship, Dearie," said another woman. "And I'm sure you don't."

"Heah, yoh honor," said the cowboy, reaching over a few heads and handing the attorney a bandana. "Be a genaman an' blindfold yohself. Th' sooner th' rest of us *men* can get outa heah, th' fasta we can get th' women out." No one disagreed.

I had barely started to grab the first guy's hand when Jess reappeared with the business end of a fabric fire hose.

"This orta do-it," he said, still playing the cowboy. "Hits attached to a spigot in th' wahl down th' haul... ya'll." He winked and laughed and handed me the nozzle of the narrow flat fire hose. I lowered it through the opening.

"Head's up," I called. "Climb on this."

As the men climbed out, those with women still in the elevator were reluctant to leave the roof. But that limited space was no place for a group to gather. One jerk even ventured too close to the edge and had to sit down abruptly to regain his balance. Once again, the cowboy made things happen. He had climbed up to be across the trap door from me, helping to pull guys out, but he gave up that position to a worried husband.

"C'mon you guys," he prompted. "This thang cud start movin' agin. Let's do this fast. Two of us by th' doah an' th' rest in th' hall. Let's go." No one seemed to mind being bossed around by the cowboy. He was doing a good job.

When the wobbly, subdued passengers finally climbed out and into the hallway, they lapsed into relief and started rehearsing the stories they would tell later on. Most of the group quickly headed toward the nearby stairway; some going down, others going back up to the tenth floor. Two guys who had started to argue in the elevator were separated by their girlfriends, but continued to bravely sass one another in the stairwell. A few people exchanged telephone numbers they would probably never call and the hallway began to clear out.

When the last woman had been pulled up the fire hose and joined with her husband, I looked around for Jess. He was down the hall talking to the cowboy.

"All cleah?" he inquired, as people disappeared into the stairwell.

"Yeah," I responded, wondering what he was up to. Suddenly the fire hose began to swell and Jess and the cowboy came striding down the hall, Jess slightly behind, mimicking the cowboy's stride. They quickly stepped onto the elevator roof and looked down through the trap door just as a stream of water began gushing from the nozzle, which was on the floor of the elevator. The reluctant lawyer, looking like a martyr awaiting execution, still had his blindfold on. But when the powerful stream of water quickly soaked his shoes, he howled in surprise, ripped off the bandana and started dancing with the lively fire hose, which was whipping back and forth between the walls and soaking him in the process.

"Jess, you crazy bastard," I yelled. I was surprised that the cowboy had gone along with this stunt. He had seemed so responsible. But the look on both their faces as they peered down through the trap door was blatantly that of juvenile pranksters. Just then the outraged attorney managed to get the nozzle back up through the trap door. Jess and the cowboy, in no position to wrestle with the flailing fire hose, hung on to the elevator cables as the hose whipped around the shaft, threatening them and sending curtains of water into the depths.

I was still standing by the door in the hallway. I started for the shut off valve, but then, like a snake preparing to strike, the gushing fire hose reared up under its own pressure and backed into the hallway, where I had my turn. I managed to get a working grip on the nozzle, and, by the time Jess and the cowboy made it back down the hall to turn it off, I had sent a couple hundred gallons of water down the polished tile floor of the hallway. As we headed for the stairwell, we could hear the attorney yelling legal threats and calling for the police. I was a bit uncomfortable about just leaving him, but we had lowered the fire hose back down into the elevator.

By the time we got our wet pants into dry lounge chairs a few blocks away, we were veteran comrades. We had shared an adventure of major proportions and were still revved up by its energy. We laughed and told stories and it wasn't long before Jess revealed his deception to the cowboy by dropping the southern accent altogether. When this happened, the cowboy was silent for a moment. I thought he might become angry.

"Not bad, Old Chap," he said. "Except for a few specifics of pronunciation." His British accent was rather good, but soon fell apart as he tried to maintain it. In spite of the fun we had and promises made, Jess and I never saw the cowboy again.

*   *   *

Later that week Jess called to tell me about a newspaper ad he had come across. It seemed that a certain San Francisco attorney was looking for witnesses to an incident that had happened in an elevator in the Mart Building the previous Saturday night. After that, Jess took a break from gate crashing for a while and we didn't team up again until the St. Francis Yacht Club party.

BUYING BILL'S BODY

I had visited my stepfather, Bill, just once while he lived in Guadalajara. He was a WW II wheelchair veteran, and, like a number of other disabled veterans, he had discovered that his money could buy a lot more in Mexico. During my visit I got into a poker game with him and a few of his veteran buddies; four wheelchairs, one paraplegic, and me. Damn, they were good. They obviously got a lot of practice. But it was also as though the damage done to their manly bodies was somehow compensated by their ruthless, aggressive skill at cards. I lost a bit more than I could afford and wound up watching and learning. Bill later offered to make up for my losses, but I declined. I think it pleased him that I was willing to pay for my lesson.

After years of marriage, good times and bad, Bill and my mother had come to an arrangement. He spent most of his time in the house he rented in Guadalajara and she stayed in the wheelchair friendly home they had built together near Petaluma, in Sonoma County. Even so, they did exchange a few visits by automobile, back in the days when long auto trips were more common than air travel.

Bill had been in Mexico a little over five years, it was 1975, when his wheelchair rolled backward off a high curb and slammed his bent body onto the cobblestones. His shoulder was broken, he was taken to a hospital, and, a few days later he died of complications. It grieved me that his family was so far away at the time. His wish had been to be buried in Mexico, so my mother and I flew down to settle things.

I don't think my dear old mom had flown in an airplane but one time before. As I tried to comfort her, sitting tensely beside me, I could tell she was stubbornly holding on, terrified but determined, silently praying for us to get safely back on the ground. She did her best to loosen up and relate to the friendly flight attendants, but she was clearly of the school that said: "If God had intended us to fly, we'd have wings."

*   *   *

Bill had married my mother, in Georgia, when I was eight years old. I liked that he wore a military uniform and told funny stories. And I have always been grateful to him for bringing me out of poverty. He had served in the Army Air Corps, had been stationed for a while at Hamilton Field, in Marin County, and, like so many servicemen who'd passed through the beautiful San Francisco Bay Area, he eventually decided to return.

My biological father had been gone since I was a baby, so Daddy Bill was the only father I knew. He had been a pool shark, a carnival barker, and a would-be criminal. In 1940, in a courtroom in Evanston, Indiana, a judge had given him the choice of joining the U.S. Army or going to prison. He had driven the getaway car in a failed gas station holdup. I can still hear fragments of the carnival routine he sometimes recited.

> "There's a great show goin' on inside, never out and never over. See JoJo the Dogface Boy, Macro the Bug Eater, and there's Little Eva, weighing eight hundred and fifty-four pounds, who will endeavor to jump into a Coca-Cola bottle without making a splash."

I will never forget arriving at the Ferry Building in San Francisco, after a continental train ride; the cold, windy trek up Market Street, the pathetic crippled beggars along the sidewalk, the punctuation of rhythmic calls from newspaper vendors, the wonder of Clinton's Cafeteria and the Crystal Palace Market. My new life began in that world.

Before Bill's back injuries finally put him in a wheelchair for good, he worked as a cook at the Marin Café in San Rafael, while my mother was a waitress at the old Mission Inn. Eventually they bought a home in Santa Venetia, just north of San Rafael. And, some years later, after a difficult go at the restaurant business themselves, Bill and Myrtle moved up to Petaluma and built a G.I. loan wheelchair home a few miles west of town. My visits with them were at intervals that gave me snapshots of their relationship. Flipping through these snapshots in rapid succession would make for a sad picture show: two different worlds, endless negotiation.

When we got off the plane in Guadalajara, Max Rodriguez, a young Mexican guy who had attended Bill on a couple of stateside trips to Petaluma, was there to meet us. His family owned a swank, urban nightclub, on the same compound of property as their large family home, so my mother and I were well accommodated. This nightclub was so dimly lit it was hard to tell exactly what all went on there. I got the feeling that Max and his family were into more than one business.

I had to pass on the traditional all-night vigil with Bill's body, as did my mother. But tradition would not be denied. A few elder Mexican women did go to the mortuary chapel that night, and I could tell they were not pleased when Myrtle and I didn't bother to join them. Regardless, I was impressed that my stepfather was being so honored. Bill attracted people first of all because of his humor, and then because of his bold, honest character. He stood pretty tall in his wheelchair.

The business of the funeral, which was scheduled for the very next day, was more than I expected. When we arrived at the large, elaborate mortuary, there were two limousines and a hearse awaiting us. Bill's veteran buddies, plus the Rodriguez family and other Mexican friends, made up quite a crowd. But before anything else could happen, I was ushered into an office for the bad news.

Sitting behind a large ornate desk was a well-dressed, heavy-set guy wearing dark glasses and smoking a huge cigar. He was perfectly cast for his role. Speaking in flawless English, in a voice that would have made the Godfather proud, he calmly told me that Bill's body could not be removed for burial until the mortuary bill was paid. Eight hundred and fifty-four dollars, American money, in cash. No checks, no credit cards, no promises; all of which occurred to me. I stared at him in deep frustration, but it was extremely clear that no deals could be made. I knew Myrtle and I didn't have that much between us in traveler's checks. So, I would have to get to Bill's bank.

I had all the documentation and had already talked to the bank on the phone the day before, but it was quite a distance across town. Fortunately, one of Max's cousins, a dare-devil cab driver, was on hand. Within minutes, I was flying down crowded streets and alleys, hanging on to the dashboard and trying not to close my eyes. Even with that scary ride, it was almost an hour before we got back to the mortuary. I couldn't avoid feeling embarrassment. I should have checked with them the day before.

It occurred to me there was something oddly poetic about using Bill's own money to buy his body, but I never got to the bottom of that particular thought. Suddenly, it was the amount of the mortuary bill that took my total attention. Eight hundred and fifty-four dollars - the number echoed through my mind. Then it came in a flash: "and there's Little Eva, weighing eight hundred and fifty-four pounds, who will endeavor to jump into a Coca-Cola bottle without making a splash," part of a carnival Barker routine Bill would perform now and then.

"Did you know my stepfather?" I asked the dark glasses.

"No, Patron," he replied. "I never had that pleasure."

"Could I see your bill?"

"Of course, Patron, your copy is right here."

He pushed an official looking document across the desk. There was slight mockery in his tone when he used the word "Patron."

The mortuary statement was professionally itemized, figured in pesos and then translated into dollars. I stared at the total. Nice going, Bill, I thought, I'll just chalk it up to incredible coincidence and keep it between you and me. But thank God you were such a damned good poker player.

Counting those bills out on the glass top of the large ornate desk suddenly became a great pleasure, an honor. Not even the dark glasses and slight smirk on the thick wet lips around the stinking cigar could make a difference. Bill was laying down his final bet, in a game he could not lose. Fat-lips nodded slightly to someone through a side door and Bill's casket was being loaded by the time I got outside.

Myrtle Lee

My mother survived for over twenty years after the trip we took to bury my stepfather Bill in Mexico. She would have lived longer had she not been addicted to tobacco. In due time she allowed her country property near Petaluma, with its out buildings and a couple of small "hidden" trailers, to become a way station for illegal farm workers from south of the border - an activity for which she never asked for nor received a penny. In fact, she sometimes provided groceries if a family with children was involved. No matter my arguments with her about the risk she was taking, she stubbornly ignored my concern. Her death was like an earthquake to me, not only a great personal loss but a disorienting tectonic shift of generations. It was a curiously significant honor when I took over her list of Christmas cards to our relatives in Georgia.

"Last night I watched my mother take her final breath and I will never be the same. It was strange, I didn't just look at her exhausted struggle as she lay dying in a hospital bed, her sunken eyes alien with morphine, her mouth gaping wide like that of a starving bird; I witnessed her, with an intensity that I'm still trying to understand. It was as though her labored breathing and the focused energy reaching out to her through my eyes were united in an effort to both hold on and let go at the same time, a tension gradually giving over to the inevitable moment.

And when it came, that final little sigh after so much hard fighting, after so much effort to breathe, beyond the frail infected lungs corroded by the poisonous vapors of several hundred thousand cigarettes; when it finally came, my heart was broken in a way that I can never explain. In that precious moment, when my mother's pale tongue curled up between the thin lips of her open mouth for a final, soft exhalation, there was a numbing noise so loud within me that only silence could express it.

In that precious moment, the mystery of life did a dark pirouette on her chin, taunting me to ask, as so many have asked before me: Where have you gone, my mother? Of what material is this impenetrable curtain that now separates us? Were you bathed in white light as you floated into the waiting arms of Jesus? Did you see your mother and father and all your dearly departed? Or did you simply fall into the final oblivion of non-existence? I will raise the better part of you up higher now, my mother. No longer will I entangle myself in the apron strings that trailed behind you. Your death is the beginning of a conversation we could never have until now."

JOE AND THE TIME MACHINE

In Northern Marin County, between Highway 101 and the Pacific Ocean, around the corner from the distant glow of city lights; we found a number of places to park and set up Joe's telescope. It was a large, expensive Unitron, equipped with an electronic tracking device to compensate for the earth's rotation, which kept our heavenly targets centered in the field of view. And, we had star maps, with precise settings for whatever we wanted to see.

We didn't talk much, except on the drive up from Sausalito and to keep each other awake on the drive back. Our viewing hours usually passed in silence. The activity of looking out into the awesome night sky had such a special quality, it was like being in a great cathedral, a liminal space of silent worship and deep, mysterious communion. And since it was usually pretty cold in that great cathedral, we brought plenty of libation, thermoses of hot coffee we generously spiked with bourbon or brandy.

"Take a look." Joe beckoned me over to the telescope. "There's a really good view of Jupiter's moons."

Something strangely wonderful happened whenever I looked into the eyepiece of Joe's telescope. It was as though my brain was sucked in through the eyepiece and out into space, to hang suspended somewhere in the void between planet Earth and our visual destination, often light years away. We took turns gazing into the eyepiece, for lengthy periods of time, but never interrupted one another.

Aside from the obvious and fascinating activity of star gazing, I had the feeling that our occasional trips into the dark countryside served some greater purpose for Joe. He would come into the bar where I worked and I could tell from his expression that an astronomy trip was due. He was more somber than usual, and then he'd ask if I wanted to go "time traveling." I never asked what, if anything, had happened. I just learned to associate a certain mood with us taking a late-night drive to gaze through his telescope.

I had met Joe where I was tending bar in Sausalito. He introduced himself with a request – could he be reached at the bar's telephone number in case of an emergency. Of course, I said. Since he volunteered no more information, and my position behind the plank involved a lot of neutrality; I didn't ask.

He appeared to be a gentle soul; short and slightly built, in his early fifties. He was a quiet and steady drinker, pleasant when spoken to, but hardly ever did he start a conversation himself. I noticed that women seemed to be drawn to him, a fact that aroused my youthful male curiosity. Looking back, I believe they were attracted by his air of quiet detachment (not indifference) as much as by his pleasant good looks. Perhaps he offered a feeling of safety, or represented that one male relative from whom they had needed approval. At any rate he was cleared by the owner to run up a sizeable tab, which he did, and promptly paid every few weeks.

I noticed that no matter how much alcohol Joe consumed he never appeared to get drunk. His demeanor would remain pretty much the same for as long as he sat at the bar. We had a couple of pleasant conversations, but I really didn't know any more about him until I answered the phone one evening and a female voice asked for a Colonel Joe Beyers. Colonel? He had given me the name, but not the title. Joe always sat just around the corner at the end of the bar, so I could easily hand him the phone. After that first call, I had to ask.

"Is that Colonel business on the level, Joe?"

"Yeah," he smiled, with a hint of embarrassment. "I'm a full Colonel in the U.S. Army, but I'm also a doctor. The calls I get are from Letterman Hospital, just over the bridge." Since my childhood family environment had always located doctors at a very high place on the social totem, my view of Joe shifted from casual customer to privileged character. Then one night, after he'd been coming in for a while, I overheard an exchange between him and another customer, who was wearing a friendly heat-on and looking for company.

"So, what do you do?" Joe was asked.

"I'm a brain surgeon," he replied. His tome was so casual I thought he might be kidding, but he wasn't. After another phone call had passed, I had to ask.

"Joe, do you actually leave here and go do brain surgery?"

"Yeah, sometimes," he answered, with a slight smile. "But don't tell anyone. I've got all the customers I can use." On one occasion when the owner was also behind the bar, I was taking a break out front on the sidewalk when Joe came out, greeted me and headed for a sleek little Austin Healy with a zippered cockpit cover. Although the night was foggy and cold, he put on a light jacket and drove away with the top down, headed for the Golden Gate Bridge.

"Why do you stay in the Army, Joe." I once asked, when I thought I knew him well enough. "Do you really like it?"

"Mainly because I get a lot of practice," he replied. "I get to do many times the number of operations than I would in civilian practice. And therefore, I learn more and get better at what I do." I really appreciated his answer. To my mind he was probably sacrificing some fame and fortune so that he could help more people.

One evening Joe surprised me with an invitation to a party at his place the following Sunday afternoon. I knew him well enough to know he was not a party animal. But then he told me there were people from work, from the hospital, who wanted to get out of the Presidio and come over to Sausalito on the weekend. He seemed just a little apprehensive.

"I'd really appreciate if you could come by," he said.

Joe lived in a little waterfront house with a huge picture window, right on the bay, near the same set of boardwalks as Sally Stanford's elegant Valhalla. There was a desk in one corner by the picture window upon which he had placed a human skull and a clear plastic globe covered with star maps. If anyone asked, he would reply that one of them contained God's brain.

He was obviously relieved to see me. As it turned out, the only other guests were three surgical nurses who seemed to me a lot like a fan club. Although he introduced them by name, from their ages and appearance I came to know them as Spring, Summer and Fall. The only one in my age range was Spring, but she was not my type. And dark eyed Summer was a bit too ripe for my taste. Straight backed Fall reminded me of the mean tempered third grade school teacher I had once known. I was a little pissed at Joe for inviting me alone into his unique medical "harem." He later explained that he had invited others who simply hadn't shown up.

They were a pleasant enough group, but I noticed that Spring and Summer quickly covered their glasses when Joe tried to pour them more alcohol. A complex undercurrent of feeling passed between the three of them about which I could only speculate.

"I think I'll coast for a while," Summer said, regarding Joe with all her heart. Then, almost under her breath: "I wish you would too." This last she spoke softly, with gentle intent. Joe said nothing. His obvious response was in the purposefully large quantity of bourbon he poured into my glass and then into his own.

Although Fall didn't drink at all, her school teacher image quickly faded as she laughed and related the story of how all three of them had been in the operating room when Joe's hastily tied surgical pants had fallen down around his ankles in the midst of an operation. It was Spring who had quickly moved in to pull them up and tie them around his waist. Joe tried to laugh, but he was obviously uncomfortable at hearing this story.

For the first time in my experience of him, Joe displayed symptoms of drunkenness. He spilled his drink and became embarrassed, even angry. I had never seen his composure so disrupted before. It was comforting for me to learn that he had these true friends who really cared about him. And certain familiarities I noticed between him and Summer indicated the possibility of an intimate relationship.

*   *   *

While one of us was at the telescope, the other would walk around, find places to pee and drink more spiked coffee. But on that last trip, as I sat in my car looking at Joe's dim figure hunched over the eyepiece, I sensed that something had changed. Joe was different. The quiet, stoic veneer behind which he had functioned for so long was beginning to crack. As a bartender I often witnessed the ugly alcohol induced changes in otherwise "normal" people. And, I was just beginning to question the myth around alcohol and having a "good time." Even so, regardless of all the warning signs, years later I was destined to wind up like Joe.

He was thin and pale when he came into the bar that night, and a little shaky as he took the first drink. My shift that day had been from two in the afternoon, so we left around ten and headed out to the universe. The night was clear and cold. We always took my Buick, with the large telescope securely wrapped in the back seat. This time, for the first time, Joe sat drinking from a bottle on the way up to our viewing grounds. His usually calm demeanor, almost Oriental in its spiritual quality, was worn thin.

"You wanna talk about it, Joe?" I asked.

"No, thanks Ray." His voice was barely audible. "I just need to be quiet. Okay?"

After we set up the telescope, I held the flashlight while Joe located the settings for our nearest galaxy, the Great Nebula in the constellation Andromeda, two million light years in the past. After he sighted in,

I touched his shoulder to signal I was taking a break and went to sit in the car.

We often stayed until dawn, which sometimes came as a surprise. But this night was different. It wasn't long after Joe ser up the scope before he turned away from it and came toward the car. Ordinarily I would have gone out to take my turn, but instead I waited. As soon as he got into the car he started crying.

I didn't learn much that night about all that had happened to him, but the fragments were heart breaking enough. Joe said that he had committed an error in the operating room and a patient had died. That much I got.

Later that month, after Joe had been noticeably absent from the bar, I wondered if he had been court marshaled and locked up. Then, I was surprised by the appearance of one of the nurses, Summer, who told me that Joe had even invited legal action against himself but was committed to treatment for alcohol dependence instead. It turned out that the patient had been near death and Joe was actually trying to save him. Summer was obviously greatly relieved and said that Joe had asked her to come by the bar to say goodbye and let me know that he would miss our "time traveling" together.

QUEEN OF BIG SUR

Wanda, the Queen of Big Sur, was thus named for a number of good reasons. She was a strikingly beautiful young woman, with long blonde hair and penetrating blue eyes, and, she was a woman of many talents. She made sandals and leather clothing of such high quality there was always a waiting list for her work (aside from the guys who just wanted to connect with her).

She was also an exceptional guitarist and folk singer, performing occasionally at local venues, but not interested in a show business career. She worked on her own vehicle, lived alone with her little boy, Damon, and occasionally gave herself a lover, who, when found out, would become the envy of other men. Her feminine beauty could be deceptive, however, for Wanda possessed a strength of character that often made her a better "man" than many of those who pursued her.

As for yours truly, the circumstances leading up to my encounter with Wanda were both at the end, and the beginning, of a long story. I had been a single parent with my own little boy, Ravi, for about six months. He was two-and-a-half years old. His mother and I had come to an agreement, without the benefit of lawyers or a court, that he would be staying with me for a while.

Ravi and I had been living in Mill Valley, in Marin County, but the influence of my previous bachelor life – with the habits and indulgences of an irresponsible free-floating freelancer – were not conducive to good parenting. We needed a change. So, I disposed of a lot of stuff, packed my son and the rest of my world into my little Renault sedan and hit the road.

We traveled through a few extended family communes, looking for a safe place to land, and wound up in Monterey, visiting friends. I had known David for years, but his recent partner, Shirley, was new to me. After a few beers, the conversation got around to what were my plans.

"Looking for a partner, I guess" I responded. "I need to get some kind of work soon and I'll need help with Ravi." My friend David got that wild, expansive look, which he usually did after a few beers.

"Maybe you should pay a visit to the Queen of Big Sur," he said, grinning. David and I had always challenged one another to reach for the stars. Shirley responded with a chuckle.

"No offense, Ray," she said. "It's just that Wanda has her pick of some pretty impressive suitors."

As a matter of fact, my feelings were a bit hurt by her attitude. So, I immediately asked if they could tell me where this Wanda woman lived. It turned out that Shirley had gone to high school with her. They gave me directions.

*   *   *

It was a long drive down the coast from Monterey. I went past her turn-off from Highway One by mistake the first time, and then, deliberately passed it going the other way. I was in a state of complexity. The idea of swooping in and capturing the Queen of Big Sur was pure fantasy. I didn't want to create a big disappointment for myself, but David and I both knew I would have to check it out. I parked the car alongside the highway for a few minutes. Ravi was taking a nap. Finally, I convinced myself it wouldn't hurt just to go see if she was home. A break from driving would be welcome.

A sign on the gate across the dirt road read: "Please remember to close the gate," which I did. The road climbed steadily up from the highway for a few miles and then leveled off next to a lush meadow.

The small house, just beyond several parked vehicles, was right out of a story book. The beautiful setting, the garden, a wide view of the Pacific Ocean - what a great place.

There was a fence around the garden, a small yard and a few scattered toys. I stood at the gate for a moment. Ravi was still asleep in the car. I had just about decided to leave when I looked across the yard to the kitchen window. The Queen of Big Sur was watching me. She opened the door and stepped out into the yard. She was barefoot and wearing jeans.

"Can I help you?" she smiled. Everything I'd heard was true, and then some.

"I'm a friend of Shirley and David's," I blurted. "And my son is asleep in the car." We exchanged names, shook hands, and she went to my car.

"Beautiful boy," she said, as she looked at Ravi through the window. "You want to try bringing him inside? My boy is taking a nap too." I stared at her, for a moment unable to utter a word. Everything about her was distracting.

"I would rather he didn't wake up alone," I managed. I carried Ravi through the little house, following her into a bedroom. I was a little startled, but not really surprised, to see three guys sitting in her living room. In the smaller of two bedrooms was a little boy, who looked a lot like Ravi, asleep on a single bed. There was plenty of room for another child.

Wanda then introduced me to a handsome, middle aged professor of biology, a fisherman-slash-poet, and a local rich kid. There was an air of competition in the room, a congestion of testosterone that made me uncomfortable. I felt somehow degraded just being male. I suddenly wished I had kept on going down the highway. This arrogant beauty, this Queen, was holding court for these poor jerks who were obviously trying to outwit and out wait one another. After a polite interval, I excused myself to get some things from my car.

On my way across the yard, I stopped to peek into a small shed next to the house. I wasn't looking for anything in particular, just curious. There was firewood stacked on one side of the shed, with a rough, double X sawhorse and a large bow saw nearby. I noticed that the sawhorse was pretty wobbly. A cross member in the right place would fix that. I really didn't want to be part of what was going on in the house. And besides, this gave me a chance to use the tool kit I had proudly packed under the lid of my Renault, an assortment of mechanic and carpentry tools, I also packed a sledge hammer, axe, hatchet, a small shovel and a small wrecking bar.

When I'd gone through the gate, I also noticed that the main gatepost was a bit loose. Some wedging and tamping should take care of that. I'd just do a couple of quick chores, take my kid and go. I selected some tools from my car and went back to the shed. There was an old plank from which I cut a piece for the sawhorse. Just as I was starting to nail it on, Wanda came out to inform me that the boys were awake and playing together. She looked at what I was doing without comment.

"I'll fix them a snack," she said, and went back into the house. I finished the sawhorse and started on the gate post. As I was finishing up with strengthening the gate, I looked up to see her again watching me from the kitchen window. On impulse, I hefted my hatchet, lightly buried its blade into the top of the gate post and left it there.

A short time later the three suitors filed out of the house and walked past me through the gate. The professor nodded and mumbled something courteous, the fisherman heartily shook my hand, and the young guy grinned and said "No fair using a kid."

Wanda and the boys came spilling out into the yard just as the vehicles of the three men disappeared down the hill.

THE SUMMER OF SIXTY-THREE

One... two... we carefully counted the dull thuds that came from the mouth of the tunnel. Three... four... concussion waves followed with a slight rush of escaping air. We had drilled and rigged six dynamite charges, carefully fused at different lengths. If we only counted four or five, we would have to wait until the following morning before going back inside the tunnel to carefully uncover the failed charges. If we went back in right away, a slow burning fuse could prove disastrous. If all the charges went off, however, we would go back in right away and check out the rocky pile of potentially rich ore we had blasted out of the tunnel wall.

My senior partner, an older hippie dropout named John, had decided to refurbish an old gold mine that had been abandoned since the late nineteen thirties. John was also a qualified engineer and a family man. He had a good front and had appropriately secured a year's lease on the property from local county government. The recorded name on the original claim was the Big Chief Mine.

There were two cabins, about a quarter of a mile apart, situated on either side of a narrow shelf of mountainside a couple of thousand feet above the American River. The shelf had been partially created by the water pressure of placer mining, which had left a scarred landscape of rocks, bare earth and stunted conifers pushing up through the broken terrain. It was a kind of stark and wild Japanese garden. The mine tunnel, where a vein of gold had been followed for fifteen hundred feet into the mountainside, was located about half way between the two cabins.

John was competently knowledgeable about restoring the mine. He had already invested in the tools and equipment we would need. My quarter share of the gold, if we struck a rich pocket, was secured by my labor. And, by the fact that my attractive girlfriend, Wanda, and our two little three-year-old boys (one hers, one mine) came along with me. John's priority for a mining partner was a matter of family; and, I could tell he was quite taken with Wanda.

There were many positive features about John's priorities that made him the model of a conscientious family man. He was creatively resourceful about providing family fun. The first thing he had done after arriving at the Big Chief was to find the optimum location for a swing. The swing he rigged, with a fifty-foot length of heavy rope (and a sturdy cross member for seating) was anchored to a branch high above a dry creek bed. Taking a turn from one steep hillside across to the other could build up some substantial "G" force near the bottom.

John's family consisted of his elegant wife, Liz, an artist of considerable talent, her daughter, Helen, who was more the functioning home-maker than her mother, and two boys, eleven and seven. Helen and the older boy, Juno, were from a previous marriage Liz had years before. The younger boy, Eric, belonged to John and Liz.

The mine was located about forty miles up the North Fork of the American River from Auburn, California. John's family had been settling in for a week or so by the time I moved my little group up from Big Sur. I was impressed with how he had managed to bring his converted full sized school bus down the precipitous dirt road to park it near the main cabin. The bus would provide a second living space for John's family and a guest room for visiting friends, of which we had many over that summer.

A flat clearing next to the bus became our community patio. And, after we had restored the small water powered generator down at the mine, we were able to produce enough electricity for an occasional nighttime party. We strung colored lights in a tree next to the bus and fired up a phonograph with external speakers. We also managed enough juice for a few hours of refrigeration on most days.

Creating our own electricity was an exciting big deal to me. I enjoyed the self-contained mechanics of the process. We had cleared the long winding ditch from a spring fed creek to fill the small reservoir above the mine. A ten-inch pipe came down the hillside from the reservoir and was ultimately reduced to a half inch nozzle that accelerated the small cups of a water wheel that powered the generator. When the water pressure gauge on the pipe read 120 pounds and the volt meter read 115, we had a steady stream of electricity. But the electric line only ran to the bus and the main cabin. I could have rigged a line to my cabin, but Wanda and I preferred the way it was.

My family cabin, a remarkably sturdy little two room, two story structure, was a short distance beyond the far side of the boulder strewn, wild Japanese garden, on a steep wooded incline. There was a square hole next to the wall in the downstairs ceiling and the upstairs bedroom floor. I rebuilt the ladder on the wall and carefully instructed the boys on going up or down, which they only got to do twice a day.

It took some time to pack everything in from my van to the cabin, but Wanda and I soon created a wonderfully functional little Hobbit home. I still get a special feeling when I remember the magic of our transition with the twilight hour. Carefully lighting and placing the kerosine lamps was one of my favorite rituals. The world outside grew smaller and more distant in its darkness as the world inside grew larger with its light. This quiet transformation of this hour soon became a treasured routine for all four of us.

Since we lived in risky terrain, the boys had a limited playground next to the cabin and were warned about rattlesnakes, one of which I killed and hung in a small tree to ward off others. Also, on the walk to the mine, or to connect with John's family, there was a deep crevasse next to a dangerous drop-off over which I had to put a wooden bridge. The crevasse was only a couple feet wide, so I secured a few heavy planks and laid them across. We started out carrying the boys over this bridge, but by the middle of summer they had learned to cross over safely in our company.

A narrow gauge set of rails ran most of the length of the mine tunnel, which had been blasted through the rocky, self-supporting aggregate of an ancient riverbed, and followed a winding course of exploration. There were hardly any timber supports for the whole fifteen hundred feet, except at a few short branch intersections and the mouth of the tunnel. John had already done some rail repair and soon an antique hand pushed ore car of solid iron was once again rolling through the tunnel, carrying loads of ore or an excited passenger on a thrill ride.

It took a few steps of faith for me to get past the first twenty feet or so of that tunnel, but then I achieved a psychic surrender to being "inside" the earth, under countless tons of potentially crushing weight. It was interesting to watch our visitors decide whether or not they would proceed. Some would take one look at the tunnel mouth and flatly refuse to enter, others would have to go through a process of convincing, while still others would just proceed without hesitation. We had enough company that summer so those of us who lived there would sometimes speculate as to who would balk and who would not.

Sometimes, when John and I were not at work, I would don my helmet and carbide lamp and go deep into the tunnel all by myself. After a thousand feet or so, I would find a relatively comfortable place to sit down and blow out my lamp. I was curious to experience the complete absence of light and sound. But I could not find total darkness or total silence because "I" was there. Nerve patterns behind my eyes or the sounds of my own blood and bowels kept me from reaching my goal. Still, after a half hour or so, I would get about as close to total darkness and complete silence as I imagine one possibly could.

The narrow rail track leading out from the mouth of the tunnel ended abruptly beside a well-constructed, heavy duty sluice box perched high above a rock pile of debris and a sharp incline to the river far below. After leaving the dark tunnel and before the abrupt stop, my roller coaster passengers in the ore car, adults or children, would make a variety of interesting sounds at their impression of flying off into thin air.

The frame and sluice box at the end of the track were made of redwood and after some soakings were still quite serviceable. Next to the sluice box was an open shed which still contained the old water wheel generator and an equally old air compressor with a large fly wheel. Both were still in pretty good shape.

Our largest, most memorable upgrade was carried down the mountainside in primitive fashion. We made a litter of long carrying poles, as indigenous people do with large game, and hauled a Ford V8 engine down to the mine in order to power the ancient compressor. There were surprisingly few leaks in the two-inch pipeline that ran alongside the tracks for some distance into the tunnel. John had a welding outfit so we soon patched the pipeline good as new. We could then generate enough air pressure to try out our new jackhammer.

Everyone was on hand after our first successful dynamite excavation, and shortly thereafter many willing hands were operating the sluice box and panning the dark residue for flecks of yellow gold. We shared a lot of excitement over the things we would all do when we struck it rich. John explained that if we could find a fair amount of gold, we would take it to Mexico and sell it on the black market. He had a Mexican connection who he claimed could sell it to the Red Chinese at twice the going price, which at that time was around forty dollars an ounce.

Here and there along the tunnel were the empty sockets and short passages that had been blasted out years before in search of pockets of high yield ore, some of which had been quite successful. There being no absolute geological science about determining where a rich pocket might exist, intuition alone was our guide. John and I put together a witching wand, with a small gold nugget at its tip, for our female companions to use in witching out our blast sites. After they had done their divining, marking sites they chose with a spray-painted X, we would go into the tunnel and start drilling.

John and I both wore carbide lamps mounted on the front of our helmets and were conscious not to get too close and suddenly turn to one another during a conversation. The flame shooting out from the lamps was only an inch to an inch and a half long, but could still do some damage. It never happened that anyone got burned, but the image was always there like a Laurel and Hardy film clip.

One day, my partner Wanda came along the tunnel (she carried a flashlight) to bring us some lunch and started laughing the moment she saw us.

"You guys look exactly like an insurance company ad I once saw," she said. "I wish I had brought my camera." John had been shoveling debris into the ore car and I was just getting ready to change a drill bit for the jackhammer. We had been working hard and were covered with dirt. We then looked at one another, more like coal miners than gold miners, and quickly joined in with Wanda's laughter.

In due time we worked our way deeper and deeper into the tunnel, and then one day the charges we set off caused a quantity of underground water to begin seeping through the tunnel wall. By the time we went back inside, the large round river rocks in the walls near the end of the tunnel were dripping profusely. Pools of water were beginning to form on the tunnel floor. It was clear we had tapped into an underground waterway and that another blast could possibly let loose a torrent.

I took one final solitary walk into those depths, to blow out my lamp and sit listening to the sound of dripping water, and also to say goodbye to the special feelings I had enjoyed in that tunnel. After getting over the claustrophobia, and the fear of a sudden cave-in, another much larger sensation had dominated. Somewhere in the depths of my genetic code there was an ancient, almost intimate feeling of trust, of safety, a connection to Mother Earth that I think is unique to the human spirit. And something else, something that was not quite human, made itself known alongside that profound silence of stone.

Our total take in terms of gold that summer was barely enough to cover John's investment, but we were grateful for even that. The total take in terms of our once in a lifetime experiences was beyond measure. Wanda and I would soon go our own ways, a not so easy experience for me; but our friendship would continue and that summer together with our boys was something we both held as quite special.

Excuse or Explanation

Disability is just a word, until you wear it as a label, as a definition of who you are. Then it takes on a power that can disturb and dominate your whole life. I was born visually impaired, at a time before visual aids for students had been developed. So, with little help, I made my way through public school; grammar school and high school (plus a couple of failed attempts at college) basically playing "blind man's bluff," finding strategies to either blend in or stand out as "normal."

I learned to survive in spite of being in denial about my vision. I refused to be set aside and labeled as inferior. In my quest to be seen as normal, I learned to depend on my acute hearing and other, more subtle, senses to pick up on what my eyesight might have missed. And, since I have no way of comparing my level of vision to that of anyone else, I had little idea of the real degree of my difference.

Now, when considering my life history and the behaviors I considered to be necessary at the time, such as driving a car, I am both amazed and disturbed by some of the risks I took; not just for myself, but for others, especially those who were dear to me. Consequently, I've had to wrestle with the subtle distinction between "excuse or explanation" and forgive myself as best I could.

I belonged to that generation of high school students who, just after WW II, had easy access to a broad market of good running 1930's automobiles, at very low cost. These vehicles were a large part of my social life, and the world around me, so I wasn't about to be left out.

I had no doubt of my ability to drive, nor did anyone else. At that time my eyesight had not been legally classified.

Practically everyone I knew had a vehicle, as I did, and driving around Marin and Sonoma Counties was no problem. Highway 101 was still a two-lane road and there wasn't much traffic in the small Marin County towns or back country rural areas. Freeways and Supermarkets were still just words to describe a world to come.

Unfortunately, by the time I flunked getting a normal driver license, I had already been driving for a few years. By then my life completely revolved around my mobility, as was the case with everyone else I knew. Although I was granted a limited license, to drive only on county roads and not on 101, it wasn't long before I violated those conditions. It took many years more and a long conversation with my guardian angel before I was finally able to give up the freedom to which I had become so accustomed.

The psychological impact of all those years, of the intense conflict between fear and faith that ruled my life, created a complicated world of both advantage and disadvantage. An intense fear of disclosure, that I would be found out for the incomplete and inferior creature I knew myself to be, was overcompensated by an almost insane degree of faith in my ability to overcome any obstacle.

From my current point of view, after a lifetime of coping with "disability," I am most of all saddened by my long-term experience of isolation. My blind faith (no pun intended) gained me a sense of enormous personal power, which often led to some bold successes. But, my brittle and fragile shell of overconfidence also caused me to be extremely vulnerable. This powerful self-deception, of which I was nevertheless acutely aware, reinforced my isolation and thus became my self- made prison.

Only later did I come to understand the extent to which I had lots of company. I sensed that we are all in some way "disabled," and our individual genius is most brilliantly applied in overcoming our perceived inferiority. It is this genius that drives us and expresses our individuality, the diversity of which drives our world.

Trapped in the illusion of an ever-threatened existence, however, I was cut off and convinced that there was a shared world that everyone else got to enjoy, but one from which I was excluded. I will never know the extent to which this is true, due to my eyesight; but I've learned to understand just how important we all are to one another, as each of us represents a unique view, an equally important possibility of life, endowed with the same validity.

*   *   *

In 1965, before I turned thirty, I was living in a cheap rental in the Larkspur hills, in Marin County, alone with my four-year-old son and without a job. The last work I'd had was as a construction laborer near the town of Tiburon. A foreman had instructed me to "go over to that blue pick-up" and fetch the cable I'd find in the truck's bed. I started out across the field in the direction he indicated, even though I couldn't see the truck toward which he pointed. I corrected course when I finally did identify the truck, but this brought unwanted attention. When I got back, the foremen questioned me and ultimately let me go, although reluctantly.

Some time before that last job in Tiburon, with realistic concern about finding long term employment, I finally applied to the California State Department of Rehabilitation in San Francisco. A condition for applying with the State was to also apply for Social Security disability, which I did, and promptly forgot about it.

State Rehab did enroll me in an IBM class in San Francisco which used the 402 Business Machine (punch cards, control panels) as a precursor to computer programming. Honestly, I did quite well with the theoretical side of the class, but when offered a pad on which other students saw the light green ink outline of a flow chart, I only saw a blank sheet of white paper. State Rehab and IBM argued over fees paid, and I was forced to drop out. I still can't help but wonder what my life might have been like if I could have seen that damned ink.

*   *   *

I had been reluctant to apply for any help on a local level, for fear that some bureaucrat would question my ability to care for my child and try to take him from me. A couple of years before, when working as a janitor in Auburn, California, I'd had an eye exam with a local optometrist and he classified me as "legally blind." I was afraid that any investigation into my status would reveal my secret and the disability label would also de-classify me as a father.

In the midst of all this came a day that marked a major turning point in my life. After descending the many steps that led down from my little flat on a deeply wooded hillside in Larkspur, I reached into my mailbox and pulled out a huge surprise. It had been a while since I had routinely followed instructions from the State Department of Rehabilitation and applied for Social Security Disability. I had gone out in search of help to find a job, not to be set aside, but here it was.

An official looking envelop contained a check for eighteen hundred dollars, which included disability back pay from the time I had applied. There was also a notice indicating I would thereafter receive one hundred and fifty dollars a month. It's difficult to describe my state of mind as I stood by the mailbox. I guess confused excitement would be one way to put it. But I also had a sense of foreboding, a sense that something was terribly wrong.

As much as I needed it, I did not feel the money was mine. I had done nothing to earn it. I had worked a variety of jobs during and since high school, always earning my own way. The State Forestry (teen fire fighter), construction labor, shipping clerk, gardener, dance instructor, liquor clerk, factory worker, bartender; some of these jobs were temporary, some I quit, and some I lost as I had the construction job near Tiburon. But, to get paid for nothing, just because I couldn't see too well, didn't seem right. In fact, I emphatically rejected the idea. There had to be a catch.

The following day I left my son with a lady friend who had been helping me as I looked for work, and paid a visit to the local Marin County Social Security Office. I showed the clerk my paperwork and had just one question.

"What do I have to do for this money?"

In spite of the obvious, I was not prepared for the answer.

"Nothing," said the representative, with a cool federal smile. "You don't have to do a damned thing."

I was devastated. What I had for so long avoided and yet somehow expected had finally come true. I was dismissed, discounted. I no longer mattered as a viable member of my society. I went home and wept for a long time.

MAESTRO

In the summer of 1965, I repaired a wooden camper shell on the back of my recently acquired '48 Dodge flatbed, and left Marin County bound for Mexico. I was accompanied by my four-year-old son, my pregnant bride-to-be, and a few books of traveler's checks. My plan was to visit friends along the way and then go in search of a violin maker, probably in Mexico City, who was willing to teach me something of his craft. I had approached a couple of instrument makers in the Bay Area, but they had assured me that twenty-nine was far too old to begin as an apprentice. They didn't even want to talk to me without charging a fee.

After spending some time around Taos and Santa Fe, we drove south to El Paso-Juarez and crossed the border. After a stop in Zacatecas to have a broken rear spring in my new old truck repaired, I decided to head for San Miguel de Allende. I had corresponded with an old friend, John, who had a home there, and was invited to stay for a while. I had known John and his gypsy-like family in several places over several years. His pattern was to spend part of his time in the United States, working and saving every penny he could, and then living it up in Mexico.

Running a household in San Miguel de Allende at that time could be pretty inexpensive, especially if you knew the neighborhood as well as John did. He had finagled a property in a fairly poor section of town, on a dirt alley called Callejon de las Animas, a large Romanesque quadrangle within high stone walls, shared on both sides as walls for other properties. The front wall, with an enclosed room on either side of a short hallway, had a massive front door that opened onto the alley.

The back end of the quadrangle, with brickwork arched openings, was twenty feet or so above an open field and offered a picturesque view of a nearby cathedral bell tower. Inside those walls, with an open courtyard that included a camouflaged outhouse, John had accomplished a uniquely hip hacienda. The dark, polished tile floor of an open Sala, with a large stone fireplace and raised hearth, a ballet bar and a mirror covered wall; these were the sights that greeted our entrance. When I first admired the place, I had no idea it would turn out to be my home for almost the next two years.

In one of my letters to John I had mentioned my plan to look for a violin maker. Shortly after we arrived, he invited me to meet a woodworker who knew how to make violins and just happened to live at the end of the alley. I politely accepted his offer, but wasn't particularly impressed by the crude backyard work-shop or the smiling little man who greeted us. John had already expressed his desire for me to stay at his house while he and his family took another trip back to the States, so I was quite suspicious that he had so conveniently found a violin maker in the neighborhood.

Since I spoke little Spanish and Juan Espinoza spoke no English, it was John who carried the conversation. Although there was a guitar and a cello hanging along one wall, in for repair, it appeared to me that Juan was mostly involved in building furniture. Thinking I had found a way out of John's apparent manipulation, I asked that he find out more about Juan's expertise, why he didn't focus on stringed instruments exclusively. Although my question was answered through translation, there was no mistaking Juan's demeanor, his casual honesty and quiet dignity.

Juan made his living by serving his community, as needed. If it was furniture, he built furniture; if making an instrument, he could do that as will. And, as I would later find out, the scope of this man's work was far more amazing than I could have imagined. When I asked more directly if he could teach me about building stringed instruments, he pointed to his head, smiled and explained that every detail of construction; guitar, violin, cello, bass, guitarrón or harp, was completely available from memory. Juan was forty-seven at the time.

I went away that day doubting what I had heard, but, considering John's request and my wife's growing pregnancy, it seemed a good idea to stay in San Miguel for a while. The next time I went down the alley to visit Juan, I went alone. I met his little round wife, Rufina, and a number of children. But, as I would gradually come to experience, the place was almost always quiet. As we stood in the shop, at the rear of his small quadrangle, the challenge of our language barrier became an intriguing enjoyment. As we experimented with simple repeated words and creative pantomime, our smiles turned to laughter.

Although I learned that "Martillo" was the Spanish word for hammer, and that we would be working in centimeters instead of inches, that was about as far as language got us. The real learning was on a more somatic, non-verbal level. In fact, upon reflection, I came to understand that our not having a common spoken language at first was probably an advantage. Instead of bullshitting, we simply did things. I learned by taking action, by imitation and osmosis. I was soon aware that staying in San Miquel de Allende to work with Juan was a decision I would never regret.

Juan had two older sons whom he had hoped would stay home to work with him, but, as he learned of their desire to find work in the city, to become owners of TV sets, and maybe even automobiles, he set them free. He did have one young apprentice, who came around after school, but it was the boy's father who paid Juan to teach the boy carpentry. I also started out paying him, but after a while he asked me not to pay him. He said that his payment was in having someone to whom he could pass on some special knowledge. And, he was also excited by my desire to experiment, to create some innovative possibilities of resonance with wood and strings. Eventually, I created my own shop up the alley at John's, and worked in both places. The neighborhood was quite pleased that a gringo was apprentice to a local maestro.

There are many stories I could tell about my time with Juan. He was maestro, guru, artist, shaman, but most of all, he was a friend. Once, when I got wrapped up with frustration and impatience, stressing out a bit over a cello I was learning to carve, Juan showed up at my door and asked if I'd like to see the latest instrument he had made. Of course, I said yes, I hadn't even known he was building an instrument. He reached into his pocket and pulled out a remarkable miniature, built on the half shell of a walnut. The spruce top fit exactly, the neck and pegs were perfectly proportioned, and there was even a tiny bridge and thin little strings.

I took off my glasses for a closer inspection of the little walnut "guitar," but it wasn't until I looked up at Juan that I really got the message. He didn't have to say "take it easy," it was in his eyes, and even in the air around him. This smiling little man, who produced such an enormous amount of truly fine work out of his crude backyard shop, seemed always to be relaxed and have plenty of time. That was amazing to me. I sometimes wondered if he ever slept, or if magical elves came in the night to assist him.

It's a fact that for all the time I worked with him, I never saw Juan in a hurry, or even break a sweat. Of course, there was always grunt work, but he did it in such a relaxed, casual manner, it didn't look like work. And, as I learned, his slow easy pace was quite deceptive, because not a motion was wasted. Over time, I understood that he did most of the work in his head. The physical activity was simply a final step, and I swear, somehow the physical world seemed almost anxious to co-operate with him. On occasion, if a problem did come up, he would set aside an instrument, or a piece of furniture, and seem to ignore it as he went about other business. Then, when he approached it again, he would immediately go into action. The piece itself, he said, had told him what to do.

In terms of the scope of Juan's work, there was the day I came walking down the alley and noticed a large flatbed truck parked in front of his door. As I drew closer, Juan and four other men started carrying two huge temple doors out to the truck. Not only were these doors heavy monstrosities, about four by eight feet in size, the panels were constructed out of hundreds of pieces of channeled wood, joined together in complex herringbone patterns. There had been a fire in a local cathedral and Juan had beautifully duplicated the doors that were lost. In due time I would come to understand how he had made those doors in just a few days.

Once, near Christmas, when I entered Juan's front door on my way to his shop in back, I glanced into a side room and was amazed to see a beautiful, Biblical mural, about eight by eight feet, on a far wall. It was a night-time street scene, with the walls of crude quiet buildings, dark shadows, a couple of palm trees, and brilliant stars in the sky. But it was more than a mural, it was a feeling, an awe inspired feeling. As I gazed at it, I more fully realized the amazing scope of Juan's talent. Anyway, shortly after Christmas, I glanced into that same room and the mural was gone. Juan explained that he had whitewashed over it in preparation for painting the next religious holiday. As I stared at that wall, I wondered how many masterpieces had been layered there.

*   *   *

Many things happened during that time in San Miguel; my son Ravi had his fifth birthday, my daughter Rachel was born, the Beatles became outrageously famous, and my learning with Juan Espinosa initiated a long and intense love affair with what's commonly known as "creative process." Once I had experienced those unforgettable states of selflessness and timelessness, I knew I had found my "drug of choice." The gift of tapping into the divine power of total participation would change my life.

About Timelessness - I well remember this one particular day because it vanished. I got up that morning, had a light breakfast, went to my shop, and after what seemed like a few minutes, wondered why the light was fading. The shaping of the instrument on my workbench was nearly done, but I had no recollection of the work. There was a plate of cold food nearby, but I had no recollection of anyone bringing it. Many hours had passed in what seemed a few minutes. I would thereafter experience many such days, but this was the first.

About Selflessness - I remember the focus of becoming the tool I was using, of being a tiny creature traveling across the landscape of wood grain as my 20/20 fingertips explored the subtle currents of fiber that spoke to my imagination about shape and sound. There was such magic in those journeys.

* * *

Aside from the skill of hand, my learning with Juan Espinoza was about attitude, courage and surrender, lessons that I carried to many aspects of wood working over the next twenty-five years. What I would like to leave you with is this: True Creative Process does not belong to the artist, nor to any one, it is a spiritual journey of participation. I'm convinced that many artisans throughout the ages understood their work as a form of worship, without ego attachment. As soon as what you are making takes on a life of its own, you enter into a relationship with it, a zone wherein the artist becomes like a junior partner, sometimes even a willing slave. But the rewards of this surrender are so deeply fulfilling, it can be a joyful bondage.

I have learned there is an eternal river of boundless energy right above our heads. It is a river of life, it is a source of power so kind, so loving, so generous, that all you have to do is plug in. The only difficulty may be in learning how to get out of your own way.

I have nothing now but a few photographs to remind me of Juan. One of the greatest losses I've ever experienced was a cardboard tube in which I had placed the drawings he did for me on the last day I saw him. We had done a lot of work during our time together, but there had never been a drawing, nor a plan, to which we refereed. As Juan had assured me on the first day I met him; every detail, every measurement, was immediately available to us from his memory.

But I didn't have such a memory, so on that last day, I brought him a roll of paper and asked him to draw me some instrument plans. And that he did. I would later show those drawings to people who would not believe I had witnessed someone draw them freehand. Clean single lines, no smudges or corrections, perfect curves, exact proportions, precise measurements; and all casually drawn while he was chatting with me. I didn't really know how special those drawings were until I took them out some time later, after I had returned to the States.

I never saw Juan again, but he did take up permanent residence in my psyche. I dream about his beautifully crafted, handmade world, from which I went on learning for a long time. It was as though he had planted seeds that would sprout some years later, in the sawdust of my own experience. And I still hear his final words to me, which he spoke in perfect English.

"You always had the courage to cut the boards and be open to whatever came next," he smiled. And that was my graduation.

Pigs

Early morning, the smell of strong Mexican coffee. I ease out of bed. A quiet, gentle train of burros move past my window, bearing wide bundles of firewood to the local marketplace. They are a silent surprise, pleasantly surreal in the red dawn – stocky little ballerinas who perform a stiff-legged pirouette at the end of the alley and disappear around the corner. With a stretch and a yawn, I move slowly through a quiet breakfast of coffee, papaya and sweet bread. Then I am drawn to the excitement that awaits in my studio.

The body on my workbench looks quite different in the daylight, smaller than I remember from the night before. I run my hands over the smooth curves, sensing for volume and balance. A thoroughly familiar landscape passes beneath my fingertips, each centimeter a sculpted memory. Today I will return to the delicate process of scooping out her belly. I glance with pride at the elegant head and slender neck that hang nearby.

I turn the sculpted body over and prepare to follow her lead. I slowly lean my shoulder into the long handle of the razor-sharp gouge, listening carefully for the cutting tones that will tell me how far it is to the outer surface. Poco a poco, the wood peels away toward a more resonant thickness. I become a mindless instrument in a timeless dance, so absorbed that I no longer exist. I have become the tool I am using... Suddenly, a rough guttural voice erupts in my ear.

"Mouf ofah, sonfa bitch." My startled reaction tips the chisel to a dangerous angle. I look around, but no one is there.

"Tut tut, Schnicklefritz," says another guttural voice. "I vass here furst. Dis corn be mine corn." I shake my head and take a deep breath. After a confused moment, I realize the voices are coming from the back yard next door – from the other side of the tall adobe wall where the neighbors keep their pigs.

"Hey, Grinko," I hear. "Get beck to vurk. You ain't got nuttin' better dan schnoopin'?" With a happy heart I turn back to the cello on my workbench. What a precious gift – Mexican pigs who speak English with a German accent. Another fine workday in Margaretta-ville.

MACHISMO

I don't think I could ever exhaust the potential for story Juan Espinoza brought to my life. Much of my time with him seems to have been spent in another dimension, a liminal threshold between two worlds. Being around him in the context of learning to build stringed instruments touched me with the easy magnitude and eloquence of his spirit. Yes, it was obvious that he was skilled, but more than that, he was "connected."

I suppose one could compare this connection to "the Force," as in the Star Wars movies. But no, it was not so much like that energy related to martial arts; it was more like "the Source," related to the universal energy of creativity. It was through Juan that I learned to let go of the illusion of control and "allow" the work to happen, to trust, to rely on the mystery of "flow." It was a learning I would try to apply, with varying degrees of success, to areas of my life other than woodworking.

One day I asked him if he had ever played pool, a game with which, due to my eyesight, I'd had an inconsistent relationship. "Por seguro," he said, he enjoyed shooting a game of pool now and then. To this day I regret that my best games of pool seemed to be the result of "allowing" the game to happen under the influence. There were times I could run the table with ease, in that zone of looseness between caring and not caring, between attachment and non-attachment, but only with the lubrication of alcohol.

At any rate Juan and I agreed to seek out an empty table that very evening. We got together around eight and strolled downtown. There was one major pool hall near the main plaza, but every table was occupied when we got there and others were waiting to play. I had thought this was the only pool hall in town, but Juan indicated there was another place we could try.

We walked several blocks away from the main plaza and came to a nondescript doorway in what appeared to be a residential building. There were no signs or other indications of a pool hall. However, when we opened the front door and entered, we were standing at the top of a wide, open flight of stairs leading down to a large room with several pool tables, all but one of which was in play. Then, as though a switch had been thrown, everything stopped.

That silent moment, with Juan and me standing at the top of the stairs and every head in the room turned toward us, is forever held in memory. It didn't take long to figure out what was happening. My maestro had brought me to a place where I should not have been. The pool hall downtown was okay for gringos, but this place was for locals only.

Most of the men in the room were younger than Juan and didn't seem at all friendly. In fact, they seemed to me like a pretty tough bunch. When I checked Juan out from the corner of my eye, it was clear he was calm and unperturbed. I can't say how long we stood there, but the invisible switch was eventually thrown again, in reverse. And everyone resumed their games as Juan and I headed for the empty table.

A History of Burma

I called my truck Burma because the previous owner had found one of those old Burma Shave signs along the road, cut off the "Burma" part and attached it to the back end of the wooden camper shell he had nearly completed. It was a 48 Dodge, one ton flatbed, which accommodated a good-sized plywood camper shell; with a cab-over deep enough for a double mattress. The roof above the cab-over was the incomplete part, since there was as yet no roof. I wound up strapping down a heavy tarp as a temporary cover.

I got a good deal on Burma because she listed to one side, due to a broken rear spring. I bought a good used, heavy duty leaf spring and new brackets, but the job would require some welding and the estimates I got were pretty expensive. After I decided to make a trip to Mexico, a friend suggested that I could get the work done there for a lot less. Otherwise, the truck was in very good running order, it just looked a bit lop sided.

It was late summer, 1965. And I was looking forward to living like a gypsy in the back of my new truck named Burma. I completed the interior of the camper, put off doing the roof, and set out for Mexico; along with my pregnant girlfriend, Bjay, and my four-year-old son, Ravi. I packed the leaf spring in the back of my lop-sided Burma, under the small bed I had made for my boy. Zacatecas was the first large Mexican town on our route, so I decided to try having the spring repaired there.

We stopped at a neighborhood store on the outskirts of town; and, after asking around, I ended up following a young guy who walked rapidly alongside the street while I tagged along in low gear. He stopped at a metal garage door in the middle of a residential block and knocked on a smaller door beside it. A thin, middle aged man in greasy overalls stuck his head out and listened to my guide. I got out of the truck to negotiate.

My limited, tourist level experience with Mexican culture made me suspicious. The young man who had directed me to this place disappeared around a corner, which surprised me. I had been certain he would expect a tip for his trouble. Then it occurred to me that perhaps he would get his tip from the worried looking man in the doorway. Too late to turn back now, without feeling like an idiot.

After I had explained my situation as best I could, the mechanic opened the noisy metal garage door and motioned me to drive in. In spite of his worried expression, which I later determined was habitual, I took comfort in his air of quiet competence. Something in his manner convinced me that asking about money right away would be inappropriate; perhaps even an insult. I followed my intuition and decided to trust him.

We got the replacement spring from its cradle in the back of Burma and the mechanic began jacking up her left side to examine the damage. I relaxed and stood at the garage door, watching my traveling companions as they took a walk around the neighborhood. Bjay, my dark complected, attractive petite girlfriend had a spirit and appearance that made her a racial chameleon. Depending on the setting, she could appear to be Asian or African, Arab or Mexican. She and my four-year-old, with his curly blonde hair, made quite a splash wherever we went.

Across the street from the garage, construction workers were laboring on a new house. There were men on the roof, on the walls and out in the yard, about a dozen of them. As I stood in the doorway, one of the workers suddenly burst into song, soon followed by another, and then another. Within seconds the entire construction site was transformed into something akin to a musical movie set. I couldn't help looking around for a camera crew. And it actually did sound as though any one of those guys could easily qualify for a professional production.

I was enjoying the music as it suddenly occurred to me that maybe this spontaneous performance was being put on just for my little family. People don't really burst into song that way, do they, except in the movies? I ducked back into the garage and squatted down to watch the worried mechanic working under Burma until Bjay and Ravi came back with the news that a neighborhood family had invited us for a visit. I closed the padlock on our camper and joined them. As we walked down the block, several houses from the garage, two of the carpenters across the street were still singing, locked in close harmony.

We were led through a heavy wooden door, down a short hallway and into a sparsely furnished, but immaculate parlor. A large, highly polished floor model Victrola occupied a prominent position in the room. We were offered sodas and directed to sit down. An adolescent boy DJ proudly installed a record in the Victrola and the commanding tones of a military march filled the air. While we sat drinking our sodas, a number of neighbors came through the room, greeting us as though we were some kind of dignitaries. Ravi's blonde hair was an apparent fascination. And, even though Bjay didn't speak Spanish, her native Portuguese Creole was close enough, beside which her non-verbal communication was delightfully universal. I gradually developed a kind of dependence on her natural ability.

We finished our sodas at about the same time the second march record was over. There was only the boy DJ and a middle-aged couple left in the room. The boy ceremoniously turned off the Victrola; an unspoken signal that the party was over. With "mucho gustoes" all around, we shook hands and went back to where the new spring brackets were being welded into place. The whole experience had lasted little more than ten minutes. Over time, I would come to marvel at the memory of how this little neighborhood had so beautifully and easily opened a space of cultural conviviality around us, and then, just as easily, had closed it.

By the time Burma rolled out into the street, proud and straight for the first time since I'd owned her, I expected to pay quite a bill. The mechanic had worked on that spring for over two hours. So, when he said "cincuenta pesos," I thought at first he must mean fifty dollars, American. But no, all he wanted was around four dollars American. That was amazing to me. I would eventually come to understand and appreciate this dignified aspect of Mexican culture, with its many good people to whom overcharging a gringo would be felt as dishonoring to themselves.

I don't think it was just my imagination that Burma seemed to run better after that. The long stretches of quiet, two lane highway between population centers gently rolled by. And, when we did stop, the sturdy flat head six under the hood was little more than lukewarm. There was only one time, much further south of the border, when Burma suffered a malfunction. The engine was stuttering, and getting worse. And after stopping for long enough to find out there was nothing I knew to do about it, I made it into a small town and asked directions to a mechanic.

I was directed to another combination home and shop on the edge of town. When I inquired with the youngster in the oily coveralls, he indicated that I should wait and went up a flight of stairs to a large residence above the shop. Presently, a distinguished looking man in a well-tailored suit, white shirt and tie, came down the stairs with the boy. He motioned for me to start the engine and quietly listened. He directed the boy to rev the engine at the carburetor a couple of times, placed a hand on the fender and listened more intently. After speaking briefly with the youngster, he came over to my door.

"We can fix it," he said, in perfect English. "A couple of hours." I nodded and he quickly went back up the stairs without further conversation. Wahoo! I had really lucked out this time. This guy was so good he wore a suit and tie and didn't even have to get his hands dirty. After a few minutes, the distinguished looking gentleman came down the stairs again, but this time with an attractive woman in a beautiful gown on his arm. He opened one of three downstairs garage doors and they climbed into a beautiful 47 Cadillac and drove away. As I learned from the young apprentice a little later, they had gone to a friend's wedding.

We had indeed lucked out. It was Sunday, Domingo. The apprentice had only been there to do some personal work on an old motorcycle. He also did an excellent job of basically rebuilding Burma's carburetor; at minimal cost. I gave him a tip anyway, which he appreciated.

After that incident, no sweeter more dependable truck ever rolled. We eventually made two eighteen-hundred-mile round trips to the border, a side trip to Paracho, and then a final drive up to Taos, New Mexico. All those miles without a hint of trouble. Travel with Burma became a pleasant routine.

Then, once we got settled into a home in San Miguel de Allende, Burma didn't get much attention or exercise; except for our every six months round trips to the border for tourist visas. Occasionally, we would roll out to the local hot springs. Otherwise, she sat patiently waiting, getting dusty, in a wide spot at the corner of our alley - Callejon de Las Animas. This "Alley of the Spirits," was an irregular dirt roadway that rambled between high adobe walls, most of which had broken glass cemented along their tops.

Countless small wonders occurred along that dirt byway, and one of the most blatantly mysterious involved Burma. Once in a while, I would go out to where she was parked and fuss with her. I'd check the fluids and start the motor and let her run for a while; keeping the battery charged. On this particular day there wasn't much traffic passing by, so I easily noticed when a drunk old man came to a sudden stop in the middle of the alley. He stood still for a moment, looking as though he had just remembered something important, then suddenly turned and headed in my direction.

I was leaning over Burma's fender, checking under her hood. The old man mumbled something unintelligible and pointed toward the carburetor. He apparently wanted to show me something. I wondered if he might not be trying to get a few pesos out of me for more booze. But I followed his lead. He pointed to the fuel line, near where it was connected to the carburetor, and pulled it slightly away from the top edge of the manifold. He pointed to that spot, said something else unintelligible and staggered away.

I got a wrench out of my tool box and disconnected the fuel line from the carburetor. I pulled it toward me, away from the engine, and saw a worn spot on the back of the line, where it had been rubbing against the manifold. I suppose it's possible that a dangerous fuel leak could have resulted; but, unless he had come in the night with a metal file and had created the worn spot himself, how could that old drunk have known about it? Unless, perhaps he'd had experience with that same type of engine. From then on, I watched out for him every time I was in the alley. But he never showed up again.

*   *   *

It wasn't too long after moving into the neighborhood that I learned the unique importance of this alley (which gave a new twist to its name) to a lot of drunken cowboys and Indians. A little beyond the far end of our Alley of the Spirits was the "city limit," a borderline creek bed beyond which was open country. Beyond this point you could safely pass out in a drunken stupor and not get picked up to do road work the following day. Even if you passed out in the middle of the creek, you would still be immune from the official early morning roundup of the cobblestone brigade. Occasionally, late at night, dark figures could be seen staggering down the alley, bouncing from one wall to the other, desperately trying to make it to the creek.

When we had first moved into the neighborhood and I started going to Juanita's, our corner store, I noticed a urinal on one wall in plain sight. I reacted as most American tourists would, viewing the public urinal as a quaint feature of a less sophisticated culture. However, six months later I would be standing at that same urinal, feeling quite sophisticated, and talking to Juanita over my shoulder. The degree of my enculturation at that time still interests me. I stood there peeing in front of Juanita and it seemed perfectly normal.

The neighborhood was quite pleased that I labored as gringo apprentice to a local woodworking maestro. And, since he and his family lived just down the alley, my little family was graciously accepted into the heart of the community. Bjay rapidly made friends and many people believed that just touching my little boy's blonde hair would bring them good luck. He became a kind of celebrity. I could hear people calling his name whenever he was out around the neighborhood.

It took me a while to share in the trust that local parents had for the culture around them; that everyone would watch out for the children. The experience of living in a loving, trustworthy village eventually sank in. Children were fed and protected wherever they happened to be. Another major benefit of this communal belonging was that Burma never got vandalized. She just sat there getting dusty.

The large, Romanesque quadrangle I had secured from my friends, who were currently in the "States," had a couple of extra rooms, so I had space for traveling visitors, which happened often. One day a tall, skinny guy who called himself Morgan came to my door looking for a place to stay. He said he had heard of me from mutual friends. He was at least six foot six, and so skinny he had the appearance of a stick man. Morgan had just escaped a Mexican drug bust of an American commune in Oaxaca.

"I don't have any money," he said, pulling a quart jar from his backpack. "But I do have these." The jar he produced was about two-thirds full of potent little pink capsules of pure LSD, made by Sandoz Pharmaceuticals. Morgan declared that he'd had enough.

"If you want them," he said. "Just let me know when you think my rent is up and I'll move on." During the time he stayed with us, all Morgan did was to work on designing his own personal deck of Tarot cards. The images he drew were powerful, some of them disturbing, but not all of them unpleasant. He often sat at a table in a corner of the main Sala, just watching, which really didn't bother anyone. Morgan's watching was friendly, and humorous, and conversations with him were always interesting.

On the other hand, I'm not so sure he did me such a favor when he handed me all that LSD. I gave some away to people I trusted, and limited myself to one capsule a week. And I did indeed enjoy those Sandoz Sundays (Sandoz Domingos) for a while. I had some truly remarkable experiences; but, by the time I left Mexico, I understood better what Morgan had meant when he said he'd had enough. There was still a large quantity in that jar when I gave it to an art student I had come to know. I was getting ready to go back to the States and not into smuggling contraband. I could easily have sold it, but, as a guest of the Mexican government, I saw no sense in taking such a risk. Ironically, before I got out of town, someone I'd never met before tried to sell me one of those little pink capsules on the street.

*   *   *

I had put off finishing the roof over the camper until about a month before we planned to leave. And then, after I finished that job, I found I couldn't stop. I had been working with a Mexican maestro, an artist in woodworking, and was inspired to turn Burma's plain plywood camper into a thing of beauty. I had purchased a good jig saw on one of my border runs to El Paso and I put it to good use cutting out artful trim for the upper edges of the camper; a flow of curves, scrolls and symbols. Burma became a major project.

An artist friend did a fabulous job of adding dimension by painting what I had applied. Burma began to look like an elegant, mediaeval circus wagon. A couple of other artists joined in and I wound up with a rolling art gallery. Across the front of the cab-over, centered above the cab, I had applied a stylized wooden cross, with rosettes at the ends. My artist friend did an especially beautiful job on this figure, a heavenly cross in silver and blue.

As we traveled through various towns and villages on our way back to the border, there were a few times when Burma made an appearance and everyone on the street would immediately remove their hats. It did occur to me that I might get in trouble for impersonating a priest, but we were just passing through. On one occasion groups of people along the road were clapping and cheering as we drove by. The groups grew larger and I pulled over to learn that we had somehow missed a checkpoint and were inadvertently in front of a motorcade featuring a local dignitary and a famous matador.

As we drew closer to the border, I did begin to wonder how Burma would be received on the other side. Typical of our experience in Mexico was the last stop we made before crossing, in the little village of Magdalena. It was night time. We ordered some tacos in a dimly lit café. While we waited, the girl behind the counter was being wooed by a handsome young man who spoke to her in soft, caressing tones. She responded with equal softness. The air was charged with the sweet natural energy of their flirtation. After our lengthy stay in Mexico, Bjay and I could look at the young couple and enjoy the family feeling of an older generation.

We took our food out to the small table in our camper, near where Ravi and baby Rachel were asleep, and had a quiet dinner. We were just getting ready to close up and drive on when a couple of transitos, local policemen, came strolling by. They stopped to admire Burma, smiling and complimenting what they saw. They were curious about the camper, so I invited them in to look around. They stayed for a few minutes, cheerfully shook hands and went on their way. I had no idea then just how much I would miss this side of Mexican culture.

The contrast between that gentle stop and the Friday night drive-in restaurant we next stopped at in Las Cruces, New Mexico, was astonishing. The young people in the drive-in were loud, insecure and aggressive. There were no gentle exchanges. And the local policemen, big men wearing helmets and dangling an assortment of weapons and equipment from their belts, swaggered and drew their own coffee from the large urns behind the counter.

I glanced out the window to where Burma sat, looking completely out of place; I felt the same. I hadn't anticipated this culture shock. We had become so completely involved in the values and rhythms of our Mexican life style, we felt like aliens here. I was oddly embarrassed, all the more because I knew I couldn't share my feelings with any of those around us. I didn't stop driving, except for gas, until we reached Taos, over 350 miles away.

Part of our extended hippie family network had settled around Taos, near the small village of Arroyo Seco. We soon found an old farm house for rent and took our place in this late nineteen-sixties phenomenon of intentional community. Aside from those I already knew, we were soon in community with a polyglot of misfits from all over the world, loosely transplanted into the ancient landscape of Northern New Mexico.

There was the magical, white haired lady from England, a story teller, who loved to have us all over every couple of weeks for a bread baking party. She'd built two of those large, igloo shaped adobe ovens in her back yard. Her son, a Berkeley math professor, who owned the house his mother lived in, showed up with his wife as often as possible. There was the Dutch artist who had been raised in India and was looking for someone to marry so he could stay in the United States; the angry black artist from New York and his beautiful Native American wife; the young couple who were always on the verge of leaving, but passionately changed their minds every week or so; the young spiritual couple for whom we all came together for a wonderful wedding in the wilderness; the amazing old Pueblo men, Tellus Goodmorning and Little Joe, with whom we ate peyote at the hot springs down by the Rio Grande; the wealthy young couple from Wyoming, with an adobe castle on the hill and a couple of aircraft at the Taos airport, who managed to employ practically all of us hippie artists at one time or another; the sweet old couple left over from a previous decade of Anglo artist invasion in the Taos area. And then, there was the distinguished looking gray-haired gentleman who wore a clerical collar, claimed to be a priest, and tried to fuck everybody, male or female. Our old friend Morgan even showed up for a visit.

Most of us found homes that were heated by wood stoves. So, before that first winter, I dismantled Burma's painted palace and turned her into a work horse, a wood hauling stake-side. In those days of community sharing, Burma was known by name and part of everyone's family. She stayed busy. She hauled lumber and firewood and made trips to Santa Fe for bulk food and other supplies.

One day I loaned her to a young friend who came back and said she had just stopped running and he had worn the battery down trying to start her again. I drove over to see her; in the used Nash sedan I had traded for at a local service station. I carried battery cables for jump starting, but Burma would not fire up and I couldn't afford to rescue her.

That was the last time I saw her; dirty, cold and alone in an empty field, backed up to a barbed wire fence. It was late afternoon. I leaned over her hood, as I had done a thousand times before, and gazed at her cold, lifeless engine. Suddenly, my mind was flooded with images of every detail of every moment we had ever spent together. From when I had first met her, a lopsided unfinished camper, to her glorious ride as the magical Queen of the Mexican Highway; from those warm days of long-distance family hauling to her hard use as a rural workhorse, Burma's life was flashing before my eyes. I slowly disconnected her battery and stayed in the field with her until twilight.

REVOLUTION

I was going about my business in the Taos Plaza one day when I heard a sharp voice behind me.

"Hey boy." I turned around and stared at the skinny little Pueblo Indian who had spoken.

"Yeah you, boy," he called. "C'mere." I was somewhere between anger and amazement as I walked toward him, uncertain of how to respond. How dare this old Indian talk to me like that. He must be drunk. He stood there patiently waiting, with his rough woolen blanket wrapped around him.

"You talkin' to me, Chief?" I asked, intending to sound tough. But the closer I got to him, the less angry I became. His wrinkled old face was as dead pan as any Indian face I'd ever seen, but his bright clear eyes were taunting and alive with humor.

"You gotta light, boy." His emphasis on the word "boy," which at first had raised my hackles, now carried some deeper message, as though he and I were characters in some sort of turnabout culture play, as representatives of something larger than ourselves. When I lit the long brown cigarillo he raised to his lips, our eyes met and I felt like laughing. It's hard to explain. I just knew everything was okay.

Such was my first encounter with Little Joe, with whom my hippie friends and I would later spend a lot of quality time, eating peyote and hanging out at the hot springs down by the Rio Grande. Little Joe told a lot of stories, a few of which had to do with "counting coup" with U.S. Cavalry soldiers when he was a boy. It was hard to tell what was literally true, since legend and historical events ran together, but I didn't doubt he was that old.

The long turbulent history of Northern New Mexico meant little to me at the time. I was too busy trying to figure out what it was I had come there to look for. It was 1967, there was a new and liberating excitement in the latest Beatle's tunes and counter-cultural communes with names like New Buffalo and Lama were sprouting up north of Taos.

My little family, living near the village of Arroyo Seco, northeast of Taos, belonged to a loosely knit community of neighbors who had traveled there from many places; Texas, Los Angeles, New York, Berkeley, and Nepal, to mention a few. We were an island of mostly Anglo outsiders in the midst of two native cultures, Spanish and Pueblo, who had lived in that sacred land for centuries.

Although we developed lasting friendships within these cultures over time, we identified mostly with the alternative back country community we were building. We got together to cut firewood for all our families. We played music and made a party of baking bread in outdoor, adobe ovens. We also made sure to meddle in each other's lives as much as possible.

One day in June of that year, I was out in the barn across from my rented farm house when I heard the distinct sound of helicopters. They were passing low over Arroyo Seco and into the nearby forest.

"Hey Bird," I called to my wife in the house. "Turn on the radio." Sure enough, the news was all about a shoot-out at the Tierra Amarilla courthouse, a little mountain town further up north. A group of armed men had raided the courthouse in an attempt to break one of their own out of jail. In a land where not much that was newsworthy ever happened, this event created a stir that was felt all the way back in Washington D.C.

The raid was in protest to an arrest for trespassing. The Alianza Federal de las Mercedes (The Federal Land-Grant Alliance) was dedicated to taking back the land in Northern New Mexico that had once belonged to Spanish Land Grants. This rebellious 1960's Alliance was led by Reies López Tijerina, a charismatic onetime minister and traveling revivalist who was then hiding out in the mountains.

The helicopters flew low over Arroyo Seco several times during the following weeks, while many of us on the ground openly cheered for the Alliance. From what we understood, they planned to take back their land and form an independent, sovereign nation in the middle of Northern New Mexico. But, rumor had it that this so-called "army of insurrection," to which the U.S. Government was trying to respond, consisted of no more than a dozen or so individuals. As far-fetched as their plan may now seem, it made more sense in the Sixties.

In due time and without further incident, the helicopters went away and the fuss subsided. Then, some time later, it came over the radio that Washington was going to deal with the recent native unrest in Northern New Mexico by throwing money at it, a reported two hundred and fifty thousand dollars. When my friends and I found out there was to be an official "public" meeting, at a savings and loan office in Taos, we encouraged a number of our native friends to attend it with us. The advertised purpose of this meeting was to discuss how to spend some of those funds.

Although by law the meeting was open to the public, only the legal minimum of advertising had been done – a single notice (in legalese) in the local newspaper and one buried in a small newspaper in Santa Fe. Nevertheless, by the time the meeting was held, we had raised quite a party of interested citizens. Aside from a dozen or so of us world traveling gypsies, twenty or so native people (both Spanish and Pueblo) showed up. Our friend Little Joe was prominent among them.

The small group of businessmen, four Anglos and two Spanish, were just getting settled with two Anglo government representatives when our colorful gang converged on the savings and loan office. The little business group was shocked and confused at the sight of so many native people, not to mention the rest of us.

There was no way we could all fit into that small board room. The businessmen and federal guys quickly went into a huddle. After a brief period of chaos, the president of the savings and loan made a phone call and moved the meeting over to a public school. Some other people showed up. A table and chairs, plus a portable blackboard, were brought onto a low stage and folding chairs were provided for us unexpected participants.

The businessmen took their seats at the table as the federal guys prepared to deal with the general assembly. The older of the two, a thin and nervous little man with a shiny bald head, moved to stand by the blackboard. He picked up a piece of chalk, a well-known symbol of authority, and turned the meeting into a classroom.

The collection of impassive dark-skinned faces in the audience represented a world about which this man knew next to nothing. He was anxious, and then visibly relieved by the timely appearance of an elderly Anglo deputy sheriff in the back of the room. Chalk in hand, he paused for a moment to gather his thoughts, then took a deep breath and raised himself to his full five feet eight inches.

"We're here to help you folks learn how to organize," he began. "Your government understands that you may feel left out, so we want to help you learn the means by which you may better participate." He drew three boxes on the blackboard, one above and another two side by side.

"First of all," he continued. "It helps to understand how to delegate responsibility. And believe me," he put on his best all-knowing white man smile. "It really helps to know how to use committees and sub-committees." The audience sat stone faced and silent as the federal guy went on. I couldn't believe what I was witnessing. This seemed like a bad joke.

"For instance," the bald head continued. "Let's say you want to sell your baskets." He drew the word BASKET in the top box. Little Joe suddenly spoke up.

"Why the hell you talkin' about baskets?" he asked. The bald federal guy looked out into the room for the source of that crackling voice. The ancient skeleton that was Little Joe stood up. He was flanked by two heavy set Pueblo men who looked as though they could stop a tank. The federal guy said something to his young assistant, who began rifling through a brief case.

"My information indicated that your people are basket weavers," he said.

"We don't make no stinkin' baskets," Little Joe replied, a twinkle in his eye. There was a chorus of chuckles and the assistant federal guy had trouble keeping a straight face as he handed his boss a piece of paper. The older man looked it over.

"Well then," he smiled. "We can help you sell your blankets."

"And why the hell would we do that," Little Joe replied. "It gets damned cold around here in the winter." There was more laughter. The federal guy was beginning to show signs of agitation.

"Look," he said. "We're just here to help you people."

"Oh sure," Little Joe said. "That always did sound like a good thing, but we heard it too many times. How much money you got left in the pot, right now?"

The confused expression on the federal guy's face was like a jumbled roadmap to how many places his mind was trying to go at one time. He mumbled "Just a minute" and stepped over to the table. After a brief huddle, he returned to center stage and addressed Little Joe, who was still standing.

"I'm glad you asked that question," he said. "But we are currently updating our budget and I'm afraid I can't give you an exact figure at this time. I wouldn't want to publicize incorrect information."

"Bullshit," said Little Joe. "Just make a rough guess. How much is left?" There was a chorus of agreement behind him. In the long history of their relationship, the Spanish and Pueblo people had fiercely fought one another; but they had also stood together, against the Apache and the Plains Indians. Their unity against the outsider Anglos was automatic. The federal guy took a deep breath. His bald head was beaded with perspiration.

"That's not exactly how it works," he began. "There's administration, consulting, a couple of studies yet to be done."

"You should be ashamed of yourself, White Man." Little Joe's voice was powerful in its condemnation, but there was also a tone of sorrow and compassion.

"About one hundred and fifty thousand," blurted the young assistant federal guy. "That's what's left." The older man wheeled around to face him

"What the hell are you saying?" he demanded.

"You don't get it," said the assistant, standing up. "We should just give them the money." At that moment the deputy sheriff in the back of the room was joined by two strangers in suits.

"Are you out of your mind?" asked the older man. The younger man nodded.

"Yeah," he said. "I think so." With that he took off his tie and went to sit in the audience. His name was John Scott. He was dropping out. He would stay and wind up living in a local commune. The older federal guy stood silent, with a stricken expression. The president of the savings and loan came to his rescue.

"Alright everyone, that concludes tonight's meeting," he said to the audience. "We'll let you know of any further developments."

"Wait a minute," said Little Joe. "We're not greedy people. How about if we just split what's left between us? Half for you guys and half for us. Think it over."

As we filed out, the men in suits were compelled to do something, so they made a clumsy effort at collecting names. After Freddy Fox, Woody Woodpecker and Buddy Bear had volunteered their names, the suits gave it up. The old deputy, who knew most of the native people, was grinning (as they say) from ear to ear.

THE BEST PLANS LAID

The various communities around Taos, New Mexico in the late 1960s were a reflection of several distinct periods of history. The oldest apartment house in the nation, the Taos Pueblo, still occupied by descendants of its first inhabitants, who had lived there eight hundred years ago. Then, during the 16th century, came the first Spanish travelers, most of whom settled permanently. Later on, in the 18th and 19th centuries, came the Anglos, mostly after the settlement of the Mexican-American War in 1848.

Then, yet another cultural "invasion" resulted from an influx of American artists, notable among them Georgia O'Keeffe, in the 1920s and 30s. This was later followed in the 1960s by yet another invasion of somewhat different counter-culture characters from all over the world. When I arrived there with my little family in the late 60s, I counted among my friends people from New York, Texas, California, a couple of young guys from England and one young Dutchman from Tibet.

A number of communes had come into being around the northern New Mexico countryside, a few of which I became involved with over a plan to form a food buying co-op, which was required by various distributors for us to get wholesale prices. Unlike the Lama Commune to our north and the New Buffalo Commune to the west of us, my immediate circle of friends was composed of individual families living in their own homes, but drawn together as a tight community. As recent arrivals in an ancient land, we naturally banded together.

Regardless of where we came from, however, we all had one thing in common. We were of the brave new counter-culture that would ultimately bring peace to the entire world. "All you need is love" was our message, and we could prove it by our example. Our hearts were true. God was on our side. And our message was rapidly spreading throughout the land. Meanwhile, we all had to eat.

The idea was to join together and form a legal non-profit so we could buy and supply our communities with low-cost food stuffs, like rice, grain and beans, beyond that which we could grow or otherwise supply for ourselves. The word we got from the state bureaucracy in Santa Fe was that we would have to appoint a set of officers; president, vice president, secretary, treasurer, etc., then pay a small fee and apply for our license to buy wholesale. No problem. We could do that.

A time and place were set for our first meeting, word was passed along and a good turnout was expected. Everyone was interested in saving that which most of us never had enough of - money. They came from the mountains and the valleys, from the Lama and the New Buffalo, long haired and bearded, costumed and beautiful, representatives of a new age, the spiritual cream of our new way of life. There were hand-shakes and hugs, bright smiles and loving words. Just what one would expect from heaven on earth.

We met at the Dutchman Hans' house, a story book cottage at the east end of story book Valdez Valley. I lived with my family on the ridge above Valdez Valley and would often pause to appreciate the natural beauty around us, especially our view of that perfectly shaped, flat bottomed, narrow little valley. Hans was a talented, outspoken 26-year-old blonde photographer-artist who had been raised in Tibet. He became my partner in building some benches, tables and chairs for a couple of ski lodges further up the mountains above Taos.

As we crowded into his modest living room, there was an excitement that reflected our perceived self-importance. We truly believed we were on the cutting edge of hope for all of humanity. If only the establishment could be made to see the value of what we had to offer, that the power of brotherly love could overcome all obstacles. How simple it all could be. We talked about the products we would pool our resources to buy, how we would distribute them, and then it was time to deal with the selection of officers.

After some discussion we all agreed that no one really cared who filled these formal positions for the co-op, which, after all, were just names on paper to satisfy "them" and their system. So, each of us wrote our names (which of course included all the women who were present) on a slip of paper and put them into a hat. The idea was to randomly draw a name for each officer and go with that choice.

The first name out of the hat for the office of president was my wife Bjay, a petite and happy young woman who was probably least of all interested in being president of anything. Next out of the hat, for vice president, was Julie, a misty-eyed girl who had shown up with an angry young poet from New York City. Although no one spoke out in that moment, I could see the pained expressions on a few male faces, especially that of a big, red bearded guy named Arnold, who looked stoic and regal in his long black robe.

Two more names were drawn, both long haired young men, for secretary and treasurer. But before we could go any further, Arnold spoke up.

"Ya know," he began, his voice deep and resonant. "I don't mean no offense." He cast a crooked grin toward Bjay and Julie. "But don't ya think our top officers should at least have some leadership experience?" The room was silent for a moment.

"You mean like you do, Arnold?" Hans responded with unveiled sarcasm. Arnold puffed out his cheeks beneath the red beard as he glared at Hans for a second.

"Well," he hesitated. "Yeah. I mean…" Another voice broke in.

"Just a minute. We already agreed these paper names don't really matter. What's goin' on here?" A freeze frame of the room at that instant would have revealed we had broken into factions. And then, it appeared as though our loving sweet layer of spiritual unity had been seriously torn and tossed aside, as other issues that already existed between certain individuals came to the surface.

"Oh yeah," I heard a taunting voice cut in. "You guys at Bullshit Buffalo didn't even have the brains to build your outhouse far enough away from the kitchen." There had in fact been an outbreak of hepatitis. The room was suddenly filled with an escalating volley of chaotic conversation.

"Just a damn minute," Hans' voice rose above the others. "Everybody settle down. Please. This is still America, right? Where people vote, right? So, let's take a damn vote." The room became quiet again. "Now," Hans continued. "How many want to stay with the officers we already got?" To my surprise only about half the people raised their hands, and that didn't include Bjay or Julie, both of whom apparently didn't want their appointed positions.

The mood in the room had changed dramatically. There was a general discomfort, a sense of embarrassment in the air, a kind of shameful admission that perhaps we hadn't come so far from the mainstream that had conditioned us after all. There was one older Oriental looking guy in the room who never spoke and whose smile never changed. I didn't get a chance to talk with him, but I had the distinct impression he was quite entertained by what he had observed.

Nothing was resolved and it wasn't long before people began to leave. The idea of forming a food buying co-op dissolved and was soon forgotten. Except by me who has now written about it.

DAYTON CONSOLIDATED

I started working on the pick-up truck camper about a month before we departed from Taos. The weather was cold, extremely cold, so I took extra pains to build a warm and solid home for my little family. I built it in the old barn next to our rented farmhouse, surrounded by a landscape under a few feet of snow. Average temperature was around ten degrees.

A two-by-two-inch stud frame was covered by a quarter inch plywood exterior layer. Fiberglass insulation was packed into the frame, which included the floor, and an interior layer of a slightly thinner ply (three sixteenths, except for half inch on the floor frame) was laid on. Every wood join was sealed with an industrial resin glue, plus a judicious number of screws and nails as needed.

The camper was large and graceful. I made building it into an occasion for artful design. There was a long horizontal, elliptical window in the front of the cabover, next to our double mattress. The sides of the cabover flared out a little wider than the rest of the body, providing a slightly larger "bedroom." There was an insulated crawlway for the kids, through what had been the rear window of the cab, and a tall oval window next to the camper's rear door, through which I could choose whatever scenery we'd like to see when we woke up the next morning.

After our first day out from Taos, headed for Nevada, we spent the night somewhere in the mountains of Colorado. When I awoke in the morning and tried to light the stove, I thought there must be something wrong with the matches I was trying to strike. They would begin to light, and then quickly go out.

Oh my God, it suddenly hit me. What an idiot. I hadn't yet opened the vent in the hood above the stove, which, I just then fully realized, was the only opening in our air tight little house except for the crawl-way into the closed cab. I am convinced to this day that we were just then on the verge of running out of oxygen. I threw the rear door open and took in a large gulp of cold mountain air. "Wake up everybody."

During all my years of woodworking, it was a fact that I had a tenancy to overbuild, but that was the one time when it might have had such disastrous consequences. At any rate, we all woke up that morning; my seven-year-old son, Ravi, my baby girl, Rachel, and my petite wife with the beautiful hazel eyes, Bjay. Looking back, those days on the road were some of the happiest we ever shared. Ravi, Bjay and I had a bit more experience than the baby, who had been born in Mexico. We had lived in a large camper on our previous truck, a one-ton Dodge flatbed named Burma, as we made a number of trips in and out of Mexico.

The joy and mystery of the open road was an almost addictive activity. I had intentionally charted our course over the lesser used highways and back roads between Taos and Silver City, Nevada. We passed through a number of small, picturesque towns and awoke to an endless array of postcard like landscapes.

Our arrival in Silver City was occasion for a party. It was the late sixties and I still had a number of friends living there whom I had known years before. An exodus from Marin County after the 1957 earthquake, which supported the rumor that California was going to slip into the Pacific Ocean, had provided a new strain of small-town citizen in Nevada. The two families I knew best lived down the same dirt road at the south end of Silver City; Walt and Barbara in the large A frame they had constructed and Dick and Rose in their remodeled old mining cabin further along, beyond where the road came to a dead end.

Walt and Barbara had come from New York by way of Sausalito. Walt was working on a novel that never ended; Barbara was an accomplished artist. Together they found local work as sign painters and did house painting as well. Dick, who came from a well-established family, was also a house painter and the only person I ever knew who had been officially exiled from Marin County.

As a quick draw artist, Dick had been a close runner up in the California State Quick Draw Competition, where grown men with six shooters and slick holsters were electronically measured to determine the quickest bullet to the target. In agreement with his family, and to avoid a jail sentence, a judge had banished Dick, who had pulled a deputy sheriff's loosely holstered weapon before anyone knew what was happening. This came on the heels of a car chase in which a drunken Dick had almost gotten away. If this incident hadn't been witnessed by other policemen, the embarrassed deputy might possibly have never reported it. And if Dick hadn't had enough sense to immediately drop the weapon he had drawn, he would most certainly have been shot down on the spot.

"I just wanted to see if I could do it," he laughed. But no one else was laughing. If it hadn't been for family connections, Dick might still have been locked away. Rose, Dick's wife, I knew little about. She and Dick had gotten together after he had left Marin. She was a tall, outspoken redhead whose name I didn't think fit her very well.

Our little family could have continued living in the camper indefinitely, but my plan was to find a place for us to live and for me to set up shop. And, as with others who had moved into this long-abandoned area, I would first of all look for a way not to be too burdened with rent payments. There were various empty places to investigate, but most were too run down to consider. However, on one of my dirt road tours around the area, I soon found what I was looking for.

A little further south of Silver City, down the highway from the side road where my friends lived, another rough dirt road led uphill to the deserted Dayton Consolidated mining complex, which was mostly hidden from the main highway. Near the bottom of the hill was a huge rundown old building that still contained all the old equipment of a gold refining operation, abandoned in the late 1930s. This warehouse sized structure took in dump truck loads of raw ore on the uphill side, ran it through rock crushers, liquified it in huge redwood tanks, ran the slurry through pressure and heat, and then, finally extracted the gold in a smelter at the bottom of the run.

I remember the feeling as I stood in the thick silence of that huge structure; the network of well-worn pathways in its sandy earthen floor; the natural incline of hillside that had simply been roofed over. It was a strange paradoxical silence, made stronger in the midst of those loud industrial memories. Then, from somewhere in the dark recesses of the high tin roof, I could hear the soft cooing of pigeons.

Further along up the hill, past another huge, but empty structure, was a collection of buildings where I staked my claim for a family compound. After removing my homemade camper, which would still serve as a temporary home (later to become the kid's playhouse), I took numerous truckloads of industrial trash to a nearby desert dumpsite. Gradually, we cleared and cleaned the yard and a small office building which would become our new home. Across the open yard was another sturdy old building in which I hoped to establish my workshop.

But first I needed electricity. It was obvious that most of the complex had been wired before, but it was also obvious that someone had stripped the external cable from the short poles that had brought electricity up the hill from the poles along the highway. When I approached the Nevada Power Company, they would only agree to put a meter on a pole at the bottom of the hill. I would have to bring electricity the rest of the way to my shop. We actually didn't want electricity at the house.

Unfortunately, when I paced off the distance from the telephone pole to the old switch box at the end of my shop building, I was disheartened. It was roughly eight hundred and fifty feet and I would need at least number six wire. From the information I gathered talking to a couple of local electrical supply houses, the cost would be prohibitive. Regardless of that reality, however, it seemed that my faith in the plan for a shop was destined to be rewarded.

About half way between Silver City and Carson City, there was a desert junkyard where an old junk dealer named Ed took me into a "twilight zone" of wish fulfillment. I swear, it was as though he was just waiting for me to show up. I stared at him, speechless. He just happened to have a nine-hundred-foot roll of number six insulated three-wire outdoor cable that I could have for fifty dollars. He also had some great furniture clamps and a few other items that made my year. It was a slow process, but with the money I had made from a couple of jobs around Taos, and selling some equipment I'd had to leave behind, I was able to get my woodworking operation together again.

Meanwhile, I learned that the Dayton Consolidated was owned by a mining company in Spokane, Washington, and wrote them a letter with my proposition to stay there. I didn't intend to put in much more work only to be asked to leave. After a few weeks, a retired mining engineer and his wife, both with white hair, came down from Reno to visit us. He had been an employee of the Spokane company and was asked to check us out. They were a gentle and loving old couple who quickly developed a heartfelt connection with my family. I think we reminded them of their own early beginnings. Anyway, it was soon agreed with the company in Spokane that I could lease the complex, as caretaker, for ten dollars a year. No cheaper rent have I ever enjoyed.

A little way beyond our home site and my shop, there were a few smaller buildings and a tall wooden triangular framework that sat atop a wide vertical shaft that I would guess was hundreds of feet deep. This incredibly dangerous hole was loosely covered with decaying plywood and a few rough planks. Needless to say, this was but one of a number of places around the property where the children were strictly forbidden to go.

*　*　*

After we had lived at the Dayton Consolidated for several weeks, a sheriff's car came up the hill one day and a tall, lanky deputy climbed out. I felt apprehensive and wondered why he was there.

"Howdy," he said, in a soft-spoken tone. "My name is Dalton and I'm the only law this side of Carson for quite a way." There was no bragging or threat in his statement, just matter of fact. He was actually there for a more or less social visit. He had heard about us and wanted to get acquainted. We walked over to my shop, where I was working on a prototype of a child's cradle I hoped to market over in California. He was a curious, intelligent kind of guy and I could tell he approved of our presence at the Dayton. Just as he was leaving, he stuck out his hand and looked straight into my eyes.

"If you ever need to shoot anyone," he said. "Just make sure to drag them inside before I get here, so I can write it up as a burglary." At first, I thought he was kidding, but I'm glad I didn't laugh. The look on his face said he was perfectly serious.

* * *

One of my favorite things about living in rural Nevada in the late sixties was the sun-drenched quietude, the great clean bowl of sky and the sense of knowing there were only a few people for many miles around. Although the highway passing by where we lived was by no means deserted, the long uphill grade from Silver City to Virginia City didn't attract a lot of traffic. There were alternate routes that were not so steep. From where I had my woodworking shop, in a sturdy old building on top of the hill, I could walk over to a steep edge and look down on a stretch of highway from the south to just where it turned into the mountainside community of Silver City.

Some memories of living with my young family on that property bring a smile, others are in a not so happy category. Many things happened, but some memories stand out for which words like synchronicity or serendipity are just not quite adequate. Such incidents were at the time a kind of everyday magic. After all, since my introduction to the Native American Church a decade or so earlier, the desert landscape, from Lake Pyramid in the north to Woodford's Reservation in the south, had held a secret dimension. I had caught a glimpse of another, ancient and magical reality behind that thin blue veil of desert sky.

One day, preoccupied with money woes, I took a break and walked down near the highway, checking the electrical line that supplied my shop. There was no particular problem, but, since I had laid the heavy cable myself, it was my routine to occasionally check it out for safety. As I approached the telephone pole where my electrical meter was mounted, I noticed a sparkling new Cadillac parked alongside the paved two-lane highway. There was a wet spot on the ground near the rear of the car. The passenger windows were tinted and reflection off the windshield made it difficult to see inside. The driver's side window quickly rolled down.

"Hey, fella," a gravelly voice extruded. "D'youse know of a tow truck or a garage nearby." I didn't like being called "Fella," but I was in a good mood.

"What's the problem?" I asked as I walked closer.

"Problem?" A flat, emotionless, dark complected face stared at me over the window's edge. "Goddamn thing won't start's the problem." In a brief flash of sight into the car's interior, I could see there were at least three other men in the car. They all wore suits.

"Release the hood latch," I invited. Premonition is sometimes a powerful thing. I knew I knew something, but didn't know what. Sure enough, one of the battery terminals had been oozing corrosion. The only tools I had in my coveralls were a pair of plyers, a rag and a piece of rough sandpaper, which is exactly what was needed. I worked the battery cable loose, cleaned the corrosion away, sanded the battery post and cable connector to bare metal and put it back together.

"Try it now," I said, closing the hood. The motor instantly purred into life. There was a brief exchange inside the Caddy (I swear in

Italian) before the driver held out a couple of bills. I accepted the tip and the big car swooshed away. Wow, Holy Crap, Thank You Jesus. I stood there staring at the two one-hundred-dollar bills in my hand. This meant I could not only make my selling trip over to California, but could also take my young wife on a dream date to Reno for her birthday.

*　*　*

My young and attractive wife, whose physical attributes did not go unnoticed by those around us, was part of a strange and memorable exchange I had one day with a red headed wild man named Finley. He lived, with his wife and two children, in a run down, formerly abandoned little house further up the hill toward Virginia City. I don't think I ever saw Finley sober. Rumor had it his wife's family provided for the children and she provided for Finley.

Regardless of his alcoholism and the wobbly nature of his character however, Finley's Irish charm made him tolerable. He had the gift of gab and humor that was usually quite entertaining. But sometimes, the drunker he got the more obnoxious he became. Such was his condition one day when he drove up to my shop and staggered through the doorway.

"Hey, Finley," I greeted him but continued shaping a headboard for one of my cradles, my latest venture for the California antique and craft show market.

"Look what I found," he said. He held out a steel spike about ten inches long, three quarters of an inch in diameter, and sharply pointed on one end. He laid the spike on my workbench and stared at me without speaking. It was obvious he had something to say, but was having some difficulty getting to it, which was unusual for Finley. I laid my wood rasp aside and turned to face him.

"What's up, Finley?" He leaned against my workbench for balance and spoke through a crooked grin.

"My dear and beautiful wife wants ta sleep wid ya," he said. I wasn't at all prepared for such a statement, but my response was immediate.

"Geez, Finley," I blurted. "Why are you laying such a story on me? I'm really not interested." His crooked grin became a scowl.

"Not interested? Ya callin' me wife ugly? She ain't good enough fer ya?" Finley grabbed the steel spike off the workbench and threw it toward a nearby wall. The spike struck a four by six timber point first and stuck there. In the time it took for me to walk over and pull the spike out of the wall, I got an inkling of what Finley was really up to. I had noticed his flirtatious attention to the shapely little woman who was my partner.

"You phony son-of-a-bitch," I glared at him. "You're trying to pull off some kind of wife swapping routine." I hefted the heavy spike and deliberately flipped it over his head. It rotated end over end and landed with a solid thud, sticking into the wooden floor behind him.

Finley, appearing a bit more sober now, turned and walked over to pull the spike from the floor.

"What's wrong with that," he insisted. "My old lady would surprise ya." He then threw the spike some distance, sticking it into a far wall. I slowly walked to where the spike was stuck and retrieved it. Without a word, I gauged the distance to the wall beyond where Finley stood and threw the spike with all the force I could muster. Finley didn't flinch as the spike sailed past and struck the wall behind him, point first, deep into the wood. We were both aware of the dangerous game we were playing and there was an unspoken challenge about the lengths to which we would be willing to go.

"What's wrong with that, you dumb bastard," I said, raising my voice. "Is I'm not interested."

"Aw, c'mon," Finley was pushing it. "What ya got against a little strange stuff. At least I'm makin' th' offer man to man." With that, Finley turned around and walked over to pull the spike from the wall. It took both hands. We made eye contact as he walked toward me. He stopped just a few yards away and threw the spike, which stuck in the floor between my feet. I reached down and pulled the spike out of the floor.

"Finley," I said, quietly. "Get the hell out of here before I do something we'll both regret." He hesitated, opened his mouth, but then quickly made his way out the door as I moved toward him with clear intention. I was through playing games. As he got into his car, I heard him call out.

"No hard feelins' hey, I jus' thought it would be worth a try."

But now, here's the really interesting part of this story. For whatever reason, Finley and I had operated for a brief time in what I would later refer to as "the zone." The following day, when I went into my shop, I tried and tried to stick that damned spike. I flipped it and gripped it in any number of ways, but not once (except straight down) did that unbalanced chunk of metal make contact with anything point first.

* * *

At first, I thought the noise was in my radial arm saw. The usual whine of the electric motor suddenly took on a deeper, guttural sound. It was only after I turned the saw off and walked over to the door of my shop that I realized we had company. Several motorcycles were weaving their way up the rough dirt road that was our driveway. As they pulled into the wide yard between my shop and our converted home, one of them noticed me. My shop was in an old building with a wide loading dock along the front, which allowed me to look down on the motorcycle gang.

"Hey, partner," a long haired, bearded biker called to me. "We thought this place was deserted."

"Yeah," I replied. "The deserted buildings down below give that impression. I like it that way." He laughed and rolled closer to the loading dock.

"How far are we from Virginia City?" he asked. I quickly counted seven motorcycles mounted by a variety of men, from clean shaven youth to the older bearded character who had addressed me.

"About three miles up the hill," I answered. The bearded one turned his bike around and rolled back to his companions. They all wore jackets with the words "Hells Angels" on the back. After a brief huddle, during which time I thought about the distance to the rifle in a corner of my shop, he returned to the loading dock.

"A few of the guys want to stay and look around," he said. "Is that okay?" I was surprised by his courtesy. I had assumed from their jackets these guys were the mythical warriors and pirates of their club's reputation. I was glad my wife and children were gone to Carson City to do some shopping, but also a little apprehensive about being alone with this gang.

"Sure," I said. "So long as they follow a few rules." After a brief conference among themselves, four of the bikers took off down the dirt road and the other three rolled over to where I stood above them on the loading dock. It seemed somehow appropriate they were the youngest of the crew.

"Just a couple of things," I said. "You're welcome to check out the old mining operation down below, but the building across the way is my home, so I'd appreciate you stay away from it. Also, stay away from that tower over there. The mine shaft beneath it goes straight down and is very unsafe." At that moment one of the young men pulled a small pistol from his jacket pocket and I felt the beginnings of fight/flight panic.

"Okay if I do a little target practice?" he asked. Once again, I was surprised by the courtesy and respect these guys were extending. It was nothing like the reputation that preceded them. I wondered if I was being set up for something.

"Yeah," I said. "So long as you fire into the hillside. Agreed?"

"No problem," he replied. As I looked them over, soon to learn they were Frank, Tony and Buzz, I was impressed with how much they appeared like a group of playful neighborhood teenagers on a country outing. My cautious sense of threat was dissipating. I even considered the idea that maybe they had stolen, or otherwise misappropriated, the jackets they were wearing.

And then came crisis. It was only about twenty minutes after I'd returned to my woodworking that Buzz came to my shop door to inform me that Tony had fallen down the mine shaft. I let loose a string of curses and quickly went with him over to the triangular framework of timbers above the loosely covered shaft. Buzz called down into the darkness.

"Hey, Tony, I got the guy who lives here." We could barely hear Tony calling back from some distance below.

"Help me, you guys, I'm really hurt." He had apparently climbed down to the first level platform, a crumbling structure with an old wooden railing. When he had leaned on that railing in an effort to see further down, it had given way.

"Hang on, Tony," I called to him. "We need to get some help."

Meanwhile, my wife, Bjay, had returned with the children and groceries. I quickly explained what had happened and asked her to drive down to see if our friend, Dick, was available. Aside from his work as an avid gun collector and dealer, Dick was also a house painter and scaffold rigger. I was aware that he had plenty of rope and pulleys. This was the quickest way I could think of to retrieve Tony.

Buzz and I kept up a calling conversation with Tony, encouraging him to hang on and not to try to move. My guess was that his fall had been broken by a deeper platform or an earthen ledge, which was probably not very wide. I doubted he could see much in the darkness and might accidentally roll off his landing place to a certain death. The labyrinth of shafts and tunnels left by decades of gold and silver mining had plumbed the depths of those mountains to thousands of feet.

When Dick arrived, with a powerful flashlight, he quickly sized up the situation. He secured a line to his truck, ran it over a pulley he attached to the tower frame and deployed it, with block and tackle, down into the shaft. He instructed me to descend the rickety ladder, while attached to another line, to the second platform about thirty feet down. From the way the first and second platforms were situated, he determined we would probably have to bring Tony up in stages.

After I had descended that treacherous ladder and watched as Dick lowered himself down the shaft, several small boards broke loose from the aging structure above and fell in our direction. Although one of the pieces bounced off my shoulder, Dick was not hit. Unfortunately, we did hear an emphatic noise from Tony in the darkness below, something between a yell and a scream. We would eventually learn that a number of his bones had been broken in the fall.

There were definitely some terrifying moments before we made it back to the sunlight above. I will never forget the sight of my friend, Dick, as he lowered himself past me and down into the pitch black, yawning mouth of that abyss. My respect and admiration for his skill and courage was established forever. Looking back, I am reminded of a saying attributed to a Native American named Ambrose Redmoon: "Courage is not the absence of fear, it is the judgement that something else is more important than fear." I could tell from the sound of Dick's voice when he finally reached Tony that he was not immune to fear. Tony was moaning loudly and then yelling with pain.

"Stop your fucking complaining, Man," Dick commanded. "I know you're hurting, but shut up and help me get both of us out of here alive." By the time Dick hoisted him up to my level, Tony had mercifully passed out. I thought he might have died, but his labored breathing said otherwise. Another couple of tricky maneuvers and we made it out.

By the time we got back into the sunlight above, my smart wife had enlisted Frank's help to get a single mattress into the back of our pick-up. This would serve as Tony's ambulance to Carson City.

*   *   *

A number of weeks later, an entourage of motorcycles surrounding a single automobile showed up in my yard and I was called outside.

There, wearing a full body cast, was Tony. He was finally on his way home to Oakland but insisted on this detour.

"I'm really sorry, Ray," he said, looking pathetic in his reclining car seat. "Thanks for pulling me out. I should have listened to you in the first place. I just wanted to come back and tell you that." I leaned into the car and placed my hand over one of his.

"Just get well, Tony," was all I could say. I appreciated that no one was stupid enough to ask about looking down the shaft, which Dick and I had covered more securely. As I watched the noisy parade descending down the hill in a cloud of dust, I was thankful that Tony was alive and that local news of this incident had stayed within my little community. I had expressed my wish to all concerned they steer clear of any newspaper or police reports and they obviously had. It just didn't seem necessary to have any more people snooping around the Dayton Consolidated.

I am forever grateful to my friend, Dick, and in my gratitude spent a lot of time on a cabinet I made for him.

SUICIDE IN SAUSALITO

There are those mornings in life when one wakes up and wonders, "How the hell did I get here?" It was the early 1970s. I awoke to the gentle rocking motion of my recently acquired houseboat, a converted World War II LCVP (Landing Craft Vehicle Personal) and wondered for the umpteenth time why it hadn't been more correctly named a Landing Craft Personal Vehicle, or LCPV. But such is the categorical military mind-set, I guess. Then I had to wonder why my thoughts kept returning to dwell on such useless trivia.

As the throbbing in my head became more synchronized with the rocking motion of the boat, I summoned the courage to sit up and immediately regretted it. I fell back onto the luxury of my warm double mattress and groggily surveyed my new home; the narrow horizontal cabin windows that looked out on dock pilings and a variety of other craft; the neat little galley with booth-like table and padded benches; the full-length mirror on my narrow closet door; the built-in head and shower. And, beyond the aft cabin hatch and a step up, the partially enclosed cockpit and after-deck, a comfortable place to spend an afternoon.

The guy I bought the boat from had done a really good job on the interior; however, when I'd had a marine survey, which I should have done before the purchase, the surveyor just shook his head and didn't even charge me for his time. There were such obvious signs of dry rot. Oh well.

Finally, I got up the nerve to get up and get dressed. I choked down some instant coffee and slowly climbed up to the dock. My boat was moored to a long, wide boardwalk on tall pilings, a finger of dock that stuck out into the bay from Gate 3, Sausalito. There were a variety of other vessels that made up my dockside neighborhood, most of them occupied full time. I walked down the dock toward land and then up a narrow dirt alleyway. I paused at the edge of waterfront city, a hodgepodge of buildings and activities in what had once been Marinship, a vital wartime shipyard during the early 40s.

A little way through the maze to my left was The Studio, an elaborate state-of-the-art Warner Brothers financed recording studio where I had been employed for the past few months. A rather large severance check would be waiting there for me. To my right, a little way through the maze and across a wide field, was the brand-new supermarket up on Bridgeway where I could stock up on the long day's supply of liquid salvation. I turned toward the supermarket.

I had come down from Sonoma County to work on the recording studio, which was built into the refurbished shell of a huge old warehouse. My old friend Daniel and I were part of a hippie woodworking art movement that had impressed a young world of entrepreneurs who were competing to find out the exact location of society's "leading edge." We had worked together on the Au Relais, a new French restaurant in the town of Sonoma. I'd had a family and a woodworking shop at that time, where we made accessories for the restaurant.

Daniel played the part of long-haired hippie artist to the hilt. He was a handsome and intense young man with a gift for talking his way in over his head and then learning how to swim. He had scored the job of doing art carpentry in the recording studio and then asked me to join him. Daniel was loose and creative, and had a lot of good ideas, but he didn't have a great deal of experience. He and I had known each other through the same extended family and had shared some time at the family compound in Mexico, where I had lived when I studied with a local violin maker. Our combination of friendship, energy and experience had made us a good team.

Our schedule, while The Studio was being constructed during the daytime, was to work from eight in the evening till eight in the morning, when the regular union guys came in; kamikaze carpentry is a term I used. This meant we had the place all to ourselves all night long. So, the first piece of equipment we moved onto the job was a good stereo system. Rock music and good weed were to us essential tools. And, we did in fact create a pretty impressive body of work; the huge inlaid sunburst on one wall in Studio A, the inlaid and curved walls in the lobby, the psychedelic wooden murals in the restrooms, and even an inlaid floor in the office.

But there was a lot more to The Studio than the areas available for our woodworking. It was the most advanced recording studio of its time in the area, designed to attract the many musicians who lived in or liked to visit Northern California and had little love for the trip to record their music in LA.

After the old warehouse had been gutted and restored, there was space enough for many extras; a sauna and hot tub, a massage room, and a round "conference room" that was one huge water bed. The philosophy I heard expressed by the radical young partners who were in charge of building The Studio was "the more you spend, the more you make."

As I came back across the wide field from the super-market, equipped with a cold six-pack of Rainier Ale and a pint of Korbel brandy, I hesitated by the alley leading to my boat and thought about going over to pick up my check at The Studio before I got too far into the day's libation. Daniel had been gone for almost a month and I had stayed on as "house carpenter" to finish up a few details. But unfortunately, the work soon began to get in the way of my drinking. With the job pretty much finished and Daniel gone, my commitment to staying sober was slipping. The break-up with my family was a constant source of weirdly delicious, insurmountable pain.

I missed her and I hated her. I missed my children and struggled with the reality that my son had been sent to live with his mom in Chico, while she and my two little daughters had gone to live at their secret address in Santa Rosa. It was only the innovative problem solving of my art work at The Studio and Daniel's company that kept me distracted enough to breathe.

Standing at the crossroads between a sizeable check that meant nothing and the lure of a cold Rainier Ale made up my mind for me. I turned toward the dock. As I walked along, I allowed my mind to slip into a warm bucket of self-pity. Although each step became a jarring reminder of my wife's betrayal, it also brought me closer to the potential relief of self-medication. Soon I would feel better. I would find a greater presence and peace of mind, the full measure of my deserving good-guy victimhood. I was almost running toward my boat.

Ah, perfect, cold ale with a brandy back. Within a few minutes I could feel the warmth and security as my body-mind settled into its chemical castle. It didn't matter to me that my fortress was a hollow kingdom of illusion, a sparkling reign of power that would peak and endure for only a short time. Like any other addict, I was seriously dedicated to protecting my right to serve that illusion.

In due time, after attempting to write yet another unsent letter to my wife, searching for exactly the perfect words to match the poetry of my pain, I decided to walk on over to the recording studio. A cool breeze was blowing. I donned my new coat of Spanish leather and my sassy leather cap and climbed up to the dock. I felt regal and powerful now, kind of untouchable. And I never stopped to wonder why the only time I felt really good about myself was when I was drunk.

I entered the small patio by the office on the far side of the warehouse and stuffed a couple of strong mints in my mouth. I still had a key to the office door, but I rang the bell anyway. The buzzer went off and I let myself in. The sight of the inlaid floor, curvy built-in desks and artfully paneled walls gave me a rush of pride.

"Hi Nellie," I greeted the attractive young woman who was the only one in the office. She, along with a couple of other efficient business beauties, had been called up from LA after the studio had opened for business.

"Hi Ray," she replied. "I've got a check for you here and Gary said to let him know when you came in." Gary was one of the partners in charge of the studio. He and Chris, the other partner, were an amazing combination. Chris wore business suits, kept his hair short, and was the corporate front man. Gary was the long-haired recording engineer who wore a lot of loose silk and patent leather shoes with no socks. He was responsible for bringing a revolutionary 16 track recording console to Northern California.

"Come on in." Gary was seated against the padded backrest, his legs stretched out on the waterbed surface of the round conference room. I took off my shoes and bounced over to sit near him, nearly falling on my face.

Gary was a unique individual. His reputation as a sound engineer brought some of the biggest names in the business to The Studio, along with a few young apprentices who would sweep floors and clean toilets just to get into the control room with him during a session. He was a skinny, oddly handsome little guy whose silk costumes and delicate manner seemed quite effeminate, but his energy around the secretaries and female groupies was anything but gay.

"Remember," he began. "When Chris and I met with you and Daniel about the possibility of building another studio in Jamaica?"

"Yeah," I responded. "But I thought that was a no go."

"It was," he said. "But now its back on. And although we haven't been in touch with Daniel yet, I wanted to let you know, just in case."

I hesitated before asking:

"Just in case what?"

"You do something about your problem," he said. "Like I can smell it on your breath right now."

"Yeah yeah," I responded, with a gesture of dismissal. "But everybody..."

"No buts, Man," Gary interrupted, as he anticipated my objection. "It doesn't matter that I snort a little coke or smoke a joint now and then, that's business. And I don't get fucked up behind it. I show up for work; you don't."

I felt angry and ashamed all at once. I thought I had been pretty cool about my drinking. I glared at him and tried to think of something smart to say. But then I just bowed my head and remained silent.

"I'm sorry, Ray," Gary's tone became gentler. "I know you're going through a lot right now, with your family and all. But please, do something about your juice habit. Okay? Your work is impressive and, until lately, you showed up as a good worker. Take a break, get sober. Let me know where you're at, okay?

After Gary left I sat alone in the conference room for a while, saying goodbye to my memories of the place. Tears of remorse-anger-confusion welled up in me and I obviously had to get back to the safety of my boat. As I was leaving, Nellie stopped me.

"Here's your check, Ray," she smiled sweetly. "And, oh yeah, Chris asked me to get your key." I fumbled with my key ring and labored to remove the office key. We exchanged key for check, which I didn't bother to look at. Then I stumbled out the door and into the chilly bayside afternoon.

I climbed down the ladder onto my boat feeling like a fugitive. I didn't want to hear what Gary had to say, because I knew it was true. And, unfortunately, I really didn't believe there was anything I could do about it. To prove the point, I crawled into myself and drank until I passed out. Oblivion was preferable to the painful confusion of a semi-sober reality.

∗ ∗ ∗

Bang! Bang! Bang! The noise seemed to be coming from a great distance, but getting closer. In my dream my boat was somehow adrift in a great forest and tall trees were falling on it. But then, slowly, I realized someone was banging on the hatch. I had automatically shut the bolt when I came in.

"Hey man, I can see you in there. Wake up." It was George, who lived in an old converted tugboat further down the dock. George looked like a mixture of Erroll Flynn and Douglas Fairbanks Jr., and, aside from being another alcoholic, he was in fact a good actor, working both local amateur theater and some occasional, more professional work in the city. He had a six-pack in his hand.

"Jesus Christ, man," he grinned. "You look like hell. Here, have a brew." I took the can and stared out one of the boat's narrow portholes. It was nearing dusk. I was right on schedule. The day's drinking was done, the evening's drinking was commencing.

"I feel like hell," I said. My croaking voice sounded strange to my own ears. "In fact, I feel like killing myself. I've been thinking about it a lot lately." The statement surprised me. I knew that was how I felt, but I hadn't yet articulated it, even to myself. I hadn't known until that very moment how serious I was about it. "I give up," I continued. "I don't want to go through this goddam struggle anymore." I was angry, but also on the verge of tears.

"Far out," George was still grinning. "You got any good shit around here I could use."

"Goddam it," I snapped. "I'm serious."

"Goddam it," he grinned. "I am too. Can I have yer leather jacket there Matey? How 'bout this boat? Ya gotta will made out yet? How ya gonna do it? Ya gotta gun? Ya gonna stab yerself? Or maybe ya could hang yerself from the dock. I can see the headline now: "Dejected Dummy Danglin' Dockside."

George's departure from his usually impeccable diction meant he was playing a role. His grin had become somehow juvenile and a bit idiotic. As I stared at him and reached for another beer, I couldn't help laughing. Then we were both laughing. The evening's drinking was getting off to a good start.

TRIO

They came together for a one-night stand, Tuesday night at a new waterfront club in Sausalito. The place wasn't quite finished. Some of the interior construction was still in process. But the owners wanted a trial run on the small bandstand and a test of their new sound equipment.

The place was quietly open to some of us locals, but the grand opening had not yet happened. The three musicians who showed up had been hastily put together by phone. They were all union members, but had never played together. I knew one of them, the drummer, and had met the bass player once before. In fact, I was there with a few of his friends. We were sitting at a table by the bandstand when the three of them arrived, a few minutes apart, casually introducing themselves to one another.

The pianist had come from the city, San Francisco; the bass player was local; and the drummer, who was also a graphic artist, had recently moved down from Reno. I had visited his studio and had seen his unique art work - amazing pieces that he created by manipulating chemical reactions on sheet metal. He made it look so easy, but when others tried (including myself) they could only make a mess. I was curious to see if he was as creative a drummer as he was a visual artist.

The bass player, a short heavyset guy originally from New York, was something of an enigma. He looked like a portly businessman, with short hair and usually dressed in tailored conservative suits. He had a large and beautiful houseboat, near Gate 3 in the old Marin Shipyard, but was often away for periods of time. A friend told me this bass player could have his pick of gigs, from New York to Chicago and LA. He was really that good. But he also made an effort to avoid becoming too well connected, or too well known. That didn't make sense to me until I eventually got to know him a little better. His anonymity and flexible schedule gave him the freedom for his chosen life style. He was a highly regarded musical guru, preferred to teach in his own studio, and had students who came from all over.

The pianist was a woman neither of the other two had met before. Her appearance was careless and messy, but her dark beauty could not be concealed. The unkempt curly black hair and loose-fitting clothes could have been a conscious attempt to distract from her sensuous good looks, but actually served to make her even more attractive.

She played a couple of clubs around the city, but was also a single mom and selfish with her time for her little boy. She worked as little as possible. And, since that Tuesday was a convenient off night, she got a baby sitter and took the drive over to Sausalito. The drummer and bass player openly stared at her, but then were cool enough not to stare for too long.

With a minimum of small talk, the trio soon started playing. And from the very first moments, it was apparent that something special was going on. As they gently explored the range of their shared vocabulary, the subtle probing of their musical intelligence was like a rising tide. Casual conversation quickly died out as the audience leaned forward to listen. Their music opened a vibrant subconscious field around us that was charged with possibility.

As the trio warmed up, the sound of their instruments took on an added dimension, flowing and blending in such a way that sometimes you couldn't tell one instrument from another. The drummer, who was even better than I had imagined, didn't just keep the beat, the tonal blending he produced on a small set of finely tuned chromatic tympani was so tight he could articulate melody or harmony. Without missing a lick, the bass and piano accommodated his unusual ability, discovering exciting new relationships as they adapted to his lead.

The twenty or so of us in the scattered audience were spellbound, drawn into the trio's excitement. Together they had found something they could only have dreamed about as individuals. And the powerful intimacy between them, the depth of their communication, made us all feel like an integral part of their musical union. We were suspended, breathless, holding the mystery of their extemporaneous flight, so turned on we could even savor the silence between the notes.

At the end of their first set, the three musicians just stared at one another, grinning and making sounds of appreciation. I noticed a few people heading for the pay phones by the rest rooms, undoubtedly to let others know of the "happening" that was going on then and there.

The break was short and it wasn't long before the trio was playing again, and this time the pianist started singing. "Are the stars out tonight, I don't know if its cloudy or bright, cause I only have eyes for you." A gently intoxicating wave of infatuation swept over everybody. When the drummer and bass player spontaneously added their vocalizing, the trio's close and unique harmony transformed an old standard into something all their own.

After about an hour and a half of peak expression, they ended up exhausted. The bass player rubbed his chubby hands together in a way that said they had become a little sore; the pianist's dark curls were clinging wet to her forehead, framing and highlighting the intelligent depths of her hazel eyes; the drummer sat perfectly still, eyes closed, in a transcendental state of mind.

It's difficult to say exactly what it was we witnessed that night. The energy that drove the trio was somehow itself alive, independent of them, an archetypal force that demanded their total involvement, as though their combination on that night was ordained, inevitable. Each musician would have told you that each of them played incredibly well only because of the other two.

We all knew that a group this good had to be shared with the world. Excited whispers planned for their promotion. Just wait until the right people heard them. A recording session would be automatic. They would become famous.

But then, in the midst of all that excitement, a dawning wave of realization began to spread throughout the room, sharpening our sense of appreciation. I'm not exactly sure at what point I began to understand the fragile and fleeting nature of the gift we received that evening. Others around me gradually showed signs of the same understanding.

With an odd mixture of joy and resignation, we realized that this music would never be repeated, or recorded, except in the memory of those of us who were fortunate enough to be there that night. To my knowledge the trio never appeared together in this world again.

ASHES TO ASHES

My son arrived from Chico that evening to stay at his grandma's house in Petaluma. My mother had the spare bedroom and all the trimmings to welcome a tired and hungry nineteen-year-old. I was living in a one-bedroom apartment in Rohnert Park at the time and planned to see him the following morning. After a brief exchange with him over the phone, I finished off the brandy I had at home and so enjoyed about a half-pint cushion as I drove around to Cotati. Sociophobic alcoholics, as I was then, usually need to get a slight buzz on before facing the terrifying world of other people.

After all these years, it interests me to think about what it was I was looking for in that crazy, dangerous world of public drunkenness. I have since accepted that addiction is simply a fantasy way of being what you want to be - braver, smarter, more competent, more likeable, more acceptable, taller, thinner, unblemished, uncrippled. It's like a bridge to other people - a way of breaking out of unendurable isolation. Strange how hard I ran away from myself while desperately trying to find myself.

As I slip into the well-worn saddle of the bar stool, I savor the gentle calm of anticipation that settles over me; I feel reassured. I am a midnight rider of long experience. Like a junkie in preparation, I can feel the effects of the gin and tonic even before I order it.

At just the right degree of euphoric heat-on, anything seems possible from a bar stool - any journey to anywhere the heart desires. My thirsty spirit dips through a kaleidoscope of alcohol bright colors, painting me an effortless empire - a warm cozy place where all my questions are finally resolved and there's nothing left to worry about. The whole wide world becomes as one bright little jewel that I can delicately hold between my fingers. With elegant, deliberate ease, I turn it over and study each facet, dazzling my absentee brain with illusive flashes of profound wisdom. I have the power of rampant imagination, a painless path to perfection. I am a natural man, an omnipotent man, rubbing elbows with God.

And then, I hear God. He is standing next to the juke box. He is wearing worn boots, levy's, a plaid shirt and a straw cowboy hat. He is short and stocky, with swarthy Native American features. What I hear is the complex rhythm he makes, rubbing his rough hands together, lightly slapping his thighs, clicking his lounge and making rhythmic guttural sounds from deep in his throat. His rhythm dances in subtle, elegant circles around the standard tune coming out of the juke box. A Redneck down the bar regards him with disdain. Others ignore him. I am fascinated by his musical mastery.

There's a pool cue leaning against the wall next to him. I glance at the bright spot of one quarter waiting on the rail of the pool table, a sign of the next player in line. Two serious young men are pushing their way toward an end game. I slip off my stool and approach the pool table, a little brighter and more confident than when I walked in. I slap my quarter on the rail next to god's quarter and glance in his direction. He nods slightly, not missing a beat, and I return to my stool to watch him play the upcoming winner.

He plays an interesting game. He's good, but occasionally blows an easy shot. Then I sense his strategy. He plays a game within a game, allowing his opponent to sink shots and gain position, but then he more than catches up, making difficult double bank shots with ease. He plays to the edge of losing, and then, however difficult, sinks the eight ball to win. Then it's my turn.

"What's yer name," I ask.

"Meda," he replies.

"Your name is Da?"

"No, Asshole, Meda, one word." He says this with a broad smile and extended hand, which is as calloused and strong as I expected.

My pool game is an unpredictable sojourn into psyche land. Because I do not see with any great acuity, I depend on instinct and some mystical form of cosmic radar. The more I drink and act with a certain confidence and abandon, the better I seem to play. I haven't the sense to recognize any limits; so, sometimes I make shots that others wouldn't even try.

"You fucker," Meda exclaims. "How'd ya do that."

"I haven't the slightest idea," I reply with a grin. But the truth is, I'm in the zone. I'm in that magical place where vividly envisioning the crazy shots I try will somehow make them happen. I'm out of my mind; which is, in fact, the absolute prerequisite.

Meda and I take turns holding the table against all comers. As the night passes, I have occasional flashes of my need to get home, but this magic is too good to pass up. Finally, its closing time. I can't believe it. By this time Meda and I have achieved a sloppy, alcoholic state of barroom brotherhood.

"Hey Rabe," Meda says. "I got at least a case o' beer at home. Come on over."

It is my great misfortune that I have no resistance. I allow the moment to rule. Besides, it I go to bed now, I won't get enough sleep anyway. I follow Meda's battered old pick-up truck down 116, turn right on another paved road, then left onto a long dirt road, then off that onto a long dirt driveway to a small two room house.

My memories of that fateful night at Meda's place are a collection of vivid images. I remember going out into the starlit night to stumble around in his vegetable garden, to reach over a high rail fence and pet a horse he has whistled into existence. It's dark. I can barely see the animal. Suddenly Meda leaps over the fence and onto the animal's back. He rides off with whoops of laughter.

Later, as we sit drinking beer and talking, I notice an interesting little painting on the wall, an arrangement of garden vegetables suggesting a cockeyed wolf face and extended paw.

"That's really neat," I exclaim. "Did you paint it."

"Yeah," he replies. "You really like it?"

"Un huh."

"It's yours."

I am surprised by this sudden gift, but then I remember, this is the Native American way. The drunken white brother admires something in his house and Meda has no choice but to offer it as a gift. I'm reminded of a story about two professor types, on a Reservation, with clipboards and pencils, who ask an elder woman to give them some idea of a Native American ceremony.

"Sure," she responds. "First, you get a whole lot of food. Then you invite everyone you know and they all eat as much as they want. And they can stay as long as they want. Then, you invite them to spend the night and provide places to sleep. In the morning you all get up and eat some more, spend time together, talk and tell stories. Then, eventually, everyone goes home." The two professors are haughtily convinced the old woman is putting them on; but she isn't.

At one point during the night, I speak of my nineteen-year-old son who is visiting me from Chico. I am too drunk to realize just how badly I am screwing up his visit by staying awake all night. While I brag about my golden-haired boy, I notice the silent tears streaming down Meda's rough cheeks. I stop speaking and remain silent.

"Tony," Meda says in a harsh whisper. "My son, Tony. He got killed last year."

I feel a rush of emotion. And the tears, made all the easier in my drunken, vulnerable state of mind, begin to flood my vision. My new friend, Meda, has lived my worst nightmare.

"Goddam stubborn kid, I warned him," Meda smacks his fist into an open palm. I can feel the anguish of this awful experience alive in him all over again. "Had to hang out with those goddam idiot bikers."

The story comes out in fragments. Tony, a tough and belligerent young motorcycle warrior, had apparently been murdered at a Hell's Angels type gathering the previous year. And his death still remained an unsolved crime.

I am silent as Meda goes through his painful recollections. I feel a twinge of something akin to guilt as I think of my own son, safely asleep at Grandma's house. We finish off the case of beer a little after dawn and Meda suggests we go shoot some more pool. I am amazed at his energy. Once again, I follow his pick-up, but this time out of our rural environment. We eventually wind up at the Eightball bar in Cotati.

It is early Sunday morning and the place is packed. I have not experienced this before. My drinking is done at home or out at night. The doorway to this bar is like a time portal. Outside it is morning; inside it is late at night. The contrast is startling.

All three pool tables are occupied. Meda walks over to put a quarter down. Where does he get the energy? He looks ready for anything. I am drunk, and exhausted. My dizzy brain leads me to a phone booth outside to call my son.

"Hi Ravi," I try to cover my guilt and exhaustion with comradery, but I know I sound like a croaking frog. "I'm kinda fucked up, Son. Could you come over to Cotati, the Eightball, you can't miss it. I'll be outside." Once I sit down on the curb, I realize how hard it will be to get up. And that's where I am when Ravi shows up. He parks just behind my little Datsun and gets out.

"Gimme a hand, Rav. There's someone I want you to meet." Without hesitation I stagger into the Eightball with my son trailing behind. I get Meda's attention and introduce him to Ravi. The bartender has a sharp eye for my son's youthful appearance and yells at me.

"Hey you, get that kid outa here." He starts down the length of the bar toward where he can come out from behind it. I take a belligerent stance. Ravi pulls on my arm.

"C'mon Pop, let's go." I pretend to reluctantly comply with an eye of bravado toward the bartender. As we head toward my apartment in Ravi's car, I tell him all about Meda, as though my story justifies my drunken, exhausted condition. When we get to the door of my apartment, it turns out I have lost my door key, and this is not the first time.

"I'm sorry, Ravi," I groan. "Would you go over to the manager's office." I see the pain and disappointment on my son's face. I sit on the cement steps and wait. As the manager opens the door, he looks down to where I sit and lets me know where I stand.

"I'm really tired of this shit, MISTER," he says, and walks away. I struggle to my feet and start to go after him.

"Son-of-a-bitch can't talk to me like that," I exclaim. But Ravi stands in my way. He firmly takes my arm and leads me back to my door. I am almost asleep on my feet.

Ravi sees me collapse on my bed, throws a blanket over me and silently leaves. By the time I wake up that evening and call my mother's place, my son has already headed back to Chico. The pain of that day sticks to my heart like napalm.

* * *

A few months later, August 7th, 1981, a week before my son's 20th birthday. I sit in that same apartment and experience a crossroads I will never forget. I had gone to the Deli for my usual Sunday morning libation of Schlitz Stout Malt Liquor; but, regardless of my severe thirst, I cannot get one of those tall, frosty cans to open.

Every time I reach for it, my mind becomes flooded with vivid images of my wasted reality. Once again, I see the pain and disappointment on my son's face. I see the confused uncertainty of my two little daughters when their occasional visits with me are riddled by my unpredictable behavior. I am, in fact, losing my children.

For over three agonizing hours, I sit at my kitchen table and stretch my hand out to that beer can, only to become, repeatedly, paralyzed with grief. The decision that is growing inside my soul is a slow process, it only dawns on me gradually. But then, the sheer terror of not knowing if I can live without alcohol leaves me breathless. Finally, I have to accept the awful truth. I am not afraid to die, I have proven that. But I am afraid to live.

It is a hot summer day. My aching head is reeling with a confused spiral of both hope and despair. I take the unopened six-pack downstairs and throw it into the dumpster. I am terrified. How I will live now, without my beer, is a frightening mystery, but more terrifying is the slow, ugly death I have been living. I have not had a drink of alcohol since that day.

CIRCLE CORNERED

I didn't record the exact date, but it was late in the year 1990. I turned the key to lock my shop, a converted barn several miles west of Petaluma, and flipped off the main electrical switch in a junction box by the front door. This day had been coming for a while. My success at arts and crafts shows had sustained my work more than enough to make it to the next show, but the bottom line seldom showed a lot of profit. After time and material, show fees, food and motels, from Seattle to Los Angeles, I was not making much of a living. Aside from all that, my relationship with my live-in driver, Ann, was going through changes. And, without her help I would be stranded.

My youngest daughter, Ruby, who had lived with me since she was thirteen, had done the driving for the past couple of years, until she turned eighteen. And then, she had to move on. Our parting was painful, but necessary. She'd accepted a job and living arrangement in San Francisco and I encouraged her to do what was best for her. After that, I depended on a network of family and friends. Until, eventually, the idea of having a live-in helper took hold and I was currently providing for a woman who had taken on the job a few months before.

How long had it been? Six years in this location? Six years of hard labor, of building up my shop, acquiring every tool and piece of equipment I needed to do anything I wanted with a piece of wood. At least I had managed to make that part of my dream come true, and I was grateful. I could wake up in the morning with a design in mind; and, starting with bare boards, have a rendering of that design by day's end. Since I had been at it for a long time, I had made every conceivable mistake more than once. I was able to accurately envision and execute every step of the process in my mind.

But, as a visually impaired, isolated woodworker in rural California, stubbornly holding my labor-intensive principles, and labor-intensive designs, I had not achieved the financial stability for which I had hoped. I was anachronism, a throw-back, a man who longed to see the artful, handmade world that had existed before the Industrial Revolution.

Over the years I'd had a variety of work places; the crude indoor-outdoor shop in Mexico, the rough out-building in New Mexico, the old mining complex in Nevada, the shop on highway 12 near Sonoma, the garage near downtown Santa Rosa, the old barn south of Santa Rosa. Each of these could be identified with the kind of work I had done there.

In the early days, in Mexico, I had learned to build stringed instruments, but later, with a family to support, I had turned to any work I could find. In Taos I had worked with a partner to provide a variety of furnishings for a couple of ski lodges; plus, creative projects for a few wealthy clients. In Nevada I had built cradles, a hand carved, old world floor model I designed that went over well with antique dealers. Periodically I would bring a truckload of cradles to California and not return home to Nevada until all of them were sold, or consigned.

In California, I started building one of a kind furniture pieces, designed and manufactured Bonsai Planters for a while, and wound up buying old pieces to restore and resell. Unfortunately, for a period of time, my work was second place to a difficult married relationship which ultimately ended in divorce. After the break-up with my family, and a period of helping to build a recording studio in Sausalito, I worked with a group of hippie carpenters under the banner of All Heart Construction and committed some pretty good art work.

Now, standing outside my current shop, near Petaluma, I looked back down those years with a mixture of regret and gratitude. I was sorry I'd ever heard the saying that all one had to do to succeed was to work hard. At some point I realized it was more a matter of "all one had to do was work smart." Regardless, of greatest importance to me was that I had experienced one of the most ancient compliments to one's spiritual life - the revealing journey of craftsmanship.

It doesn't matter what the medium, the process of three-dimensional creation will, if you're lucky, bring you face to face with the mystery of yourself. Depending upon the depth of your involvement and your willingness to cooperate with and learn from the material, to approach the work in a thoughtful, sequential way; you will find that the more you give over to the creative process, the more you will develop a sense of spiritual collaboration, that you are not alone.

I've written about this before, because it was for me an astonishing discovery. In the midst of my work, when I had given myself over to the project, when the selfless experience of becoming the work itself was all I knew, then things would happen through my hands, through my attention, that were given from somewhere beyond my will. I can understand how artisans in ancient civilizations might experience their work as a form of worship. Throughout the centuries, until the time of the Renaissance, the idea of an individual claim to art work was, I believe, rare.

*   *   *

Several years before this fateful day, in 1984, I had turned another key in a final transition. The guardian angel that had seen me through 35 years of illegal driving had given notice. So far, as a driver, I had not hurt myself or anyone else, and my guardian angel wanted me to keep it that way. So, as difficult a life change as it was, I chose to quit driving while I was still ahead. After that, in order to keep working, I'd had to hire drivers.

Now, as a result of placing an ad in the local newspaper, I shared my narrow, rented two-bedroom trailer with a live-in driver who seemed to be happy with room and board and a percentage of proceeds. Unfortunately, she also considered our relationship as going somewhere much more involved than I was prepared to accept. Life had become a bit more complicated than I wanted to maintain.

As I turned away from my shop door, I could feel a familiar knot in my stomach and a buildup of moisture behind my eyes. I thought back to all my shops, to all my work places since Mexico. Here I was again, turning a transitional key, but this time I was ending my long, long love affair with woodworking for good. The loss of that relationship was like losing a limb.

It didn't seem possible. Something that had become so much a part of me, so second nature, would no longer be in my experience. I was proud of what I had done, of all my designs; my children's furniture, my inlaid coffee tables, my various one-of-a-kind projects.

Everything I did was unique, and long lasting, but also uniquely time consuming. I knew how to jig up and replicate items, but manufacturing required a capital investment I couldn't find. As I've written about elsewhere, funding for a small disability business was not made directly available to the disabled, it could only be administered through complex bureaucracy. Unfortunately, regardless of my viability, I had found no program (especially in the Reagan era) that could help my business. So, I sold myself as a struggling artist, devoted to the principles of old-world craftsmanship.

As I stood there lamenting, keys still in hand, my greatest regret was that I would not be able to pursue the dream projects I had put off into the "someday" category, but one of which I had already started on the side.

The possibilities of my musical therapy chair, for which I had begun to work out the problems of laminating a frame, still fascinate me. Imagine a free-formed, hollow bodied chair suspended between two arm rest harps mounted on rockers. Imagine pendulum stroked strings with autoharp chord change buttons at the ends of the arm rests. Or, you could rock and strum the strings yourself. Imagine the feeling of resonance, of sitting between two harps filling the hollow sound chamber beneath and behind your body.

Another important dream project was what I called the "Wind Ax," a construction that will always live in my mind, if nowhere else. Imagine a collection of pipes, reeds and strings built into a twelve-foot-high sculpture-like framework which is activated by the wind. The whole construction is mounted on a ball bearing dais with a directional wind vane at the top and placed in a windy public site on the Pacific Coast. Can you imagine a huge singing sculpture placed where busloads of school children can come to listen and learn about the phenomena of sound?

Lost in thought, still holding the key to my shop, not wanting to go to the trailer right away, my mind went to the plans I would now pursue. Letting go of my shop was not only about stubborn principles and money, plus an entangling, unfair relationship I couldn't honor; it was also about another dream I'd set aside some years before. I had tried to enter a regular college program more than once, only to have my eyesight provide enough challenge to stop me. Now, I was determined to go back to school, full time. My last show had been exceptionally lucrative; so, I had given myself the gift of a large screen TV and a Commodore 64 keyboard, plus a clumsy old used printer. This electronic set up allowed me to write in a way and with greater ease than ever before. I also learned that my old enemy, the card catalog, was gradually disappearing from college libraries and being replaced by computer access. Now, at age fifty-five, with a computer and large monitor, the lifelong dream of higher education was within sight.

Did You Get to Become
Who You Wanted to Be?

There was a time when what I valued most about myself, and others, was that vague and illusive quality known as "authenticity." I had more a sense of congruity then, a sense of being in harmony with myself. But lately, my experience has been off key, out of tune. I am troubled by the dissonance in my daily life. To be truly honest about who I am right now requires an examination of my motivations, and a willingness to be open to the possibility of some painful learning. Why am I living this life which only I have created and then find myself complaining about?

I once wrote a poem with the title - "My Childhood Was Limited by The Desire to Grow Up." I think of that title now because, as a visually impaired individual since birth, I have always been limited by the desire to be accepted as "normal." Although I managed to get through public high school, class of '53, further attempts at formal education were drastically curtailed by the lack of any facility for the visually impaired in the education system at that time.

I'm asking that you to look at this reality with me, not in sympathy for the poor near-sighted kid; but, with some understanding for the feelings of any minority. What I've tried to overcome, as a member of the disability community, has much in common with the feelings of any other minority; gender, race, sexual orientation, economics, or whatever. Only later did I understand that in my desire to belong, I was at risk of allowing the unrealistic standards of a market driven society (radical hedonism) to determine my sense of self-worth. I was tragically at risk of believing that individual value can actually be measured against the supposed greater value of an idealized mainstream model.

Since childhood I have lived with an intense need to become someone; not necessarily an important someone, not a superstar, but an acceptable and normal someone who belongs. My vision of this someone, through adolescence and young adulthood, was the man in a suit carrying a briefcase. He belonged. He had important work to do. He was who I wanted to be.

From the time I finished high school until I approached college with the intention of earning a degree, there was a lapse of thirty-eight years. I spent a portion of those years as an underdog alcoholic and as a struggling woodworker, barely able to survive; however, I did manage to achieve sobriety and didn't hesitate when the opportunity for higher education came into view.

My re-entry was made possible through the discovery of computer technology as a visual aid and a federal disability grant. Although there were many advantages to being an older student, I sometimes felt like an anachronism. There were assumptions built into the education system that reflected this. On the surface, things like dealing with forms that had spaces for parental signatures; on a deeper level, dealing with academic courses, teaching habits and attitudes, that were developed for college students who were decades younger. However, my age and experience did allow me to develop casual relationships with instructors, which was definitely an advantage.

By the time I achieved my B.A. I was fifty-eight years old. I earned an MA at sixty and was done with coarse work and most of my internships for a Ph.D. in Clinical Psychology at sixty-two, an age at which many professionals would be getting ready to retire; but so what? Many people achieve graduate degrees late in life and go on to successful careers. My problem was (and this gets tricky to explain)

I had also reached an age of dawning elder awareness. A by-product of my graduate education was that my innate, "natural" self had been undergoing an accelerated developmental process at the same time.

I cannot speak for anyone else, but my survival over the past several decades has been a gradually expanding journey, from black-white naiveté to moral complexity. Along with the academic subjects required for my university and graduate degrees came a growing awareness of humankind's failure to avoid corruption and violence. As an elder anachronism with a newly remodeled mind, I was distracted by the flaws that riddled our imperfect world, particularly in the field I had chosen to pursue.

So what? Be realistic. Many professionals have learned to overlook the small nagging voices of ethical consideration; or, they just don't have ears to hear. In the field of psychotherapy, a career for which I felt experientially qualified, my education and training had been ponderously influenced by the legal, pharmaceutical and insurance industries. I understand the need to be aware of a professional connection to these industries, the protection connection involved with making a living within the "system;" but, it seemed to me the categorical bible of psychotherapy, the Diagnostic and Statistical Manual of Mental Disorders, was developed much more for the needs of these peripheral industries than for the actual practice of psychotherapy.

Although we practice within the complicated context of our current society, it is often the ills of that society and not those of the client that underlie serious problems. I have, in fact, made this statement more than once: "You are not the problem. You are simply having a sane reaction to an insane world." It is the therapist who must reconcile the sacred healing art of facilitating emotional change with compliant consideration for the needs of legal, medical and insurance regulation.

As an older person, I'd had the distinct advantage of life experience and an intuitive understanding for many of the "pathologies" I encountered. I had over two thousand hours of supervised practice and a span of time at grief counseling with Hospice. Unfortunately, through all this experience, the mobility restrictions due to my not driving had become more and more a problem, greatly limiting my range of activity.

Then, to make matters more difficult, a family emergency concerning my precious daughter, Rachel, required me to ask for a leave of absence from my graduate school. To my surprise I was told that if I did so, there was no guarantee I would be reinstated when I re-applied. The school was in paranoid turmoil about its standing with WASC accreditation and pushing hard to graduate more students. Nonetheless, their rude and unfair treatment in my case was hard to take.

I had been a faithful member of the founding class for that school, supportive and patient with its growing pains. My hurt feelings caused me to join with a group of students, in the next class behind mine, in a legal complaint with the appropriate board in Sacramento. By the time I regretted that impulsive move, it was too late.

I finally realized that my exhaustion was far more than a matter of physical energy, I had come to an impasse with my own nature. I wished I was younger, not for the obvious reasons, but for the sake of a certain willingness to believe. The flip-flopping changes I had endured due to the school's dissertation process were truly ridiculous.

Tears came to my eyes as I struggled again to discern the difference between excuse and explanation. It was indeed a gut-wrenching experience to abandon the idea of completing my PhD. The knowledge and experience I had gained had been costly, financially and in terms of time, but the destination I'd arrived at was only another crossroads.

The visually impaired child still wanted to be accepted as "normal," and the elder he became was still seeking to satisfy the child's need. Nevertheless, the combination of exhaustion with the school's constant changes and the legal hassle (which didn't turn out in my favor) were a sufficient enough setback to derail my plans.

Fortunately, the education and training I'd received did contribute to a journey into the mysterious territory of the great un-planned. At some point in my complex education, I had begun to understand psychotherapy as a sacred trust, as a contract to help others get in touch with the divine within themselves, to understand that our best answers are often found in the way we ask our questions. It seemed to me this spiritual element didn't fit very well with the usual financial reality of client-therapist relationships. My work as a grief counseling volunteer at Hospice has been deeply rewarding; and, the Universe occasionally sends me the blessing of a naturally occurring pro-bono client, someone in need whom I can actually help.

According to long ago Cicero: "For mortal to aid mortal - this is God, and this is the road to eternal glory." This goes along with the saying that "being of service is the rent we pay for being alive." However, such lofty pursuit does not pay the rent, nor does it buy groceries. So, I have had to remain under the umbrella of my disability label, receiving the blessings of subsidized poverty along with minimal Social Security.

Let me be clear that I am grateful for my survival; and, for the amazing opportunity of a fairly sophisticated education. Over the years I have had the freedom to attempt to repay the federal disability grant that helped to finance my education by doing the community work I would have been called to do anyway; and, I was better equipped than I would have been otherwise.

The following two paragraphs are from my letter of retirement from the ten years (2010 -2020) I served as an Advisory Council member for my local Area Agency on Aging. The parentheticals are added to better explain the programs.

"Looking back over this past decade, I am indeed grateful for the opportunity I was given to create a driving to non-driving transition program for older adults and their families. I believe that "Driving Safely as We Age" was a life-saving enterprise while it lasted. I am also grateful for the opportunity I had to work with Jane Eckels on the early stages of "My Care My Plan" (promoting and assisting older adults with Advance Health Care Directives), and also to join with Diane

Kaljian in the early days of "Aging Together" (a committee including two members of the Board of Supervisors to work on elder issues) when I was blessed to give a major PowerPoint presentation on the "History of Aging" at SSU. Another great opportunity for meaningful involvement came through working with Marrianne McBride and Mona Khanna for "The Collaborative on Positive Aging (COPA)," a year-long Longevity Revolution program of significant presentations for older adults.

"I will continue my current grief counseling practice at Memorial Hospice, where the blessings of compassion and learning through grief cradle the broken heart, and the generosity of healing grace spreads to all concerned. I will also continue to explore the profound mysteries of conscious aging, complete a legacy book of poems and short stories, while at the same time doing whatever I can to ease the suffering of older adults who are afflicted with Internalized Ageism."

*   *   *

I walked away from my potential career as a psychotherapist with great uncertainty; but, by the grace of this mysterious Universe, I was still able to achieve a good deal of work that was important to me. I have one regret - my attempt to bring effective attention to the Hidden Epidemic of alcohol and prescription drug misuse among older citizens. The failure of interest in funding for that particular project still rankles me, but the post-post graduate education of those ten years volunteering for a government agency have granted me an invisible and invaluable post-post PhD Degree.

INTERGENERATIONAL CALLING

After trying for some time for an intergenerational event here in Santa Rosa, my efforts were finally rewarded. With former mayor Jane Bender's help, I arranged with the director of the Teen Council, Ellen Bailey, to invite a group of elders to a meeting with twenty teen members on the Council, for an intergenerational conversation. The event took place from 7 to 8:30 pm, on Monday, April 23, 2007, at City Hall.

There were 20 older adults, average age 80, and 20 High School Seniors, average age 17. When they had settled into random pairs for a personal introduction, the energy in the room was charged with excitement. A 'natural' magic emerged when these two generations came together. It was a blessing to behold. The entire evening was an intergenerational success. I later learned of a few continuing relationships, one especially based on regular tennis matches.

I'm not aware of how those tennis sessions turned out, but I do know there was a time when the knowledge and skill- sets of grandparents were of practical value to their children and grandchildren, and passed on within meaningful, working relationships. Although personal family relationships are still based on traditional roles and assumptions, the tools and toys of accelerated technology profoundly widened generation gaps. Due to rapidly changing technologies, each generation has had its coming of age in substantially different worlds.

Historically, elders were not only the repositories of wealth and wisdom, they were also responsible for the continuity of tradition and cultural values. Regardless of the enormous practical advantages we have gained since the Industrial Revolution, how does a species grounded in the authority of traditional generational relationships deal with the disintegration of that natural order? Like it or not, we are currently engaged in a rapidly moving, largely unconscious and mysterious process of evolving postmodern adjustments. How do we bring this process into greater consciousness, from the point of view of all our generations, so that we may explore and influence our future for the benefit of all who are concerned?

* * *

It would be a few years before I was appointed to the Area Agency on Aging Advisory Council, where I was able to become more effectively involved in a number of elder advocacy issues. My intergenerational ambition settled into the background of things I actually could accomplish, but then a time came for me to make a play for what I really wanted to accomplish.

The following is a proposal I submitted to a couple of Sonoma County Supervisors who applauded my ideas but had the same response I so often heard - it's a matter funding.

Proposal for an Intergenerational Advisory Council In Service to Sonoma County

"The generation gaps that have traditionally existed in our society have been grossly compounded by accelerated change. At no other time in our history have such rapid advances in world changing technologies moved through multiple generations in a single lifetime. Although we are keenly aware of how our daily lives have been changed, the ways in which we ourselves are being changed remain to be seen.

"There are currently six living generations in Sonoma County, with at least four of them in the workplace. The formative years of these generations were greatly influenced by very different technologies; from listening to the radio (Traditional Generation), to watching television (Boomer Generation), to using computers (Generation X), to being globally connected on mobile devices (Millennial Generation). Growing up with these progressively different technologies has contributed to substantially different world views from one generation to the next.

"Older adults often make the mistake of assuming the young know little because of their lack of experience. They are unaware of the youthful brilliance that sees the world "as it is," through a clear lens of possibility, unencumbered by the past. Youth often make the mistake of assuming that the past experiences of older adults are irrelevant because the elder's lack knowledge about current trends and technologies. They are unaware of the wisdom gained through years of problem solving, pattern recognition and painful learning. Imagine bringing the strengths of these generations together, as they discover the deeply meaningful reciprocity in learning from one another.

> "We are not what we know,
> but what we are willing to learn."

The quote above, from Mary Catherine Bateson, is the essential spirit of "Intergenerational Learning Community." A further statement of hers brings the point home:

> "We are convening a new reality when we invite the generations
> to sit down together and apply their collective intelligence to
> issues of common concern."

Such an Intergenerational Advisory Council as this will be of great value to our community. Participants will carry with them the seeds of a new egalitarian attitude between generations - a willingness to consider the needs of all ages when discussing community projects and policies and their implementation.

"This ideal can be achieved in an Inter-generational Learning Community, through the process of Dialogue; a creative inquiry that liberates participants by identifying and transcending the defensiveness often embedded in our opinions and assumptions about one another. The challenge will be to create an inter-generational understanding that transcends ego identity.

Such is the dream of this 21st century elder."

LEARNING COMMUNITY CAMP-OUT

I attempted college a couple of times back in the mid-fifties, first at the College of Marin, in Kentfield, and then at San Francisco State. But in both cases my college career ended with the fact that my "blind man's bluff," although appreciated as courageous, was not sufficient to overcome the problems raised by my lack of visual connectedness. The well-meaning faculty at San Rafael High School had passed me through without a lot of pressure, so I believe I might have developed a mistaken sense of confidence. All I remember is that I wanted to go to school.

Over the years I did manage an occasional return to some lightweight classes, exploring psychology, and various writing classes, but the core requirements for a B.A. still remained beyond my grasp. Then, in 1991, I discovered the miracle of computer technology as a visual aid and rejoiced. My dream of being able to complete college course work finally came true and a profound period of complex learning took me on into graduate school.

What all this information leads up to is that I entered the full-time college experience at a much later age than most. And, because of my age, the experience was made all the more meaningful. Additionally, during my second semester at Sonoma State, I discovered the Learning Community, an experimental, alternative mode of education launched by a few of the tenured faculty in the Psychology Department: Red Thomas, Bill McCreary, and Art Warmouth.

I will not attempt a lengthy explanation of Learning Community here, except to say that I became so dedicated to this alternative educational experience, I returned to SSU after graduating, as volunteer faculty, and facilitated with the Learning Community for a number of semesters.

*   *   *

The following page is from my journal about the experience of an off-campus weekend camping trip. Although some of the fun may sound silly and radical, and Learning Community was definitely not for everyone, the tools that were gained for responsible self-inquiry and self-motivation played a most important role as many of our students went on to achieve highly successful careers.

SSU Learning Community Camp-out at Frog Pond

It was near the end of August, 1994, I came home from the weekend with a lot of moonlit sky wrapped inside me. On the night before, a few of us had taken a midnight hike through the magical realm of full-moon terrain. We had climbed down into the shadow-dark trees of a small valley, moved through crackling tunnels of dry vegetation, dangling on the ends of our flashlight beams like puppets on the strings of our narrow senses. We were as children, trembling with delicious, scary anticipation as we taunted the great unknown behind the shadows.

Then, as we moved out into a clearing, we lifted the wings of our arms and called out to the veil of night, howling just for the thrill of howling, echoing like a long-lost friendship into the distant hills. We waded through the tall, undulating grass of rolling fields, flooded with silver moonlight. There were subtle currents of mysterious, foreign air all around us, gently stirring ancestral memories. We were kissed with eagles' breath. We dreamed with our eyes wide open.

Eventually, after experiencing a few slippery slopes, we came to the abrupt wound of a dirt road. This we followed, sometimes pausing to examine moonlit animal tracks in the soft earth, or to rest in the soothing joy of moonlit laughter. The dirt road eventually led us winding back up to the rim, near where we had started.

When we got back to Vista Point, two other Learning Community members joined us and one of them amused herself by shining a small flashlight up her nose. This caused her nose to glow. Without a word it was understood that every one of us would have to take a turn. Another small mag light was produced and inspired more explorations; shining the bright little beams through our noses, our cheeks, our earlobes, our fingers. Then we all took a turn with my large flashlight, which each of us put in our mouths. Our cheeks and eyes glowed red from the tinted plastic rim around the bulb. There was a lot of laughter. We shared a deep joy in making those glowing masks for one another. We were sharing our souls.

In our state related group memory, we reminisced about the "foot flower" of the semester before, when a number of us laid in a circle on our backs and raised our bare feet, heels touching close together, arching our toes back into a foot flower. We understood that the value of Community was in being Community, not just talking about it. We knew we felt good in Community because that's how our species was designed to function - to laugh in the moonlight and lie on our backs making foot flowers.

FRANK

They had all served prison terms, had been released on parole, had substance abuse problems, and had been mandated by the court to be in this treatment group. As I looked around the circle of six men, I realized that all my book learning, mock sessions and class time, had not adequately prepared me for this. My supervisor, an addiction specialist of many years, was supposed to be there with me for this first session, but he'd had a last-minute change of schedule and said he trusted me to go ahead. I appreciated the trust, but wasn't that sure I could handle such a crew.

I'd never served time in prison and didn't know what to expect from these men. I only knew about prison life from the movies, and most of that had been pretty brutal. As I looked around, I wondered what each of them had suffered, in terms of sexuality, in terms of self-respect and integrity. But I had to accept that I would probably never know, not really, and that bothered me a little. But then, as I settled into my first session plan, to get them talking about themselves and what they expected from this group (since they had to be there anyway), my first ninety-minute session went by pretty fast.

I had started charts on each of them, but didn't have a lot of information with which to begin. I could have learned a lot more by reading over their records, but I felt that my job was about the present, and how they would do in the future. For the time being, I intuitively preferred to keep a clean slate for my impressions.

I have been in and facilitated different groups and I still wonder about the way people choose to sit, again and again, in exactly the same seats. Is it about territory, familiar location, predictability, or simply just one less thing about which to make a decision? At any rate this group was no exception.

On my immediate right there was always Stanley, a fast-talking evasive little black man with an impressive gift for street rhetoric. Next was Dwayne, a belligerent young man who called everyone "Bra" (short for Brother) and seemed to border on mental retardation. After observing him for a time, however, I decided his mental deficit was an act, a means of trying to fool others and perhaps find some advantage in so doing.

Then there was Frank, whose broad shoulders and huge muscles made him about as wide as he was tall. There was a dark, impulsive quality about this man, a potential danger we all felt. One was instinctively careful around Frank. Next there was Sam, a quiet grey-haired man with sad eyes. He had seen it all and was tired of what he saw. Then there was Phil, a man of average looks and average build who went out of his way to agree with everyone. All Phil wanted was to get by in the easiest way possible.

Finally, there was Gordon, an incredibly intelligent, highly educated homosexual who didn't fit in with the rest of the group at all. At first, I expected some kind of trouble due to his presence in the group, but that was because I didn't know better. There was an understanding among these men that made me feel like an outsider and sometimes left me guessing. I was impressed by the acceptance and respect Gordon was shown by this macho group. They wisely responded to who he was, not what he was. Of course, his wide range of readily available knowledge and his non-judgmental attitude of calm assurance was definitely a plus.

I learned a lot about myself during the six months I worked with this group. Fortunately, it didn't take long for me to realize the scope and accuracy of their "bullshit detectors." So long as I was open and honest with them, and not afraid to identify the elephant in the room, I received the cooperation I needed to be effective. But if I started using academic jargon or expressed the slightest hint of unfair authority, I would lose them.

Our topics of conversation tended to be widely dispersed, but I usually managed to integrate the material with a focus on Anger Management or Relapse Prevention. That was my job. The miracle of group work is that groups "work." The trick is to get out of your own way, to do as little as possible and trust the process. Facilitators who have a problem with this approach, who are hooked on power and control, will usually stay too near the surface for any real work to get done.

My novice anticipation about problems I thought I might have with ex-cons soon evaporated. In fact, these guys were undoubtedly more available to the work of group process than most people. I got to know them all pretty well, gradually filling in their charts with the usual brief notes about their progress, or lack thereof.

Facilitating this group was only one aspect of my work at the agency. I also conducted intake assessments, classes in the residence treatment program, and one on one counseling in the outpatient department. Frank, whose nickname in the group was "The Hulk," showed up one day after a group session and filled my office doorway with his wide torso.

"They told me maybe I could get some one-on-one time with you," he quietly growled.

"Yeah," I said. "But we'll have to disclose it to the group."

"That don't matter to me," he said. His voice was as hard as the muscles that threatened to break through the fabric of his shirt.

Frank often told the group stories about his violent past, but it was not so much that he was bragging as he was unloading; in fact, as though he had to unload. It was a complicated process to witness. On the one hand, he seemed to be expressing regret; but, at the same time, there was an attitude of uncaring detachment. Frank was a scary individual.

It was a policy of our group that what happened in group stayed in group. It was only after Frank made the declaration that he would not "thump" anyone for being honest with him, so long as it stayed in the group, that the others began to trust it was safe enough to say anything to him at all. I could tell Frank was trying not to hold back, but old habits can own us whether we like it or not. It was apparent Frank had been a fortress unto himself for a long time.

"How can I help you, Frank?" I asked, after he was seated for our first one on one session.

"I dunno. Jus' listen I guess. I'm so fuckin' tired of myself, tired of the same old shit." He paused; his voice was flat, lifeless. "Sometimes I feel like I'm crazy. I wanna do one thing, but then I jus' go right ahead an' do the opposite."

"Give me an example," I ventured. "What are you tired of? What makes you feel crazy?"

"Well, in group I talk like all that stuff about hurtin' people is in the past, but it ain't." He hesitated. "Can I tell you stuff without getting busted?"

"Depends on what you tell me, Frank," I said. "Like if you've killed someone, or tell me you're going to, or, if child abuse is involved, or elder abuse. Yeah, there are some things I'd have to report."

"What about jus' thumpin' people?" he quietly asked.

"No, I don't think I'd necessarily have to report you for fighting," I said. "Depends on how serious it is. And if you're looking to change." It occurred to me that he could do serious damage without really trying. Frank was thoughtful for a moment.

"Well," he began. "I hurt people, but not really bad. I jus' go out and hurt people that I don't know and then I go home and cry about it." I stared at him in silence.

"You mean," I hesitated. "You actually shed tears?" He glared at me.

"Ain't that what I jus' said," he growled. Then, with a sudden change of mood, his massive shoulders slumped and he retreated.

"I'm sorry, Doc," he moaned. He seemed to shrink before my eyes, folding his large hands in his lap and bowing his head like a small boy in the principal's office. Then, little by little, that which he had held back for years began to find its way out. But he spoke almost in a monotone.

*   *   *

One night when he was eighteen years old, Frank had been drag racing, a girlfriend in the car with him, when an elderly couple pulled out from a side street in front of him. The resulting crash killed everyone except Frank, who suffered only minor injuries. From the hospital emergency room Frank was hauled off to jail.

He had no money or immediate family who cared, and the girl's influential father, who held Frank totally responsible for his daughter's death, was vehemently determined that Frank should be severely punished. He was convicted on three counts of manslaughter and sentenced to a long prison term. From the county jail to the courthouse to prison, Frank's grief was locked away deep inside, in a prison far stronger than the bars that had surrounded him.

As this nightmare of a story unfolded, there was not the least bit of emotion in his voice. When he had finished, we both sat silently staring at the floor. This guy never had a chance, I thought. Any one of a million people could have wound up in his shoes. How many eighteen-year-olds had I known who drove too fast? Finally, after several moments of silence, I ventured a question.

"What was your girlfriend's name, Frank?" I asked. "You didn't mention her name." He stared at me for a long time, his face as immobile as a statue. Then, gradually, his expression changed into something akin to panic.

"I can't remember," he said. "Goddam it, I don't want to remember."

"Try to remember, try to say her name, Frank," I urged. "And try to remember her face. Tell me what she looked like. Try to remember all you can about her." He glared at me from inside his agony. I braced myself for what might follow.

"Fuck you," he said, in a hollow tone. But he remained seated and bowed his head once again.

It started with a slight sniffling sound, and then his great shoulders started shaking. He tried to fight it, but the emotion was more than he could hold. Seven years of prison, seven years of numbing pain. His sobbing increased into a flood of relief and mourning.

"Dolores," he whispered, bringing his hands up to clutch at his head. "Dolores, Dolores," he moaned her name louder, his voice finally cracking with emotion, his soul finally cracking the frozen denial and awful rage that had swallowed his heart. At last, he could work through the torment, in the only way he could ever escape the deeper prison that still held him captive. He cried and cried, until he could cry no more.

MELANCTON SMITH
AMERICAN PROPHET

You've heard the old saying about how "youth is wasted on the young." Well, after I returned to school in 1991, at age fifty-six, I soon felt the same could be said about how a certain degree of higher education is wasted on the young. Not that I blame the young people, that would be unfair, many of them are truly brilliant. But it seemed to be just as one of my professor friends acknowledged, "These kids just don't have the experiential hooks upon which to hang a lot of ideas."

My experience with older students, however, bears out their much greater interest in the fullness of education, in the classical sense, beyond the level of superficial exposure and memory testing. Every class I took was like a banquet, but the more I consumed, the more I wanted – the deeper I wanted to go. Nevertheless, I soon had to accept that we were merely skimming the surface. A professor was committed to covering X amount of material within X amount of time, all crammed into a sixteen-week semester full of many other powerful distractions. So, I had to set aside some fascinating inquiries in order to keep up with the skimming.

Fortunately, I also learned the word "heuristic" – a self-educating, trial-and-error method of exploration that gave me permission to follow my intuition. Soon I heard myself saying such arcane things as: "You can't really learn what you don't already know."

My previous efforts at serious college work, from the late 50s till '91, had been frustrated by my visual impairment. But the education technology revolution brought on by personal computers ultimately led to my discovery of a large monitor, my magical window into a previously unavailable world, and I've been playing "catch up" ever since. As I learned more about the external universe, I also experienced a universe expanding inside me. The thrill of learning sparked such passion and curiosity that I truly felt like I was born again.

This was my state of mind when I first discovered Melancton Smith, in a Political Science source book. Maybe he was someone I should better have learned about when I was eighteen, at a time when naivete and idealism usually hang out together; but, even now, I get excited about his existence in American history.

On June 21, 1788, this prominent businessman gave a speech at the New York Ratifying Convention for the U.S. Constitution which reads like prophesy. He pointed out that representation and political power under the proposed Constitution would automatically flow to the wealthy class, thereby "depriving the government of valuable and realistic input from the 'middling class' and the poor."

> "The great easily form associations," he said. "But the poor and middling class form them with difficulty. If the elections be by plurality, as probably will be the case in this state, then none but the great will be chosen, for they easily unite their interests. The common people will divide, and their divisions will be promoted by the others."

Interesting use of "great" to describe the wealthy, and such accuracy about purposeful division. Although there was undoubtedly some real intelligence and ability combined with affluence and education, I wonder how apparent Melancton Smith's predictions were to others of his time. How obvious was it that wealth would buy political power and promote issues of self-interest that could distract and divide the public; or was that a given?

> "But I may be asked," Smith continues. "Would you really exclude the wealthy class in the community from any share in legislation? I answer, by no means – they would be more dangerous out of power than in it – they would be factious – discontented and constantly disturbing the government – it would also be unjust – they have their liberties to protect as well – and, the largest share of property. But my idea is, that the Constitution should be so framed as to admit this (wealthy) class, together with a sufficient number of the middling class to control them. You will then combine the abilities, and honesty, of the community – a proper degree of information, and a disposition to pursue the public good."

When I first read this, I had to slowly go over it again. What a wonderfully simple, articulate view of representative government (although I have since considered other forms of proportional representation). Hearing these words gave me a utopian vision of what government might have been – a public trust imbued with the ideal that everyone's well-being would depend upon protecting everyone else's. Essentially that our individual survival depends upon the survival of saving one another. Melancton Smith continues –

> "We ought to guard against the government being placed in the hands of this (wealthy) class – they cannot have the sympathy with their constituents which is necessary to connect them closely to their interests. Being in the habit of profuse living, they will be profuse in the public expenses."

It has been some time now since I first discovered Melancton Smith, and maybe there's not much more I can know. I haven't had the time nor inclination to research his family history. It just impresses me that this one man, the only dissenting voice at the New York Ratifying Convention, looked at the Constitution, in 1788, before it became the law of the land, and correctly identified our government's most critical problem today.

A little further along in his speech, Melancton quotes a Marquis Beccaria, an 18th century Italian philosopher:

"In every human society," said the Marquis. "There is an essay continually tending to confer on one part the height of power and happiness, and to reduce the other to the extreme of weakness and misery. The intent of good laws is to oppose this effort, and to diffuse their influence universally and equally."

We human beings seem to be incredibly good at designing systems we cannot live up to.

MY YUMMY MYTH

I was fifty-eight; she was thirty-two. She was a student in an SSU Learning Community experiment I was facilitating as volunteer faculty, part of my graduate internship program. It was not the first time a younger female student had flirted with me, which, although not a common occurrence, was one I usually had little trouble defusing. However, this particular young woman would have none of my psychologizing. She was intellectually understanding, but otherwise impervious to my efforts at reframing her feelings.

"How was your relationship with your father?" I asked. But she just gave me a knowing look and shook her head.

"I'm sure you can feel it too," she said, with a confident smile. "I see it in the way you look at me in class." She was right. I wondered if other people were aware that this young woman actually glowed. She had thick and curly, golden blonde hair, stunning blue eyes and incredibly full lips. She was Puerto Rican, with a cultured, classy quality about her that made me think of Royalty. To make matters better, or worse, she was highly intelligent, extremely well read, and there was an honest boldness about her that simply turned me on.

It was during the first week of school, after class. We had walked to the parking lot and were standing next to her car. It was near twilight.

"I can't deny the attraction," I said, momentarily avoiding the blue search-lights of her gaze. "But I have a responsibility, a matter of professional integrity." When she reached out to touch my arm, it tingled, like a mild electric shock.

"I know," she said. "And I honor you for it. I love you for it. But you must understand, what's happening between us cannot be avoided." Her matter-of-fact certainty about our relationship was a thrill, and a warning. It left me breathless.

When I recall her appearance at that moment, as she leaned back against the trunk of her car, I have to forgive myself for falling. She was in partial silhouette, against a street light that cast a misty halo around the wildness of her bright, gossamer curls. The play of light around the outline of her shapely body aroused yet another dimension; a mysterious, powerful image of the goddess Aphrodite. I felt as though I was standing at the edge of a great storm – a silent, invisible storm.

"Did you feel that?" she asked. Without knowing how it happened, she was in my arms. And yes, it felt as though the earth had moved, but I knew the earthquake was just between us. I held her only briefly and then stepped away.

"What's wrong?" Her eyes reached out to mine.

"I'm sorry," I said. "But this is moving too fast." The truth was that I was shaken by the potency of what just happened. The experience was disturbing, like a sense of displacement – a feeling of "where am I?" She was indeed beautiful, but there was a hint of something dangerous in her presence. I could feel an ancient, masculine alarm rattling deep inside me. She smiled as though she understood and gently reached out to hold my hand while we talked. I didn't have a chance. She was simply irresistible.

By the time I glanced at my wristwatch, we had been standing in the parking lot for well over an hour. That didn't even seem possible. We had been on our way to a local coffee house, but had been so intent in our conversation we forgot to get into the car. Subjectively, hardly any time had passed at all, but I knew my watch was correct. This distortion of normal time would always happen when I was alone with Katrina. Several hours could pass like minutes.

After I came home that first night, I sat quietly in the living room of my apartment for a long time, not quite ready to believe what was happening. I had managed to behave like a panting school boy. I had lightly touched her lips with mine and barely brushed the hidden blossoms of her nipples with my fingertips. These moves were completely unexpected, impulsive, and powerful. And that's what bothered me. I was too old and too wise to be having these feelings, especially for this young goddess. But woe is me, it felt as though something irrevocable had already happened.

Eros and Pathos, the inevitable duo. How could I ever forget? We are made flesh and we all face this same lesson. There can be no love without suffering. A love affair can bring up our deepest hopes; and our deepest fears, tipping a balance scale that seldom comes to rest. I'd been there before. And now I was putting myself in a position to face the same agony all over again and it could be just as devastating as the first time. Or, maybe I could still get out of it. A large part of my rational mind still struggled to save the day. When Katrina gave me a ride home after class a few days later, and came up to my apartment for the first time, I gave it one last shot. I sat her down and made my case.

"I'm flattered by your attention," I began, easing into lecture mode. "But this isn't real. This is a prime example of projection. I'm not who you think I am. Take another look, at the gray hair, the gray beard, and the glasses. I'm this old guy over here. I'm fifty-eight years old and as near sighted as Mister Magoo. What does a young woman like you want with an old geezer like me?" I wish I'd never asked.

She was sitting straight and still, in dignified silence, her expression a delicate blend of patience and excitement. As I looked at her, I felt elated and fearful at the same time. Even though I was trying to talk her out of it, the idea that this magically beautiful young woman could actually be interested in me was beginning to have a narcotic effect. My sense of well-being was headed up Mount Olympus.

"I'm sorry if this is scary for you," she said. "And I'll back off if you really want me to, but at least give me credit for seeing what an incredible man you are. Please, understand, I'm mostly just grateful that I met you." I started to respond, but she raised her hand. "Something definitely happened between us in the parking lot," she continued. "We have been blessed with one another. We both know it. And as for the age thing, it's just a freaking number. Besides," she paused, and smiled seductively. "You wouldn't have been ready for me before now anyway."

Damn, she was good. I felt like running, but my heart was nailed to the floor. An age difference of twenty-six years was bound to cause problems. And considering my relationship history, how could I keep myself from becoming mistrustful, and jealous, especially with this gorgeous creature? But reasoning was futile. I knew I could be walking into a potential disaster, but I just couldn't stop walking. It was too late. My lustful heart was doing back flips, cheering me on.

I convinced myself that a trans -generational relationship was better than okay; it was divinely inspired. I barely noticed a flood of rationalizations, loaded with half-truth, that leaked through my shaggy armor. I pretended that I was such a cool, wise guy I knew exactly what I was doing. Hey, what the hell, it probably wouldn't last, and I'd probably get hurt, but it would be worth it.

And I guess it was. We spent endless hours in a sweetly invincible, love crazed bubble, like children in a perpetual state of discovery. Inside that bubble was an energy that focused us both through the same lens, into one magical world view. Old familiar places became new and exciting. Everything was more intense; colors, music, words, ideas, all had deeper meaning, and deeper mystery. Words of joy came swimming up from the well of my subconscious.

"When she speaks, my hands lift to caress her words. When she smiles, my soul moves, without hesitation, to dance with her soul. I whisper in her ear that we are the wild, wild reflection of a time before fear or reason."

These periods of symbiosis were such an intoxicant it was difficult to tell exactly when things began to change. But the inevitable couldn't be otherwise. The bubble continued to form now and then, but I had to face the fact that it was her bubble; I was a guest. As our relationship and the semester rolled on, there were signs that the magic was beginning to fade. And I became haunted with the feeling that something essential was missing in the relationship.

She was there but not there. And the huge ego boost that had made me the envy of other men no longer mattered. Things were okay so long as we were welded together, but, at arm's length, our differences began to come on strong. When we made love, it was more like we were both making love to her. She was selfish, and, in spite of her beauty, could leave me feeling deeply, emotionally ungratified. Her power was that of initial seduction; not follow through.

Our intimacy took on a frustrating, sterile quality. It must have been that way all along and I'd just been too infatuated to admit it. By now it was as though I had become addicted to the suffering. I just couldn't accept that the generosity of my love for her was not being reciprocated. In spite of everything I thought I knew about psychology, about narcissism and masochism, it was not enough to save me.

Yea verily, to risk love is to risk death. Karena was openly affectionate with one of the male students in my class and I had to talk to her about it. It was a rainy day. We sat in the campus cafeteria. She was upset.

"I told you I'd have male friends," she said. "If I have to change my behavior because you're in the room, then I'll begin to resent you. Is that what you want?" At least she didn't lie to me. Instead of offering a verbal band-aid, she just made it clear that my feelings were my problem. She would not be held responsible.

"I told you at the very beginning," she continued, "I need my space, I don't like someone hovering over me. The only promise I made to you is that we would always be friends."

"But," I heard myself saying. "A real friend would be sensitive to my feelings." She just glared at me.

"If this romance has to end," she said, her voice cool and distant. "It's only because you wanted more." I just stared at her, in grief. Of course, I wanted more.

In spite of all that, I would still stand in awe as I watched her walking from one campus building to another. It didn't help to remind myself that I had gone into the relationship with my eyes wide open, the pain was no less. In fact, the extent of my awareness was itself a painful confirmation of my stupidity. And yet, now that it was over, I still couldn't help but be proud of myself. It just took a while before I was once again grateful for the experience.

On Art and Such

It burned in my mind like a statement struck on the fiery tablets of Hollywood's Moses in the Ten Commandments – a single sentence that came back to haunt me. But I couldn't remember the exact wording or where I'd read it. I reviewed the books I'd had open over the preceding days and finally found it, on page 19 of a psychology text by Marie-Louise von Franz: "In the unconscious the inner world and the outer world are not differentiated." And so, reviewed in black and white, I reflected on why it had struck such a responsive chord. Then, I understood once again its unique importance to me.

My experience with learning about art has been filtered and modified through my troubled assumptions about the fact of my visual impairment, which includes a diagnosis of "color blindness." Because I must assume that others are in touch with visual cues and color frequencies that are beyond my physiological scope, I have further assumed that my capacity to appreciate or learn about art is also limited; even restricted. But, over time, I have brought this idea into question.

Of major importance in the sentence I cited above is that it implies the sheer magnitude of the inner territory from which art draws its raw material – a territory of unknown dimensions. And I remember that only infants and psychotics are known to experience this lack of differentiation between internal and external reality, which becomes a seamless and boundless continuum.

I wonder about color, about our emotional attachment to it. Color can be defined as a physical frequency - an external phenomenon. Yet when perceived and internalized, it is also our sensory-emotional response that defines it. Regardless of my physical diagnosis, I have seen color, vivid internalized color, but I cannot always prove it by naming it. So, I must assume that the importance of color, for me, is relativized in the psyche, and therefore, in my perception of art. However, since I know that the language of the psyche is imagery, and imagery is not altogether dependent on color, then I am assured that my capacity to understand and work with imagery is at least as in tact as that of anyone else; at least I like to think so.

*   *   *

My approach to art has been predicated on the belief that Divinity defines and reveals itself through the very nature of our existence. I believe the "work," or the function, of art is to open us to ourselves. And, by the very act of this opening, we will come into contact with the Divine. For example: We do not directly grasp a question that is asked of us from the outside, we can only grasp it through our response to it, on the inside.

Between the universe we apprehend with our intellect and the one we perceive through our senses, there is an intermediate universe; a world of images, of archetypal figures, of immaterial matter, of subtle body. I bring myself into this intermediate world (where the spirit becomes body and body becomes spirit) through an authentic connection. The sense organ with which I make this connection is the active imagination, the place of visions, the screen upon which appear visionary events and symbolic histories. And, it is of the greatest importance to understand that the active imagination is not the same as fantasy, or the imaginary, since these are merely inventions that remain near the surface of conscious expectation. Active imagination means that the images are autonomous, that they have a life of their own; and, that the symbolic events develop according to their own logic. Conscious interference with these images will only impede their process.

The bottom line, I believe, is that the magnitude of the unconscious far exceeds the magnitude of what we perceive as external reality, and that, in there (in the unconscious) we are all made whole. I remember the amazing experience of working with a professional psycho-dramatist. When I first engaged with her group, I could feel the raw potential for a deeper connection with ourselves through one another. Here I sought the opportunity, and the courage, to freely express the archetypal impulses that inform my earthly journey. By virtue of my willingness to go un-edited, immediate and spontaneous, I thought I might witness a version of myself that had long been held in reserve. I wanted to gain a deeper joy of self-possession, as in the words of Florida Scott Maxwell: "You need only claim the events of your life to make yourself yours. When you truly possess all you have been and done, you are fierce with reality."

* * *

In his book "No More Second-hand Art," author Peter London describes an art exhibit he attended while in college. The work was done by college art professors, some of whom he had studied with, and so, he expected the very best. But his experience of the exhibit was like walking through a textbook. The paintings were all about technique; they were not about being alive. In spite of the quality of their technical excellence, the paintings were actually lackluster - without courage.

Peter London and a few classmates were ultimately disappointed by what they saw. They went home to lament amongst themselves about the emptiness, the lifelessness of technical excellence. If you admire the work of Monet, you can learn to paint like Monet, but the price is dear. Not only would you need to spend twelve hours a day for twenty years, when you were done, you would only have learned to paint like someone else. Those artists (Monet, Cezanne, Degas, etc.) developed their particular techniques to satisfy the needs of their own peculiar expression, not to instruct others.

To my mind the very question about what art IS somehow threatens its existence. Separate from the experience, art is nothing but history. Unless we can somehow become a part of what we sense (see or hear), for us the work will always be incomplete. As I mentioned earlier, you can only perceive the question from within your response, not from "objective" reality. And yet, how we decide to interpret the art work of the ancient world may have little to do with what was originally intended. Perhaps the ancient "artist" did not see the work as separate at all, but as direct communication with the gods, or God.

I am reminded of the "Great Waltz" in old movies - reflections of a grand old time that may never have actually existed, but was always a wishful fantasy, a dream of lost culture and better days. We can re-write history in our own image, as we filter it through our current interpretations, but we may never know exactly what was felt or all of what really happened.

When I witnessed the King Tut Exhibit some years ago, I had the strange feeling of being in the presence of a truly alien culture; not just the difference of a few thousand years and several thousand miles (on the same planet), but a difference in the essential experience of being.

Exactly what was it that had motivated those strangely powerful images (not to mention the incredible amount of work involved)? Was it enslavement, money, prestige; or does the work represent a worship of craftsmanship dedicated to the gods' perfect world, a Platonic ideal which must exist somewhere?

Later, when I reflected on the exhibit, I thought of its beauty only as a by-product of its deeper meaning. In my life's experience, the power one encounters while engrossed in creative activity provides bio-chemical feedback to the brain. In such a concentrated state, in the presence of powerful and mysterious forces, Deity is an obvious conclusion.

I remember an occasion, long ago, when I was living in Mexico. I was lying on my bed, listening to the music of Bach and looking up at the patterns of candlelit brickwork in the vaulted ceiling. It suddenly occurred to me that all of "art" must already exist - just waiting to be discovered. Its true essence had to be something akin to memory, a re-collection. Otherwise, how would we recognize it?

At that time I was involved with learning from a local Maestro of violin making - a wonderful guru who didn't know he was a guru; which made him that much more a guru. I augmented my time with him with many hours in my own studio. As I explored the cutting and carving of violin parts, something in the very quality of their shapes began to inform me, to instruct me. The activity itself took on a separate life - a power that directed me.

The image of a perfect instrument grew in my mind, I could feel it in the wood beneath my fingertips, a flawless form that seemed within my reach; but somehow, at the same time, I knew that no one ever had, or ever would, quite get there. Such perfection could never exist in this - our most imperfect world.

Could I live with that - sensing and working toward something I could never quite achieve? No matter my ability, or that illusive thing called talent, no amount of work would ever achieve the ultimate goal. Throughout history, I wonder if this understanding might not have driven a number of artists quite mad; or quite sane.

* * *

Over the years of dipping into the creative power of the unconscious, I made an unfortunate discovery - mind altering dis-inhibitors seem to work all too well. It is a complex challenge to discuss the connection between chemical access to the power of the unconscious and the phenomena of creativity. On the one hand, is the intense validity of this connection; otherwise, it would not have found so many adherents. On the other hand, is the distorting psychic damage such chemical shortcuts can produce. Many artists, in various fields, have discovered and become addicted to this means of unconscious connection; and, many have suffered the reality of unfortunate consequences.

Although I engaged in a variety of substances, including LSD, heroin, methamphetamine and mescaline, it was that substance I used to get off the illegal hard stuff that cost me the most. Although I successfully left heavy drug use behind, it was alcohol that finally punched my ticket to hell.

Looking back, it still bothers me deeply that the only time I could really relax and sing with a group of musicians was when I was just inebriated enough - when all my doubts and fears were submerged in alcohol. In that warm, confident state, I managed to access my deepest connection to musical expression with artful abandon. I once picked up a saxophone mouthpiece, just the upper neck, without the body and keys, and with the motion of my cupped hands at the end of that tube, held a small audience spell-bound with impromptu blues.

But I dearly suffered for those alcohol induced moments of fearless creativity - my personality short-circuited. Giving over to the unconscious labyrinth of the larger Self, the "god within" so to speak, I was plunged into a river of boundless energy without a paddle. The ultimate result of such intensity is burnout and alienation. Such periods of grace are fleeting at best, and terribly unreliable.

I have worked with addicts as a group facilitator and counselor. I understand the magnificent appeal of those seemingly magical powers. Such is the trap of addiction. In order to become available to those magical moments, one becomes enslaved to whatever substance will do the job; even if it only works a small percentage of the time. This leads to the insanity of ever-increasing payments for ever diminishing returns. Fortunately, the sober demands of keeping all ten fingers while working with sharp tools and woodworking equipment allowed this area of my creativity to endure with independence from substance.

Nevertheless, the attachment of so many aspects of my freedom loving creativity to drugs is a memory with which I still struggle.

I understand those moments of raw power as brief visits to an authentic unconscious, which, no matter the means of chemical transportation, are still valid, although sometimes lead to nowhere land. I also remember Carl Jung's statement that one's complete and sudden exposure to the unconscious would be so overwhelming as to be fatal.

And so, as with many aspects of life, it's a matter of balance. In all these years since abstaining from chemical shortcuts, I have maintained a sobriety that covers my once naked passion like a soft glove. What I once could only hold in a tight grip of impassioned ferocity, I can now gently hold with a more sustainable and sober caress. Whether an insane tap dance on a tightrope above the abyss, or a casual stroll along the precipice, ultimately becomes a matter of choice.

JADE

My granddaughter, Jade, is ten years old and a source of wonder to me. We recently went on a camping trip with her mom and dad, my daughter and son-in-law, up near the Mendocino coast. Due to a long-time relationship between my son-in-law and the owners, our secluded campsite was on a private ranch near the Navarro River, in a particularly beautiful spot next to a small lake. It was a rare treat to have that sense of privacy in such an idyllic setting. What follows is based on some notes I wrote about Jade that weekend.

She moves through the forest with a courage born of innocence, and curiosity, a way of being as old as the forest itself. She examines the natural world like a scientist, but one who belongs there as much as the things she studies. She explores her surroundings with the impunity of her connectedness, except that she's well aware of the consequences of poison oak.

Jade had invited me to join her on a walk through the "enchanted forest," a name she and her parents had given to a nearby stretch of natural beauty. We went past the dam at the end of the lake and down into a steep canyon. We hiked along the dim-lit canyon bottom through thickets of lush fern, surrounded by a natural cathedral of redwoods. The soft lighting reminded me of stained glass, or a primeval forest scene in a natural history museum.

There was a deeply cut creek bed meandering along the canyon floor. This we crossed over several times. After a couple of fairly agile broad jumps, I found myself stretching a little to keep up. Jade had moved ahead, but then waited for me.

"Do you want to stop and rest, Grampa?" she asked.

"No," I replied. "But maybe we could go a little slower."

At one point, after we had crossed over the creek once again, the ground quickly became exceedingly soft, spongy with moisture and a thick layer of humus.

"It seems a little squishy here, Jade," I commented.

"It's alright Grampa," she smiled. "I know where I'm going." She forged ahead with apparent joy in her role as a natural scout. But then the way got deeper, more tangled and harder to negotiate. She looked up at my higher perspective above the tangled brush and quite logically asked me to take the lead. I proudly trampled the undergrowth aside through a wide, marsh-like area, and then, when the way was much less obstructed; Jade became the guide again. As we walked along in the relative silence of the deep forest, I witnessed my granddaughter in a whole new way. I saw the mythical wood nymph, an ancient and ageless spirit that moved through her. She was ten years old – plus 10,000.

Finally, as the canyon walls began to separate a little, we climbed a shallow bank onto a seldom used, overgrown roadway, layered with leaves and grass and occasionally cut across by the erosion of a deep rut.

"That way leads to the Navarro River," she announced, pointing with her left hand. "And that way back to camp." She stood there like a road sign, with her arms outstretched, pointing the way in both directions.

"How far is it to the river," I asked.

"A little way," she said. But I could tell from her smile that the river was further than we'd go on that day. She turned and started back up the road toward camp, with confidence that I'd be right behind her.

Jade has two modes of movement, the kind she thinks about and the kind that flows through her faster than a thought can percolate. Sometimes she moves in response to one of the small creatures she loves to track; frogs and butterflies are her favorites.

"Look Grampa," she slowly opened her cupped hands, just far enough for me to see a little green frog. She was so excited about the introduction I wouldn't have been surprised if the little creature had started talking.

We continued along the overgrown roadway as it wound along the canyon wall, not far above the same trail we had just taken in the other direction. Tall cool redwoods still flanked us on both sides. A little further down the road, which was littered with materiel blown down by long ago storms, Jade and I selected a couple of walking sticks. We enjoyed the feeling that we were among the very few people who had ever passed that way.

As Jade moves ahead of me, I imagine her as a native child in this same forest, hundreds of years ago. I imagine she has heard stories about the origin of things, stories to explain the living world around her. I imagine she knows the names of many creatures, and has learned how to use a variety of plants for food and medicine. Her people reside within the land, not just on top of it. And even so, with all that, I wonder if she could possibly have felt any more at home back then than she does right now. She is such an integral part of her environment, living the unconscious and total involvement of childhood, before "maturity" of mind separates her from nature and makes a mere object of the world.

As we walked further along, Jade started finding feathers. These she tried to stick into the rough broken end of her walking stick; but they kept falling out. I saw a chance to use the hunting knife I had brought along, which I hadn't used in years. My sedentary lifestyle had not included many camping trips.

"Here Jade," I said, excited to help her. "Let me cut into the end. That'll make it easier to put the feathers in."

"I don't think so Grandpa," she replied. "The wood is too hard." But she gave me the stick anyway. Sure enough, the wood was so dry and tough that when I tried to cut a deeper channel, it was apparent that I might split the stick, or cut myself instead. I wondered how she knew that already. I must admit I felt a little embarrassed.

Suddenly Jade had an idea. She pulled a few long stalks of grass and quickly braided the flexible strands together. With this she tightly wrapped the feathers around the end of the stick, which I was still holding. As she carefully knotted the braid, I was filled with pride by her handiwork. When I handed the stick back to her, she put her small hand over mine and looked up at me.

'Thanks Grampa,' she smiled.

That same morning her dad, Karl, had baited her hook with a live worm and then took off to his favorite fishing spot on the other side of the lake. I stayed with Jade; who soon caught a small bluegill. She lifted the poor wiggling creature to my face.

"Take it off for me, please Grampa," she asked. The little fish had become exhausted and hung limp at the end of the line. But then, just as I reached for it, the damned thing started violently wiggling. I jerked my hand back, and immediately regretted it. I hadn't grabbed a live fish since I was around Jade's age, when I had often gone fishing with my long-departed stepfather. I tried to grab the fish again, but couldn't get a hold. Then the healthy little creature struggled so hard it managed to unhook itself and fall back into the water.

After we got back from our walk in the "enchanted forest" that afternoon, Jade decided to go fishing again. She knew the little bluegills would be thrown back, but she was trying for one of the hard to catch striped bass with which the lake had been stocked. I had just settled down in a comfortable folding chair and put my feet up on a log when I heard her, a little way down the bank, calling me.

"Grampa, Grampa, I got another 'Bloogie.' Without hesitation I jumped up and headed down the bank to where she was waiting. I was being given another chance. With absolute Grampa confidence, I grabbed the damn fish, removed the hook from its mouth and threw it back into the water. She looked up at me with a wide grin.

"Thanks Grampa."

DRIVEN HOME

It was during the week between Christmas and New Year's, 2001, and I was taking a trip on a Greyhound bus to see my son and his family in Chico. I should have known better. This time of year was usually busy enough, but with more and more people opting not to fly (after 9/11), the ground level corridor between Los Angeles and Seattle was overwhelmed with new passengers. My portion of that corridor was usually to board a bus in Sacramento and get off in Chico; but this time my son's family had been visiting friends in Marysville, about forty miles north, and agreed to meet me at the Marysville station.

My frustration was reaching a memorable level as I stood in front of a pay phone trying to use a charge card number that kept leading to dead silence on the other end. I had just been informed of a two-and-a-half-hour delay and couldn't get through to my son's cell phone (I didn't yet own one), knowing that he would be waiting for me in Marysville.

The ride between Santa Rosa and Sacramento had taken over three hours and arriving behind schedule in Sacramento set me up for a hard time. The station was packed, the lines of waiting passengers so mushed together it was difficult to tell which line was for what gate. The line for the northbound bus, Gate 7, snaked through the station and almost to the main entrance on the other side of the building. There must have been a couple hundred people in that line.

I had taken my place in this standing marathon, which occasionally moved, and finally, with just one person ahead of me at the gate, the line stopped for a long time and we were told that another north-bound bus would be formed in about two and a half hours. Hence, I wound up angrily staring at a dead pay phone. And, for the ten thousandth time since I'd quit driving, wished I was still among the blessed, automobile citizens out there on the freeway.

In April of 1984 I had turned off the ignition in my Chevy Van and sat behind the wheel for a long, long time. I knew I had just finished my last drive. After thirty-five illegal years behind the wheel, throughout California, Arizona, Mexico, New Mexico, Nevada, and back to California; my freedom of mobility was finally over.

No one had told me I had to quit, I hadn't seen a traffic ticket of any kind in years, but the feeling had been building inside me that quitting would be inevitable. Traffic in Sonoma County had greatly increased and so had the demand for visual acuity. For a long time, I had felt that my mostly rural routes were well within my visual range and I posed no threat, but that feeling was slipping away.

I had started driving before high school, shortly after WW II, when a decent nineteen-thirties vehicle could be had for fifty dollars. The transformation of San Rafael High School during those years was a reflection of the times. My freshman year, 1949, saw very few student cars, mostly bicycles. But, by 1953, when I managed to graduate, a large dirt parking lot had been leveled at the edge of the campus. Practically every high school kid I knew had a car. It was a community supported rite of passage.

For a brief period, after I had failed to pass the eye test for a driver license, I tried to give it up; but I couldn't. I later managed to get a limited license, restricted to Marin County roads, only to school or work, and only during the day. I drove in violation of those conditions for quite a while before I was caught and my license taken. Once again, I tried to quit, but I couldn't. I didn't have the will to commit social suicide, nor did I have the kind of support from friends and family that might have made a difference. Everyone else was a driver and I couldn't stand not being like everyone else.

Driving had become second nature. But more, although I would not have used this term at the time, driving had become an addiction. When I was in high school, I would wait until my parents were asleep and sneak out to drive around all night. I explored many back roads in Marin and Sonoma Counties, sometimes getting lost, sometimes getting home barely in time to pretend I was just getting up for school. I recall being reprimanded more than once for dozing off in class.

What a time that was – the early fifties. We young people with our old cars had the run of rural Marin County after dark. We could easily take over the top of Mount Tamalpais, or the Mountain Theater, for an all-night party. We had access to the rich and diverse back country of rural Marin and no one was there to bother us.

What had formerly been the domain of wild creatures in the woods now saw an invasion of freedom crazed high school kids. There were night time country drag races, drunken car parties, laughing and yelling to our juvenile heart's content. It was a very long time before the Sheriff's Department began patrolling the countryside at night, and even then, it wasn't difficult to figure out their scheduled routes.

In the mid-century car culture of my youth, we were all mechanics. Major engine overhauls in the driveway, garage or backyard were commonplace. Most of those vehicles were much simpler, pre-electronic, built before the industry began to produce more complex machines. But what stays with me more than anything is that our precious vehicles were soulful extensions of ourselves - so identified with our freedom and independence they were almost sentient in their importance. I suppose such personal connections were just as important to succeeding generations, but our greasy palms worked on the last of the purely American vehicles.

These are a few that I remember driving: '29 Model A, '32 Ford Coupe, '34 Ford Sedan, '38 Plymouth Sedan, '38 Century Buick,

'47 Chevy Coupe, '48 Studebaker, '48 Dodge Truck, '49 Chevy Truck. For a while I even owned a '47 Diamond T Pick-up. To say that I "cared" about my vehicles would be an understatement. Each one, right up to the Chevy Van that was my last, was a unique relationship of countless idiosyncrasies, and a mysterious extension of myself.

So many thoughts coursed through my mind as I stood by the pay phone in that crowded bus station in Sacramento. Amazing how much history was unpacked in a flash of images; and, I can clearly remember the emotional changes I allowed myself to go through while standing there.

First, I let out a deep sigh, hung my head and gave in to the victim. I was tired, my trip was delayed, my phone card didn't work, I had to take a stinking bus, I deserved better. Woe is me, goddammit, no one ever had it so bad. What's the use, I give up. I might as well walk out into the street and get run over by one of those stinking buses.

Then, I took another deep breath and allowed myself to feel every frustration I had ever experienced, about anything, but most especially about not driving. It was easy to get in touch with anger about my eyesight, about a body that could be labeled "disabled." I gave in to anger, to rage. I clenched my fists and imagined the pay phone in front of me glowing white hot before it exploded and blasted a large jagged hole clear through the wall and out to the sidewalk. Passers-by stared in wonder as I stepped through the jagged hole, raised my arms and lifted off from the sidewalk on my solo flight to Chico.

Finally, after satisfying my daimons, self-pity and rage, a sense of peace came over me - a soothing calm that brought me fully into the presence of my extreme good fortune. I was alive and well and going to see some people I dearly loved. For anyone who might have witnessed the man by the pay phone, the transition from victim to raging super-hero to grateful grandfather all happened within a matter of seconds. I'd had enough risk and diversity in my life to know the value of options, and sometimes, I could even inhabit a future of my own choosing.

As it turned out, my family was already on their way to find me in that crowded bus station. And, later that night, riding in the back seat with an arm around each of my two young grandsons, I was deeply grateful for the man behind the wheel, who had been my passenger for a long time, years ago. I was grateful for the faithful guardian angel who had been my companion for so many, many miles, and had finally warned me when it was time to quit.

I had in fact been guilty of breaking the law and risking lives, and God knows I'm grateful not to be sitting in prison after a fatal accident. But, in spite of it all, I am also grateful I had a chance to play my part in the automotive history of the American Dream. And yet, a soulful part of me will always carry a burden it can never quite resolve.

MY SAECULUM

When I was a child in Georgia, I had the impression the American Civil War had just happened. The adults around me still used terms like "Dam Yankee" and spoke of Sherman's march across Georgia as though they had witnessed it themselves. I later realized that perhaps a few of them had, since the span of time between the Civil War and the Second World War was just eighty years.

Eighty years is the span of history I have witnessed, about the length of what the ancient Romans called a "Saeculum," a measure of time in which a single long life may bear witness to history; or, equivalent to complete renewal of a human population. Olympic Games were bound to happen at least once in a Saeculum.

Truly, I have witnessed the crawl of history - from the joy of one decade to the agony of the next, from the fear of one decade to the fantasy of the next - I have seen the ashes of what once mattered and shared the dream of what might be. Looking back over my lifetime, my Saeculum, I see an acceleration of technology that pulled us into a future for which we were not prepared - a fragmented world of fearful mis-information disguised as reason, of subtle and powerful micro-targeted manipulations and distortions of manufactured consent.

Regardless that we human beings are a product of earth, of nature, our own technology has taken us away from our relationship with that from which we came. We have been insulated from the realities and responsibilities of our origins, from the grounded wisdom of our intrinsic participation. I pray for the possibility of a corrective recovery, a kind of reclamation of what never was, but always could have been - a healing balance of nature born out of our deeper, spiritual potential.

I have also witnessed a Longevity Revolution that some of us had hoped would change the world, bringing with it the calming influence of a mature lust for sanity. Everybody dies, but not everybody receives the transforming gifts of old age - a time of profound self-discovery and healing resolution; a time of fearless integrity and a waking up to the essential nature of one's being.

Yet many are so intimidated by the anti-aging attitudes embedded in our culture they cannot bring the righteous benefits of old age into conscious living. People of all ages are indoctrinated into a system supported by the myth that old age is mostly a disease, adulthood in decline. Although it is true our physical being does diminish, aging is actually a reality of gains as well as losses, a subtle and complex balance of powers just waiting to be explored. I can imagine a world in which becoming old is anticipated as a positive experience.

The powerful truth of a new old age lies in one's ability to occupy questions without grasping for answers. Walking off a map of the known world into unknown territory can be terrifying, but trusting the Universe opens us to a journey of unlimited potential. The challenge is to relax into the mystery of becoming an integral part of advancing human evolution.

CPSIA information can be obtained
at www.ICGtesting.com
Printed in the USA
LVHW080718300322
714785LV00019B/530/J

9 781662 918131